THE ASTROLO

An astrology ha
Age of Aquarius.

Also in this series:
THE ASTROLOGER'S COMPANION
John & Peter Filbey
ASTROLOGICAL COUNSELLING
Christina Rose
ASTRONOMY FOR ASTROLOGERS
John & Peter Filbey
THE BOOK OF WORLD HOROSCOPES
Nicholas Campion
CHART SYNTHESIS
Roy Alexander
CHINESE ASTROLOGY
Derek Walters
DARK STARS
Bernard Fitzwalter & Raymond Henry
DRACONIC ASTROLOGY
Pamela A.F. Crane
FORECASTING BY ASTROLOGY
Martin Freeman
HARMONIC CHARTS
David Hamblin
HORARY ASTROLOGY
Derek Appleby
HOW TO INTERPRET A BIRTH CHART
Martin Freeman
HOW TO RECTIFY A BIRTH CHART
Laurie Efrein
JUNGIAN BIRTH CHARTS
Arthur Dione
MUNDANE ASTROLOGY
Michael Baigent, Nicholas Campion & Charles Harvey
NATAL CHARTING
John Filbey
SOLAR AND LUNAR RETURNS
John Filbey
SYNASTRY
Penny Thornton
THE TWELVE HOUSES
Howard Sasportas

THE ASTROLOGY OF KARMA

How our past, present, and future lives
are revealed by the birth chart

by

Pauline Stone

THE AQUARIAN PRESS

First published 1988

© PAULINE STONE 1988

British Library Cataloguing in Publication Data

Stone, Pauline
The astrology of karma.
1. Astrology, Indic   2. Karma
I. Title
133.5'8122   BF1714.15

ISBN 0-85030-728-7

*The Aquarian Press is part of the Thorsons Publishing Group,
Wellingborough, Northamptonshire, NN8 2RQ, England*

Printed in Great Britain by Biddles Limited, Guildford, Surrey

3 5 7 9 10 8 6 4 2

CONTENTS

This book is dedicated to all who suffer.

INTRODUCTION

As we enter the New Age of Aquarius, each of us is challenged to break down the barriers which isolate us from the rest of creation. We are challenged to abandon the separatism which lies at the heart of all personal and international conflict. As we achieve greater unity with others, we make a personal contribution to world unity and ultimately to world peace.

Astrology has an important role to play in helping us to achieve the necessary self-change. Our birth chart can provide us with insight into those obstacles which cut us off from others. It can show us where we need to develop a greater sense of closeness to others in terms of our thoughts, our feelings and our actions.

The personal rewards of self-change are twofold. On the one hand, as we overcome the barriers which separate us from others, we also overcome the loneliness and pain which are linked to isolation. We thus set ourselves free from karmic suffering.

On the other hand, as we become more at-one with creation as a whole, we become increasingly receptive to psychic energies and thus awaken our intuitive and healing faculties.

This book provides a new approach to interpretation, suitable both for beginners in astrology and for those with a deeper knowledge of the subject.

'. . . [the] birthright given each soul [is] that it may know itself to be itself and by choice become one with the Creator . . .'

The Edgar Cayce Readings
(Reading No. 2571–1)

PART ONE

1.

ASTROLOGY AND THE AGE OF AQUARIUS

What's New About the New Age?
One of the most exciting messages spelled out by astrology is that concerning *Time*. There is clear indication that *now*, the dawn of a new era generally known as the New Age, is when man can and must implement major changes in himself and his environment.

Astrologically speaking this new epoch is referred to as the Age of Aquarius, one of the twelve divisions of the Great Year, each some 2,000 years in duration, which mark the gradual movement of the equinoctial points (where the Sun appears to cross the Equator) backwards through the constellations.*

The significance of these epochs is that they represent different phases of consciousness for mankind. So that with the dawning of the Age of Aquarius we are about to enter a totally new cycle of experience to that which was associated with the departing Age of Pisces.

Each Great Age is governed by a general spiritual awareness linked to the Zodiac sign by which it is ruled. Inasmuch as Pisces is the sign associated with emotional inspiration, this was reflected in the spiritual mood of the past Age. Consequently the spiritual leaders who incarnated some 2,000 years ago to set the tone for the Era of Pisces founded religions which depended entirely on emotional response. The function of Jesus and the other masters who lived around the start of the last Age was to act as an inspiration (Pisces) for man to live up to. Their lives were to serve as an example of the selfless ideal whereby love, peace and world unity could be achieved. The doctrine of Christianity perfectly reflects the essence of Piscean altruism, and indeed its very symbol was that of the fishes.

But neither Christianity nor the other great religions provided a reasoning approach to spirituality. For the fulfilment of his soul

* This phenomenon is known as the precession of the equinoxes.

man depended only on his faith and his love for the ideal represented by the master of his chosen religion.

This may well have been satisfactory at the time, but is obviously no longer adequate for man's changing needs. There is clear indication that the old spiritual attitudes of the Piscean Age are being widely rejected. The reputation of religion in its old form has fallen to an all-time low. The old definition of God, in terms of an ideal to be blindly followed, is utterly outworn. Indeed that three-letter word has latterly become something of a taboo — small wonder when one considers how the various churches have dragged the name through the mire in the bloody pursuit of this or that power game.

Yet, now as never before, mankind is in need of spiritual fulfilment. Materialism is being recognized as the breeder of discontent rather than the bestower of bliss. Human beings are desperately searching for soul satisfaction, and this is reflected in the growing interest in all forms of the occult.

The time has come when spiritual values must be presented in a new language. A language which takes into account the scepticism resulting from the misuse of religion in the latter part of the Piscean Age. And a language which reflects the ambiance associated with the notion of Aquarius, the new mood of the New Age.

The Significance of Aquarius
Whereas Pisces was concerned with emotional inspiration, Aquarius is the sign connected with *intellectual* inspiration. It represents man's potential to absorb all knowledge, to tap the source of universal wisdom. Like every other astrological factor, the sign has its egotistical manifestation and its spiritual. It can be expressed to bolster man's self-centered greed for power over others; or to enrich his search for peace and joy with creation as a whole.

To become all-knowing, to gain intellectual mastery of ourselves and our environment, is clearly the challenge of the New Age. New-found access to the source of universal knowledge has resulted in the springing forth of new ideas in all areas. At the level of matter we are aware of the imminent arrival of a 'brave new world' dominated by technological wizardry, an age of machines without regard for the soul yearnings of man.

Considered from another standpoint, however, the super-intelligence of Aquarius promises a far more exciting development. Here is the opportunity for man to use his heightened reasoning faculties to gain understanding of his spiritual nature, his reason for existence, and his relationship with his fellow men and with the rest of creation. Here is the chance to gain intellectual understanding of how division can be overcome, how peace on earth can come into being.

The key to the assimilation of this understanding resides in the fundamental principle of Aquarius which can best be described as interrelatedness or wholeness. New Age diet is directed towards whole foods. New Age medicine treats the whole person rather than the isolated symptoms. The human race thirsts for a knowledge that will bring understanding of the wholeness of creation, in terms of man in relation to both matter and spirit. By teaching us to develop a universal sense of at-oneness Aquarius holds forth the promise of a brotherhood of man, held together by unity and mutual respect.

In order that we may take our place in the Aquarian Era it is necessary for each of us to become attuned to the theme of wholeness. Basically this involves learning to play our own special role not so much for self-glorification as for the well-being of the common world we share. It is this task which represents the extraordinary and exciting goal of the New Age of Aquarius. And an important aid towards the mastery of this goal consists in the study and practice of astrology.

When Does It All Start?
If we're waiting for the New Age to begin, we may be in danger of missing the boat, for the fact is that this great new era is already dawning. It is difficult to define precisely the divisions of the Great Year and thus to pin-point accurately when Aquarius commences, but just as the Age of Pisces is considered to have started around 0 AD with the birth of its greatest personality Jesus Christ, so it is generally believed that the Age of Aquarius will date from about 2000 AD. Nevertheless, there is every indication that the initial stages of the New Age began as long as 200 years ago: the entering of a new era is a gradual process and the very first step towards Aquarius may have occurred in the year 1781.

1781 — The Crucial Turning Point
On its discovery in 1781 the planet Uranus, in its own characteristic way, shouted out loud and clear to mankind to *wake up!* To wake up from the state of stagnation which had come to pervade our spiritual attitudes and to be ready for some mighty big changes in consciousness. The sighting of the planet Uranus was, as it were, the bugle call to the Age of Aquarius, the sign of which it is the natural ruler.

It is only in retrospect that we can see the significance of the development; two further planets, Neptune and Pluto, needed to make their presence known before the true pattern of events could be understood. But even at that time, the upsetting of scientific and indeed astrological thinking caused by the sudden addition to the hitherto unquestioned set of seven planets was a tremendous stimulation to reassess ideas.

Later, following the discovery of Neptune in 1846 and Pluto in 1930 it became clear that something rather extraordinary had occurred. After thousands of years during which man had been aware of only seven planets, all at once, within the space of a short one hundred and fifty years, three further bodies had been spotted in the solar system. And in spite of their vast distance from the earth, astrological research soon indicated that these three new planets were associated with energies far more powerful than any previously acknowledged by astrologers. What is particularly interesting is that the intensity of their power increases in accordance with their order of appearance, so that the last discovered planet, Pluto, is related to the most powerful energy currently known to man.*

Of course there is no doubt that prior to their discovery the three outer planets existed, albeit hidden from our view, and doubtless they exerted some degree of influence upon our thoughts, feelings and actions. But with the dawning of the New Age, man was now in a position to assimilate these three planetary energies on a much wider scale and on a much deeper level than had been possible in the past. If one considers that physical manifestation only ever follows a previous spiritual awareness, one might say that man's sighting of Uranus, Neptune and Pluto in the form of matter was symbolic of his fuller consciousness of the energies represented by those planets. We couldn't perceive these planetary energies in concrete form until we were on the right wavelength. Just as a television set can only pick up a picture when it has been tuned to the correct frequency.

And so it is that the human race has begun to 'tune in' to the New Age. Relatively new urges have started to manifest in men: new modes of thinking, new forms of feeling, new styles of behaviour. In accordance with the mood of Aquarius, the motive power behind the new ambience is that of brotherhood, unity, holism. Division is intended to be left behind as an outmoded state of being which man is now to turn from. A process of coming together has begun,

---

* An additional body, Chiron, was discovered in 1977 between the orbits of Saturn and Uranus, but appears to be only a temporary visitor to our solar system rather than a permanent member thereof. Too little is as yet known about its characteristics to be able fully to assess its significance but as one of its associations may be with the process of giving birth and the adjustment this necessitates, its manifestation may well symbolize the challenge to mankind, in the last quarter of the twentieth century, to come finally to terms with the powerful energies of Uranus, Neptune and Pluto as the 'birth pangs' of the New Age reach a peak.

as a natural sequence to the phase of disunity which began long ago in the legendary Garden of Eden.

The Path of Return

Since its 'fall' the human race has been engaged upon a long and lonely journey away from its original union with the Source. Man's desire to partake of the Tree of Knowledge has led him along the isolated path of separation whereby he has developed his ego, his sense of individuality clothed in matter, and has delighted in the experience of functioning alone. But at the appropriate time he begins to feel the sorrow of disunity and is ready to set out on the return route to the oneness from whence he originated. In other words man finally becomes ready to absorb that knowledge in whose pursuit he long ago separated from the Source. This exciting path of return and the various aspects of new consciousness connected with it are represented by the vibrations of the three outer planets.

Uranus, as the higher vibration of Mercury, symbolizes man's spiritual intellect which allows him to understand the concept of oneness and the comparative insignificance of the ego. It may be considered as providing access to *universal truth* and is particularly connected with the New Age study of astrology.

Neptune, as the higher vibration of Venus, allows him to experience a sense of at-oneness with the rest of creation, and thus to transcend the ego by practices such as meditation and yoga. Neptune is the planet associated with *universal love* (rather than personal love) and *universal beauty*.

Finally Pluto, as the higher vibration of Mars, gives the potential for spiritualization of the basic life force which, when allowed to flow up through the chakras dedicated to the Light and unhindered by ego desires, has vast transformatory potential. Here is the symbol of *universal force*: the healing power which can change each one of us and eventually change the world. Here is the wrath of Mars used for a spiritual goal.

The energy of Pluto has manifested along positive lines in the comparatively recent upsurgence of psychic healing, just as the other two outer planets can be linked to a simultaneous new wave of interest in astrology, yoga and meditation. It would appear that an extraordinary outpouring of energy from the outer planets has been taking place since mankind became conscious, in every sense, of the correlated vibrations.

This influx of energy has been variously described as 'new consciousness', 'Christ consciousness', the 'manifestation of the Holy Spirit' or 'the Second Coming'. Some say that man is about to start to use the much neglected intuitional half of the brain to receive these different vibrations. But whatever their creed or denomination, many people are aware of an exciting new atmosphere in the world. Astrology, as an important spiritual science of the New Age, describes this new atmosphere in the non-sectarian terms of the cosmos. Its advantage consists in that the notion of planetary energies can be assimilated by anyone, from whatever religious or cultural background.

Astrology as an Intellectual Gateway to the New Age

Astrology represents a superb medium whereby to explain the remarkable happenings of recent years. The planets, grouped into three basic units, are symbolic of three different states of human consciousness.

The Sun, Moon, Mercury, Venus and Mars represent man's sense of ego or individuality, the level of consciousness which has ruled largely unchallenged prior to the dawning of the New Age. These first five planets focus attention on our uniqueness and our awareness of ourselves as separate entities. Taken purely by themselves, however, they reflect the loneliness and sense of isolation man feels when he is disunited from others.

The next two planets, travelling out from the Sun, symbolize the laws, both mundane and spiritual, which govern man's existence. At the worldly level Jupiter and Saturn represent man's morality or beliefs (Jupiter) and his life structure or civilization resulting from these (Saturn). But for the New Age these two law-related planets assume a new significance as representatives of universal rather than mundane law with which we must co-operate before we can truly move into the new.

Finally, Uranus, Neptune and Pluto may be considered as symbols of a new state of awareness available to all those who seek it as we enter the New Age. Now, with the new consciousness of these three outer planets, a glorious opportunity presents itself to mankind: the possibility of thinking, feeling and acting in unity with universal forces and thus in the interests of the whole; the chance to become master of its own fate.

The point to note is that the key to this new awareness is the intellect; it is through accurate understanding that we unlock the door to wholeness and peace. Astrology, geared as it is to Uranus and access to universal truth, is an important first stage towards assimilation of the new consciousness. With the detachment this study provides we can take a cool look at the changes taking place within us and in those around us. We gain the vital objectivity so necessary for a balanced outlook.

Astrology and the Edgar Cayce Readings

However, if we are to gain maximum benefit from our study of astrology for the New Age, we need to overcome some basic misunderstandings and to approach it along new lines. In particular, we need to clarify our comprehension of its working mechanism and its significance as a spiritual tool.

A New Age source which throws light on these questions is the work of the American psychic/prophet Edgar Cayce (1877–1945) whose life-work is collectively known as the Edgar Cayce Readings.* In a self-induced hypnotic trance, Cayce gave inspired teachings on a variety of subjects, including astrology, crucial to our understanding of the purpose of the Age of Aquarius and to the self-transformation we must effect if we are to play our part therein.

According to Cayce, our fundamental failing in our current approach to astrology is our tendency to imbue the planets with powers which they do not possess and to view man as a weak and helpless being whose fate is inexplicably ruled by the heavens. In this way we are prone to use astrology as an excuse to discharge responsibility for our thoughts or actions. Whatever befalls us, we can put it down to the stars! But Cayce's teachings suggest that this is far from the truth.

The most important point to emerge from the Readings is the idea that our destiny always rests in our own hands. Thus the birth chart is the way it is solely as a result of an individual's own doing. The 'native' must accept full responsibility for his horoscope and come to understand that it has been shaped entirely on the basis of his past actions during lives on earth lived previously to this one. In other words we have only ourselves to blame, or to thank!

The Solar System as a Spiritual School

Cayce thus implies that astrology is quite meaningless without an acceptance of reincarnation; he also goes on to extend the usual idea of reincarnation in a way that should make a great deal of sense to astrologers. He explains that the soul not only undergoes various experiences in a physical body but alternates time spent on earth with 'sojourns' in other dimensions of consciousness, the focal points of which are the planets. Thus it is not just the earth but the entire solar system which provides experience for the soul.

* The Edgar Cayce Readings are on file at the Edgar Cayce Foundation, PO Box 595, Virginia Beach, Virginia 23451, USA, an international organization established to research into and publicize the teachings of Edgar Cayce.

According to Cayce the solar system can be viewed as a vast spiritual school in which the vibrations associated with each of the planets provide instruction in the theory of a specific spiritual quality, while the earth itself constitutes the 'laboratory' or the place where such theoretical knowledge is put into practice.

This notion of the 'planetary sojourns' is closely allied to the idea of the 'halls of learning' referred to in Spiritualist teachings and writings.*

Cayce sums up the cycle of experience in the solar system rather as follows. After a life on earth during which certain actions will have been committed, certain emotions expressed and certain attitudes of mind held, the soul, on leaving the body, has a period of time in which to review its recent life. On the basis of this review it will be attracted to the specific planetary vibrations it needs to assimilate in order that its further needs can best be met. A number of dimensions of consciousness, as symbolized by the planets, may need to be visited before the next return to earth and indeed all the planetary vibrations will be assimilated at some time or other. On our return to earth, the extent to which we embody that which we have imbibed between lives will differ in accordance with our ability or willingness as 'students'.

On this basis the birth chart may be considered as a record of the soul's study programme in the spiritual school represented by the solar system. The arrangement of the planets in our horoscope would seem to indicate the spiritual lessons which we have studied between lives in response to past-life behaviour patterns and which we are now to put into practice. Thus planets in various positions will not *make* us this way or that, but simply reflect the purpose of our coming life. If we accept Cayce's ideas there can be no question of passing the buck. We must accept responsibility for our destiny.

The Question of Free Will

In the light of the Readings there can be no doubt concerning the existence of our free will. And it is a sad fact that while astrologers continue to disregard or rather fail to stress man's freedom of choice and persist in the notion that the stars rule us or compel us to behave in a certain way, they will never derive true benefit from their study. It is essential to move away from the idea that the planets represent some sinister governing force beyond our comprehension or control. Indeed Cayce explains that the planets, and in fact the entire solar system, were created specifically for man's use. According to Reading

---

* See Maurice Barbanell, *This is Spiritualism* (Tandem, 1967).

No. 5757-1, '. . . the sun, the moon, the planets — have their marching orders from the divine . . .' and the function of the solar system is to provide a unified field of learning for mankind. The master Jesus is cited as an example of one who had successfully completed the course of study.

In astrological circles Cayce may become best known for his controversial statement that far from the stars ruling us, we actually rule them! The Readings insist that the power of the soul is such that mankind's activity for good or bad can in fact produce changes in the universe. Sun spots are but one example of this phenomenon and indicate how defects in man's character are manifesting as flaws in the sun — the source of his vital energy. The intricacies of how this process works may be explained by considering the endocrine gland system which represents a transmitter/receiver system for planetary energies and which not only picks up vibrations but itself emits energy of a like nature. Acceptance of this fact can help mankind to realize the immense potential of its power and is interesting when considered in connection with Cayce's predictions regarding the forthcoming earth changes which will reflect man's changing consciousness at the advent of the New Age.

Free Will versus Karma

Free will is one of the most important issues to be raised in the Readings, which constantly stress that '. . . the will must be the ever guiding factor to lead man on, ever upward' (Reading No. 3744-3). The growth of peace in the world is dependent upon each person's realization that there is no limit to the heights he or she can reach; each of us has the capacity to become totally peaceful if we so desire. Astrology is a tool which can reinforce this realization but which conversely very often denies the notion of free will by suggesting that man's fate is controlled by the stars. The reason for this misconception may well be the confusion between the role of the planets in a soul's development and the vital issue of *karma*.

The notions of reincarnation and karma have long been accepted and understood in the East, but only recently are they starting to be taken seriously by Westerners. In fact one of Cayce's greatest services to Western society as a New Age teacher of holistic philosophy was to place the idea of karma — the theory that every action results in a reaction of a nature similar to itself — within the context of Christianity and indeed within the scope of astrology. He pointed to the many references to karma in the Bible such as 'he that leadeth into captivity shall go into captivity, he that killeth with the sword must be killed with the sword' (Revelation 13:10), and suggested that original Christian doctrine did in fact embrace karma. Similarly he put the record straight regarding the relationship between astrology and karma: both are valid, being irrevocably interlinked with one another.

According to the Readings karma is something that happens exclusively in the earth plane — in the laboratory of the solar system 'school'. Karma stands for action and reaction which can occur only in the realm of matter, i.e. the earth, so any deeds committed in our three-dimensional world must bear their reaction here also. Thus karma cannot be actually redeemed during 'planetary sojourns', the function of which is simply to build up strength and learn new techniques which can be put into practice when we return to the earth plane to 'face the music' of our past. Gina Cerminara, author of *Many Mansions*, a commentary on Cayce's teachings on karma, gives the analogy of a game of tennis: if we must leave the court (i.e. the earth) having reached a certain state of play with our opponent, no matter what we do or where we go in the meantime, when we finally resume the game (i.e. reincarnate) the score will remain exactly the same. We may well have read up on new techniques or taken a little coaching but the state of play on court (the earth) remains unaltered and must eventually be continued.

Thus karma is an immutable law to which each one of us is subject. As we have sown, so shall we reap. In this respect our lives are in fact 'fated', but certainly not by the intervention of any outside source, be this God, the Devil, or the heavenly bodies! The Readings stress repeatedly that we ourselves have created our present destiny on the basis of past-life actions, emotions and attitudes of mind. We can't shift the blame — we are responsible for ourselves. In this sense our experiences on earth are indeed predestined by virtue of our own past behaviour.

Given the irrevocability of our karma, the planets should be seen as sources of knowledge and wisdom which will help us to put matters to right. After all, Cayce specifically states that the planets exist solely for our benefit and are part and parcel of our path towards spiritual perfection.

When considered in depth, Cayce's teachings open up the vast and wonderful potential of the human soul. Although subject to spiritual law, the soul enjoys almost unlimited freedom of choice in terms of its growth and development:

1.   The soul enjoys freedom to choose which planetary dimensions of consciousness it will visit following an earthly incarnation in order to absorb knowledge for 'resumption of play'.

2. The soul may choose to what extent, if any, it will learn between lives.

3. And — of the greatest importance — it is also possible to choose to what extent we will put this learning to good use when we return to the earth plane. *Thus we have free will in respect of how we will meet our karma.* We may have no choice in that we must face what is due to us, but our reaction to that fate is vital. The mode of our reaction will be shaped by the wisdom gained from our 'planetary sojourns', and will itself govern (a) our future karma and (b) the spiritual curriculum to be studied during the next series of 'sojourns'.

The Timing of Transits

The question of transits is closely bound up with our misunderstanding of the role played by the planets. It soon becomes plain to any student of astrology that crisis points in one's life indisputably coincide with the movements of the planets to critical positions in the birth chart. Not surprisingly, until recently the obvious conclusion was to assume that the planets themselves were responsible for the dire consequences that often came to pass. Nowadays astrologers are for the main part hesitant to adopt this outlook, if only due to fear of the scathing comments of scientists.

The truth may well be that transits as such do not bring about events in a person's life but merely coincide with karma which had anyhow to be met. It seems that this coincidence between the timing of karma and transits exists in order that the part of man which is attuned to the vibrations of the planets* may react to the energy of the transiting planet and be put in mind of the necessary quality or knowledge needed to face the karma. It would appear, however, that we are able to react to the movement of a planet only because we have already familiarized ourselves with its vibration during a 'sojourn'. The energy we pick up from a transiting planet can be compared to the revision notes we hurriedly glance at prior to the actual test (karma). We will react to the transit to a greater or lesser degree and in a more or less positive fashion according to our experience of the 'planetary sojourn'.

The occasions when transiting planets form angles with natal planets would seem to represent the 'examination dates' when our practical tests have to be sat, and these are the opportunities for the soul to translate into three-dimensional action that which it has absorbed during its experiences between lives.

* Cayce stated that each of the endocrine glands represents a focal point for one of the planetary energies.

Astrology Must Not Become Our Scapegoat

Thus we see that the current tendency to define astrology as a
'correlation' between the positions of the planets and the destiny
of mankind would appear to be valid. This notwithstanding, a
fundamental change of attitude towards astrology is undoubtedly
needed. Firstly it is essential that we should accept responsibility
both for the condition of our birth chart and the circumstances of
our life. It is only too easy to blame the planets for a situation which
in reality is a karmic challenge of our own making.

In addition, if we are to achieve a positive approach to astrology
it is important that we see the planets as friends rather than as
potential bringers of doom. In particular, we should realize that our
birth chart does not 'make' us good or bad, joyful or wretched. We
ourselves are responsible for our present condition; the positions of
the planets in our horoscope merely indicate the means whereby
we can improve our state of being if we so choose.

As yet traditional astrology in no way recognizes this point, in
that one of its most basic features is to imply that human misfortune
or human failing observed to be associated with a particular planet
result from the misfunctioning or misuse of the planet — rather
than from the misfunctioning of the human being himself or herself.
Because of our general tendency to look for a scapegoat there has
somehow been the implication that the planet is responsible for our
misdemeanours.

The view presented in this book is that the vibrations of the planets
should be considered to be essentially uplifting, in that the entire
solar system represents a school of spiritual study for the benefit of
mankind. Let us look upon the planetary energies as positive in
nature; whether or not we avail ourselves of that positivity depends
upon our own motivation. That which is negative in our experience
or behaviour may be considered to result not so much from the
influence of a planet as from our own karmic inheritance.

The 'planetary sojourns' provide us with opportunities to acquire
positive qualities which we have shown the need to develop. But
whether we will take advantage of these opportunities and will put
our learning into practice during an incarnation, or whether we will
simply repeat the old patterns which actually led to the 'sojourn'
in the first place is not something that can be discovered from the
birth chart. All we can glean from the planetary positions in our
horoscope is that we have created specific forms of karma in specific
areas of life — that these have led to experiences in the dimensions
of consciousness represented by the related planets — and that these
experiences have provided us with the potential to put matters right.

Probably the greatest unknown factor in astrology is whether an individual is responding to the corrective influence of his between-life experiences or is stubbornly re-enacting old earthly behaviour patterns.

The True Potential of Astrology

In summary let us accept that we are here on the earth to meet our karma — the results, both good and bad, of our own past actions. This we do with the help of planetary learning, gained for the main part prior to this incarnation, but also to some extent at the times of transits, those 'revision notes' which provide us with a helpful energy boost.

Let us also be aware that at this very special time in history we have before us the opportunity to implement boundless self-change if we so desire. The New Age offers the potential for attunement to universal law (Jupiter and Saturn) and to the source of universal truth, love and force (Uranus, Neptune and Pluto) and thus the rejection of that isolation which has represented the root cause of our karmic suffering. As we work with the powerful healing energies symbolized by the outer planets we have the chance not only to clear past debts with greater strength and understanding but also to avoid future negative karma. For when we are attuned to universal energies, there is no longer the experience of personal suffering, there is no longer the experience of painful karma.

The challenge consists in the moderation of ego. Not, let it be stressed, the dissolution of self, but a truly Aquarian acceptance of one's own role as an equal part within the whole.

In order to use astrology as a tool that can help up towards this goal, we can approach our studies in two stages. Firstly, by assessing the arrangement of the planets in our chart we can recognize and accept the physical, emotional and mental dis-ease which represents our negative karma. Secondly, by aligning ourselves with the outer planetary energies we can take steps to change the karmic patterns which have resulted in this dis-ease. In so doing not only do we achieve greater peace in ourselves but we also make our own contribution to world peace. And of course we also minimize our liability to further 'hard' karma.

The first part of the book will analyse the significance of each of the planetary energies together with their associated signs and houses. We shall begin by considering the personal planets, those urges and drives which constitute our individuality. We shall also be considering the sorrows created by the personal planetary energies; sorrows which occur when a personal drive becomes over-emphasized; sorrows which are overcome when a personal drive is uplifted by universal energies.

This will be followed by an analysis of the important role to be played by Jupiter and Saturn in the New Age as the guardians of universal law, and a study of Uranus, Neptune and Pluto, the three planets which represent our passport to the transcendence of self, to at-oneness, to peace.

In the second half of the book, by taking a penetrating look at the various ways in which personal planets can combine in our chart with non-personal planets, we shall reflect on how best we can bring our 'selves' into alignment with universal energies. Links in our chart between the personal planets on the one hand and Jupiter, Saturn, Uranus, Neptune and Pluto on the other hand spell out the major karmic challenges with which we are faced in this lifetime. We shall seriously assess the choices before us: to go *with* the powerful and uplifting vibrations of the New Age or to struggle blindly against them, trapped in our old karmic conditioning.

Finally, by considering the link between astrology, meditation and healing, we shall consider practical methods of implementing self-change.

2.
THE INNER PLANETS:
SYMBOLS OF PERSONAL ENERGY

The notion of unselfishness is often misunderstood as an annihilation of self, a disintegration into nothingness, but this is not the purpose of New Age transformation.

The fact is that each soul entity is essentially indestructible: the soul may be considered as an eternal spark of life which possesses, inherent in itself, a unique individuality by which it is distinguished from every other soul. We should indeed be proud of our own uniqueness; we each have our own special role to play which no one else can undertake for us and which we are eternally assigned.

As we enter the New Age, our goal is to retain or more particularly to enhance our own special qualities, but to express them in a way which takes into account the well-being of the whole.

The function of astrology is to throw light on the personality traits which make us the unique human beings that we are, and to indicate ways in which we may transform those personality traits so as to achieve a greater sense of at-oneness with others.

The three outer planets — Uranus, Neptune and Pluto — represent the powerful New Age energies which are currently challenging so many of us to adopt new attitudes of mind, of heart and of action as we learn to overcome the barriers which separate us from others at each of these three levels.

The influence of Jupiter and Saturn is to instil us with a sense of universal law and order whereby we can find the faith and the self-discipline to embark on the vast personal changes which the outer planets involve.

In contrast, the five inner planets — Sun, Moon, Mercury, Venus and Mars — together with the Ascendant and Midheaven — represent the crux of our individuality, our ego, or what makes us 'ourselves', and as such deserve very careful attention.

The word *ego* today carries derogatory connotations implying an unhealthy absorption with one's own importance. But to know oneself to be oneself, apart and unique from the rest of creation, has represented the entire rhyme and reason for mankind's descent into the world of matter and has motivated much of our experience up until the present time. Problems have arisen simply because we have got our sense of self-importance out of proportion. Individuals, groups and nations have become totally absorbed with themselves to the point of alienation from others. Instead of giving emphasis to our 'selfhood', we must now learn to look beyond it.

The ego may be considered to be the physical manifestation of that which we term our soul, i.e. the spark of eternal energy which carries within it the seeds of all our potential self-expression. And in terms of that physical manifestation of our soul, we may differentiate between five separate ego functions which we refer to as the Sun, Moon, Mercury, Venus and Mars.

The Sun and Mars have been traditionally termed 'male' in respect of their characteristics, standing as they do for recognition from the outside world and the assertion of our physical strength. Likewise, the tendency of the Moon energy to nurture and care for others and that of Venus to create harmony and provide sensual satisfaction has led to these two planets being labelled 'feminine'. In contrast, the function of Mercury to reason and communicate has been placed beyond sex classification and presumably considered common to both men and women!

However, before we readily accept these gender labels, it is necessary to acknowledge that it is rare to encounter a man who is wholly male or a woman who is totally female: the majority of us embody the sort of sexuality which comprises both male *and* female drives. It is the balance between these drives which determines the extent to which a man is noticeably masculine or a woman is visibly feminine. The scientists will explain this as a question of male and female hormone balance.

A vital facet of New Age thinking is to go beyond the notion of maleness and femaleness. Sexual labelling results in limitation and segregation — 'us and them' attitudes which can never engender the sort of togetherness and at-oneness upon which Aquarius must be based. Losing our awareness of each other simply as 'men' or 'women' allows us to see each other primarily as spiritual beings who for this lifetime may have incarnated as a man or as a woman but whose eternal identity is sexless.

Let us bear in mind that our sexual identities are never cut and dried. Each of us must acknowledge and provide an outlet for both our masculine and our feminine urges. As souls, we have played and will continue to play sometimes male, sometimes female roles, so that in assessing their 'ego', men and women alike must take into account all five of the personal planets.

For the New Age the challenge for each of us is to get into proportion our sense of ego — as represented by the personal planetary energies. For so long we have been quite simply 'full of ourselves' to the exclusion of a sense of unity with others. Now is the time not to destroy but gently to adjust the functioning of our Sun, Moon, Mercury, Venus and Mars drives. Our aim is not to denigrate the self but to elevate these five planetary expressions of our individuality. As to how this can be achieved, we must look for links between the five personal planetary energies (Sun, Moon, Mercury, Venus and Mars and associated signs and houses) and either the law-and-order planets (Jupiter and Saturn and associated signs and houses) or the outer planets (Uranus, Neptune and Pluto and associated signs and houses).

'Links' are to be understood primarily as a personal planet forming an aspect with Jupiter or Saturn or with Uranus, Neptune or Pluto; secondly as Jupiter or Saturn, or Uranus, Neptune or Pluto, falling in a house or sign ruled by a personal planet; thirdly, and of lesser importance, as a personal planet falling in a sign or house ruled by Jupiter or Saturn, or by Uranus, Neptune or Pluto. Part Two of this book will focus on the specific challenges we face in terms of these planetary interrelationships as highlighted in our birth chart.

The following descriptions of the personal planets and the signs and houses which they rule should clarify the nature of these five vitally important facets of our ego. However, our interest in the personal planets is mainly in the manner in which they may be transformed by association with more powerful outer energies. It is by virtue of such associations that we as individuals may learn to free ourselves from karmic suffering — the outcome of over-emphasis on the inner planets — and take up our rightful heritage of unity, peace and joy.

The Sun — Leo — The Fifth House:
The urge for recognition of one's personal worth

The Sun
Although all five of the personal planets each constitute facets of our individuality, the Sun is most representative of our ego in the generally understood sense of the word. The Sun stands for our urge to express our true selves, the real 'us' as opposed to the mask or outer personality represented by the Ascendant. The Sun is therefore our desire to establish our identity as an individual, our need to show who and what we are, and to make our own special mark on the

world. In the symbol of the Sun, the dot at the centre of the circle indicates the seed of our unique individual expression.

The need to feel that we, as individuals, are of some essential worth is vital to survival. Without a sense that we are needed and that we have something to contribute to life, the will to live simply disappears. We all need to feel that we are valued in some way or other, and this is the urge symbolized by the Sun.

The development of our sense of self-worth is vitally dependent upon recognition. Without applause from the outside world, we have no yardstick whereby to gauge our potential. We need this positive feedback from others in order to build a healthy self-image.

When the Sun principle is over-emphasized, however, we risk overplaying our desire for self-esteem. In this case our ego needs can develop out of all proportion, to the point that we can hardly function without constant reassurance and acknowledgement. As a result we may become so obsessed with our personal image that self-pride is truly our Achilles Heel. The location of the Sun in our chart can throw light on possible tendencies towards excessive self-absorption which could prove detrimental to our general well-being.

In contrast, when the Sun is manifesting in a balanced way, the question of recognition will not be of paramount importance. Thus the qualities of the self will be given generously for the sheer joy of self-expression, regardless of whether acknowledgement from the outside world is received or not. In addition there will be the ability to recognize and praise the individual talents of others; at its highest level the Sun is a great cheer-leader.

The need to be recognized as an individual of some worth is essentially masculine in nature since by tradition it has been the male sex who have enjoyed the greatest opportunity to go out into the world and receive acknowledgement of their intrinsic qualities, whatever these may have been. For this reason, in a woman's chart the Sun has traditionally stood for the male partner. Until the emancipation of women, females had little opportunity to express their Sun urge in their own right and therefore would frequently subconsciously attract towards themselves a partner who embodied the characteristics, for good and for bad, of their own Sun placing. Although this is still the case to some extent, nowadays with the New Age appreciation of the *whole* person as a complex embodiment of both masculine and feminine drives, many women are beginning to use their Sun drive in their own right. As a result of their new-found self-expression they are less likely to become unwitting victims of their own ego hang-ups through the behaviour and lifestyles of their menfolk.

For men and women alike the Sun is considered as representative of our father and the significance of our relationship with him in learning to develop our own self-expressive urge. His influence, for good or bad, serves to shape our own self-image. The location of the Sun in our chart can thus mirror the quality of our relationship with our father and the challenges it may have presented.

In more general terms, the placement of the Sun in our birth chart in terms of sign, house and aspects will indicate the areas where we need to experience a sense of self-worth and where it is important to us to gain positive feedback. However, these are also the areas in which we must guard against excessive self-pride, over-dependency on recognition, and the negative psychological processes which can accompany such tendencies.

The Sign Leo

In accordance with its ruler the Sun, the sign Leo expresses itself with a need for recognition, and most notably so when the Sun or Mars falls in Leo. Whatever its environment, Leo needs to feel appreciated if it is to develop any sense of self-worth. It is also important to note that Leo can express itself with the ability to give recognition to others, and it is this capacity to give praise and encouragement that makes Leo such an inspiring leader. When over-developed the Leo need for recognition can involve an insatiable quest for acclaim and ostentatious behaviour in the pursuit thereof.

Especially when the Moon falls in Leo self-pride is pronounced although this need not represent a problem since the root of the word 'proud' means 'to be of value'. To be proud of onself is to be aware of one's worth as an individual, which after all sums up the essence of Leo. However, a negative facet of the Leo temperament is that it can develop conceit, implying an over-inflated sense of its own worth. In that case it will also be unhealthily dependent on applause, susceptible to attack by blows to its pride, and a foolish victim to those who prey on its vanity.

The Leo intellect operates with a need to make its mark on the world. In particular when Mercury falls in Leo, the mind can operate with great creativity in the pursuit of recognition. Speech and writing are likely to be exceptionally self-expressive and whatever the situation there is a remarkable talent to delight the audience. On the other hand there is a very real danger of allowing the need for acclaim to influence the quality and integrity of one's communicative faculties.

Relationships are of vital importance to Leo since it is only through others that it can build up a positive picture of itself. Consequently, and most particularly when Venus falls in Leo, a loving, reassuring partner can provide immense fulfilment to this sign, whereas a failed relationship is quite simply a blow to the pride and the self-confidence. Problems occur when Leo becomes unable to function within a relationship without continuous ego bolstering.

The Fifth House
The Fifth House rules our self-expression and all activities which give opportunity for recognition, such as:

— the performing arts, which represent an obvious source of applause and positive feedback;
— sports and games, another important means of earning applause and playing to an audience;
— love affairs, which bring the admiration and flattery of the beloved and thus boost our sense of self-worth;
— children — for many of us procreation is the most obvious form of self-expression in terms of leaving our own special stamp on the world and indeed many of us live out our own urge for self-expression solely through our children's lives; in addition children are a natural source of feedback, at least while they are young, providing the sort of admiring love which makes us feel we are 'special'.

The Moon — Cancer — The Fourth House:
The urge to feel emotionally secure

The Moon
In contrast to the traditionally masculine urge for self-expression represented by the Sun, Leo and the Fifth House, the Moon stands for a more feminine, gentle aspect of our make-up. This is the desire for emotional security, the desire to feel serene, to feel safe, and to feel protected from pain or harm. The Moon symbolizes a need which is present in both sexes, although traditionally men have been encouraged to disregard the feeling side of their character. Whatever our sex, the Moon will indicate the form of our emotional needs and the sort of activities and lifestyle which will enable us to meet these needs most satisfactorily. The location of our Moon will also highlight any stress we may suffer due to lack of emotional fulfilment.
    Tranquillity of mind is perhaps the most essential key to the general well-being of our body and soul. Increasingly there is the realization within orthodox medicine that all forms of disease originate from dis-ease of the mind, a fact which has long been acknowledged by

practitioners of alternative medicine. For this reason the Moon is of importance in the birth chart by virtue of the clues it gives us as to how we may stabilize our emotions.

For most women the problem is that of over-emphasis of the Moon principle, leading them to experience excessive and unreasonable emotional insecurity and anxiety in their lives. The situation is different for the male sex, however. Having been traditionally urged to repress their emotions, most men do not so much over-emphasize the Moon function as ignore it entirely and for them the challenge is to learn to accept responsibility for their feelings as a vital facet of their expression as a whole being. Unless they are able to do so, they are likely to meet continuously with females who embody their own unconscious feeling nature, including their unrecognized emotional hang-ups.

Not only does the Moon represent our need to feel secure in ourselves, but it is also associated with the urge to fulfil others' emotional needs. However, unless we are ourselves reasonably self-secure, we will find it difficult to care genuinely for others. Where our own emotions are unstable, mothering becomes little more than an exercise whereby we bolster our own emotional needs. Smother-love reflects an attempt to obtain from those in our charge the emotional fulfilment we have been unable to achieve of our own accord; and all too often it can degenerate into a degree of over-concern and possessiveness which will ultimately alienate those we love and further deplete our own security.

Representing as it does the urge for emotional security and the urge to nurture, it is natural that the Moon should also symbolize that person in our life who provides us with our very first emotional comfort — our mother. The location of the Moon in our chart by sign, house and aspect can throw light on the nature of our relationship with our mother and any challenges it may have presented. It is through our contact with her that we learn to modify and refine our own emotions. Because of the law of karma, the nature and quality of the maternal care we receive as a child is directly related to the state of being of our own Moon and thus to the way in which we have expressed the nurturing urge in past lives.

In general terms, the placing of the Moon in our birth chart by sign, house and aspect will highlight our emotional needs and the factors which may influence our emotional security. In so doing it will point to possible sources of psychological stress which may result from insufficient emotional expression or excessive preoccupation with our emotional needs. At the same time the Moon's placement will underline any lack of balance in our urge to nurture others and can help us to learn to care more lovingly for our dependants.

The Sign Cancer

In accordance with its ruler the Moon, the sign Cancer expresses itself in a need to experience and provide emotional security, primarily for itself, but also for others.

Especially when the Sun or Mars falls in Cancer, effort will be given to building up a secure home base and family life; the larger the family the greater the sense of 'belonging' — hence the Cancerian clannishness, interest in ancestry, etc. In some cases Cancer restricts itself to caring for itself and its family members, but in others there can be the desire to 'mother' the world at large through occupations such as nursing, community care, social work, work with children or in the catering profession. But however it expresses itself, difficulties can arise for Cancer when it becomes over-dependent upon being needed by others.

Cancer very much *feels* its way through life and in particular when the Moon falls in Cancer this sign experiences a real concern for its own emotional well-being and that of others. It goes without saying that this sort of temperament will be worrisome, especially when faced with a threat to its stability. It is also likely to be extremely sensitive to the condition of others within its 'unit' and fret about the happiness of those close to it. Here Cancer must keep a careful check on its emotions since when over-developed this sign can easily turn into a neurotic worrier.

The Cancer mind operates not on the basis of reason but rather of feeling. Especially when Mercury falls in Cancer the intellect effects an emotional rather than a logical analysis of any situation and the memory will tend to recall sentiment rather than cool facts and figures. Since it is highly tuned to the emotional functioning of self and others, at best it will tend to assess the emotional impact an idea will produce in others and will generally take into account how the other person might react. But at worst it will be hypersensitive to criticism, whether meant or otherwise.

In relationships, and most noticeably when Venus falls in this sign, Cancer will both give and expect mutual caring support, an invaluable basis for love provided the Cancer function isn't over-exerted, in which case mother-love degenerates into the proverbial smother-love, and relationships are used exclusively as a means of gaining rather than giving security.

The Fourth House

The Fourth House represents the place of our emotional security, in other words the home. This is to be considered primarily as the early childhood home since this is where our future sense of emotional security is moulded. The Fourth House is indicative of the parental influence, as the 'feel' of home is what our parents make it for us, and here we're concerned only with the atmosphere rather than the bricks and mortar. Later in life this house will represent our self-made home — usually the place where we feel safest from the big bad world. It also symbolizes our ability to nurture, comfort, and care for others' emotional needs.

Mercury — Gemini — The Third House: The urge to reason and communicate

Mercury
Mercury is the only one of the personal planets which has escaped labelling as traditionally 'male' or 'female'. It stands for a drive which all of us can readily identify with; indeed in this day and age logic and reasoning enjoy a disproportionate status in relation to the other personal urges.

Mercury represents our brain and its agent the nervous system. The brain is often referred to as our personal computer, and this is an excellent way of describing the Mercury function. To be precise, however, we should add that Mercury rules only one half of the brain — the part concerned with logical rather than intuitional activities as in itself Mercury is bereft of sensitivity.

The Mercury process consists of the input of information, the classification thereof in specific categories, the comparison of newly input data with already stored facts, and the output of an appropriate response on the basis thereof.

If the brain is our computer, the nervous system can be considered as the unit of communication lines linked to various parts of the body via which input data is fed to the brain and along which the responses of the brain are output to the outside world. Thus the eyes, ears, mouth and limbs are all associated with the Mercury function.

Apart from the Moon, Mercury is the most continuously used of the individual planetary functions since the brain must constantly analyse perceptions. The speed at which Mercury operates is quite phenomenal and again can be compared with that of an electronic memory bank.

Despite the impressiveness of its skill, Mercury is a dull fellow considered by itself, and just as social dependency upon computer technology could result in a lifeless and stereotyped existence for us all, so over-emphasis on Mercury can result in a robot-like individual, void of all imagination, feeling or compassion.

The pre-eminence of science (derived from *scire* = to know (Mercury)) is a reflection of our preoccupation with pure Mercury and our disregard for its higher vibration Uranus. The lack of acceptance in the scientific world of any idea which cannot be proved by a logical process — including astrology — is a sad testimony to the God-like status which Mercury currently enjoys. In actual fact this function will not return to playing a more balanced role until it is uplifted by the outer planetary energies.

In the same way that Mercury represents our thinking function, so also it symbolizes our urge to communicate, mainly by speech and writing but also through body language. It will also describe the characteristics of the nervous system as a whole.

Thus the position of the planet Mercury in our birth chart will highlight our potential mental abilities and the ease with which we are able to communicate with others. Equally this planet points to any difficulties we may experience in terms of our capacity to think clearly and logically, or as regards our capacity to express ourselves verbally to others either through the written or the spoken word.

As with other facets of ourselves we are often unaware of the impact our ideas or our speech have on other people, imagining that our communication problems originate from others' inadequacies rather than our own. The birth chart cuts through this blind spot and provides a clear-cut analysis of the sort of mind we possess and the way we pass on our thoughts to others. By becoming aware of the positive and negative manifestations of our particular Mercury placement we can do much to improve our thinking and communicating skills.

The Sign Gemini

In accordance with its ruler Mercury, the sign Gemini expresses itself with reason and with a desire to communicate. Thus considerable time and attention will be devoted to learning, although not necessarily of the academic variety, and to passing on information to others either formally in the sphere of teaching or informally at a social level. Like a fast computer, the sign measures its efficiency by the quantity and speed of its accomplishment. Accuracy is also important, but quality or depth of research is not a prerequisite: hence this sign's tendency to have many irons in the fire. At its best Gemini has the capacity to function as a one man/woman data centre, adept at both the input and output of information, and in particular when the Sun or Mars falls in Gemini can experience greatest personal fulfilment in work in teaching, writing or the media, in secretarial, clerical or reception work, or in telecommunications, advertising or selling for example. But at its worst it is a jack of all trades and master of none, a dabbler who is never able to complete anything it starts and consequently experiences a perpetual state of frustration.

In particular when the Moon falls in this sign, Gemini tends to be free from random outbursts or unexplained moods and can usually be relied upon to take a reasonable attitude to any situation. As they do, so they expect to be done by and the cool analytical disposition of this sign is often puzzled and disturbed by less logical reactions on the part of others. Conversely, more sensitive types can find it hard to cope with the infuriatingly 'sensible' outlook and seeming heartlessness of Gemini.

Because of the computer-style speed of this sign's reactions it's invariably a jump ahead of its companions, and boredom is usually a challenge to be dealt with. But even more of a problem is the fact that Gemini is often unable to switch off its rapid thought processes at will. When the intellect becomes over-emphasized it never knows when to stop and insomnia, tension and nerve problems are the likely outcome.

The Gemini intellect operates solely by reasoning. Thus, and most noticeably when Mercury falls in Gemini, any impression will be very rapidly evaluated in relation to existing information stored in the computer (brain). The function of this sign is to gather as much information from as many sources as possible and, following processing, to output the conclusions through the greatest possible number of channels. Speech is fast and clear-cut and there is the ability to make high-speed comparisons and interconnections between ideas, hence 'wit' (derived from Latin *videre* = to see (the connection)). But when this sign is overplayed there is no provision for any form of emotional reaction or intuitional response, which actually limits its social skills despite its inherent talent for communication.

Gemini conducts its relationships at a mental level. Generally when Venus falls in Gemini the motivation behind contact with others is the exchange of ideas and opinions and this provides the basis of every form of relationship — even of a romantic nature. As always the emphasis is on quantity rather than quality, which necessitates a sufficient number of contacts to fulfil the mental craving. However, those who criticize this sign as flirtatious imply a sexual motivation which does not exist in the pure Gemini function. Indeed a major Gemini shortcoming is an overly matter-of-fact approach to relationships in which logic is allowed to assume undue importance at the expense of passion.

The Third House

The Third House rules activities which involve:

— reasoning — the general functioning of the mind and also elementary education, i.e. the ability to grasp facts; note that the nature of Mercury means that the type of mental activities ruled by the Third House will not relate to deep thought or study, these coming under the rulership of the Ninth House;
— communication — writing, teaching, lecturing, media work, selling, clerical and secretarial work, telecommunications, short journeys (whereby contact is rapidly achieved); also the general nature of our speech.

Virgo and the Sixth House:
The urge for purity

Although Virgo is currently considered to be linked to Mercury, which thus assumes responsibility for the rulership of two signs, this is an unsatisfactory state of affairs and worthy of some comment.

At the moment, whereas we have the tradition of twelve Zodiac signs, we are aware of the existence of only ten planets. Virgo is one of the unhappy misfits having to make do with a planetary energy which does not suit its character in full.

The same situation applied in the past with regard to the signs Scorpio, Pisces and Aquarius which were considered to be ruled by Mars, Jupiter and Saturn respectively until their true rulers manifested at the material and at the spiritual level.* A planet will not be 'discovered' until human consciousness is ready to assimilate the energy connected therewith; similarly a sign cannot be seen in the full light of its potential until that shift in awareness takes place. Until that occurs, the sign in question is likely to be undervalued by a society that lacks the vision to see its true worth.

If one considers the example of Scorpio, only gradually since the discovery of Pluto has this sign really come into its own, and it is only now that it is starting to receive the respect it truly deserves. Nevertheless, it still suffers something of an 'evil' reputation and has not yet become a popular member of the Zodiac.

The same applies to an even greater extent as regards Virgo, the very last sign anyone wishes to confess to, or so it would seem. The

---

* The stance taken in this book is that Pluto, Neptune and Uranus are the sole rulers of the signs Scorpio, Pisces and Aquarius respectively; however, some astrologers believe that these signs are now co-ruled by their respective new rulers and traditional rulers.

reason for this bad name could be that our consciousness is not yet tuned to the point at which it can appreciate the qualities of the sign. It is the old story: when we don't understand we condemn.

The essence of Virgo is *purity*, a state of being from which we are so removed that it is small wonder we cannot accept it. Purity of thought, and in turn of all form, could only be achieved by virtue of a vast transformation in our attitudes and behaviour. We are talking about changes greater than any on record, changes that cannot occur until mankind has brought itself into alignment with universal will. Surely this sort of transformation could only take place in the wake of the activity of Pluto.

It could be that the Virgo planet is located outside the orbit of Pluto and will make itself felt, in all senses of the word, at the appropriate time in history. On the other hand, the asteroids, situated between Mars and Jupiter at a point where a planet should lie according to Bode's Law,* are believed by some to be connected with Virgo. If these asteroids are indeed the disintegrated remains of an ancient heavenly body, then they could well stand for a personal planetary energy which was once but is no longer part of man's nature. Could it be that when this planet was whole, purity of matter did once prevail on the earth plane? Was there once a time when there was no disease or decay either of our physical bodies or within nature? Is it possible that the break-up of this planet coincided with man's spiritual fall and an associated corruption of matter?

The notion of purity forms the foundation for the basic Virgoan qualities of discrimination and criticism which are directly related to a respect for perfection — we can't judge quality unless we can compare it with that which is flawless. Also fundamental to Virgo is a keen interest in wholesomeness of diet and a healthy state of body — and in some cases an urge towards celibacy — traits which can likewise be considered as reflections of an inherent desire for purity. Virgo is further associated with the urge to accomplish practical tasks to a high standard of efficiency, and is considered to 'rule' techniques and crafts which call for an eye for detail. The diligence and accuracy it demands of itself in work of all types likewise stem from the essential perfectionism of the sign.

It seems unlikely, however, that Virgo will manifest its full potential until the notion of purity is thoroughly understood. The greatest issue is that of *gauging* purity. What is to represent the flawless yardstick whereby the Virgo discriminatory powers can operate? For

* Bode's Law postulated that the positions of the planets in the solar system correspond to a regular progression of their respective distances from the Sun.

many at this time our *own* standards are often taken as the ultimate degree of perfection; when Virgo says 'this isn't good enough', the big question is good enough in relation to what or whom?

Whatever our beliefs, it is well to accept that the desire for purity is a great deal more than a discontent with minor details of matter. It is not a question of nit-picking over trivial inadequacies in the world around us as is often the custom of Virgo. Rather it is a question of longing for a new state of physical being which is founded upon spiritual ideals, as ruled by Virgo's opposite sign Pisces, and which becomes possible primarily by positive thinking.

The major part played by the mind in bringing about this state of purity probably accounts for the traditional rulership of Mercury. For however much we attempt to purify our bodies by means of New Age diet and medicine, if our thoughts remain troubled then health may still elude us; it seems necessary to respect the interplay between mind and body. It is here that the real meaning of the age-old Virgoan maxim of 'mind over matter' becomes clear: the notion of bringing the mind to bear on matter with a view to achieving perfection is indeed feasible — but only when considered in the context of spiritual self-change.

Here it is interesting to note the similarity between the glyphs of Virgo and Scorpio. Clearly associated with the same basic principle and considered by some astrologers to have been originally one, it could be that they are each expressive of a different aspect of the transformation process, in that Virgo represents the reformed outer lifestyle we must adopt if we are seriously considering inner self-change. There is an essential interdependence between purity of body and purity of soul, an interdependence symbolized by the mythical goddess Vesta, considered by many as ruler of Virgo, whose pure, celibate lifestyle entitled her to act as keeper of the sacred flame of the temple — probably symbolic of the soul (flame) dwelling in the body (temple).

As far as the interpretation of the birth chart is concerned, we can assume that any personal planet falling in Virgo will express itself in a need for purity and perfection both at the mental and physical levels, and with highly developed powers of discrimination.

When the Sun falls in Virgo the individual's self-esteem will be governed by the standards of perfection he or she is able to achieve. The problem here is that either Virgo's self-esteem must suffer due to accomplishments not coming up to standard, or else little is accomplished since the self-esteem demands unrealistic levels of perfection.

The discriminatory powers of Virgo can nevertheless be the greatest asset of this sign, and particularly when the Moon falls in Virgo the ability to assess and to classify can prove extremely useful. When overplayed, however, the critical faculties never know when to call a halt and can alienate others by a negative nit-picking attitude. Here the urge to nurture is linked to an interest in health care, expressed either within the family (where health mania is a likely pitfall) or, more satisfactorily, in work related to health.

Mercury in Virgo produces a mind which is highly analytical and well-suited to any form of critical work. There is a special ability to bring the mind to bear on matter, whereby mental concepts can be translated into a material form, so that scientific or mechanical subjects are found to be of interest. Often, however, there is also a fascination for numbers or words, leading to aptitude in maths or languages.

When Venus falls in Virgo, it is important to provide an outlet for the critical faculties in some form of artistic activity, as otherwise they are likely to be expressed entirely in the sphere of personal relationships, where they are usually of a destructive nature. If, however, the powers of discrimination can be used creatively in the form of arts and crafts which call for an eye for detail, there is less likelihood that the critical eye will fall upon unfortunate friends and relations. With this Venus placement the ear is often finely tuned, giving musical ability.

This sign channels its energy into the achievement of high levels of perfection, and particularly when Mars falls in Virgo work will be of primary importance. The area of work is of less significance than the standard to which work is accomplished, although frequent areas of interest are the health sector, techniques and crafts, and all types of critical work. Balance is vital with this placement, as when overplayed Mars in Virgo can produce the workaholic.

The Sixth House
The Sixth House rules the purification of matter under the influence of the mind, thus:

— our job of work, in particular techniques and crafts, whereby we seek to construct and perfect a finished product in accordance with a mental concept;
— our health — our day-to-day well-being is dependent upon the extent to which we discipline our body (diet and exercise) in coordination with positive mental attitudes ('healthy mind — healthy body').

Service to others along practical lines whereby we seek to bring about a physical or material improvement in their circumstances — in particular in work within the health sector — also falls under the rulership of the Sixth House.

Venus — Taurus — The Second House; Libra — The Seventh House: The urge to experience sensual pleasure and the urge to form relationships

Venus
To return to the notion of 'male' and 'female' planets, Venus has always been considered a feminine energy, concerned as it is with the experience of beauty and pleasure, in particular through the medium of the five senses — sight, hearing, touch, taste and smell. By tradition it has been women's role to bring sensual fulfilment to those around them and in particular to satisfy men's appetites. Nowadays, however, with the growing ornamentation of the male, we see a revived trend for men to identify with their own Venus urge rather than project it onto the women in their life.

When we speak of sensual joy we refer to the happiness available to us through physical sensation in this three-dimensional world. Thus Venus is associated with a wide range of pleasures which include the beauty we behold with our eyes and that which we perceive with our ears and our other senses. In its purest form the joy of Venus is that associated with music, with art and with Mother Nature inasmuch as the best things in life are free. However, it is also symbolic of all material pleasures, such as food, drink and possessions through which we achieve sensual satisfaction. For this reason it is obviously also linked to money and resources since these are representative of our potential to acquire material goods.

Venus is one of the most fundamental of the personal urges. After all, the need to be happy, to have fun and experience joy would be cited by many as their main reason for living, and everyone needs a certain amount of enjoyment in life, or else existence becomes a pretty intolerable affair.

However, it is when the urge for enjoyment is overplayed that mankind encounters sorrow. An over-exercised Sun leads to preoccupation with pride; a preponderance of the Moon factor brings with it a perpetual state of anxiety; and when Mercury is over-emphasized, mental problems are the end-product. But the excessive use of the Venus principle is responsible for some of the saddest plights in which we find ourselves.

Over-indulgence of our sensual appetites has on the one hand threatened our health by producing obesity and diseases linked to a pleasure-orientated diet and on the other hand is responsible for spreading venereal disease, whose very name derives from the planet of sensual pleasure, Venus. Worse, man's ravaging of the planet earth in order to satisfy his material desires has resulted in the serious pollution problems which are currently destroying so much of nature.

The location of Venus in our chart by sign and house placing and by aspect will throw light on our attitude to the material world — to nature, to the earth and its resources, to sensual pleasures including music and art, and to our own personal resources — and can bring our attention to any adjustments we might wish to make in our outlook in these areas.

Another fundamental meaning of the planet Venus is that of *relationship*, since it is only by relating to that which lies outside ourselves that we can experience beauty or pleasure. The question of relationship not only concerns self in relation to matter or that which pleases the senses, but also self in relation to other human beings. Therefore how we get along with others, what we can establish in common with them with a view to coexisting in harmony, also falls under the rulership of Venus.

It is probably true to say that everything we do in life is based on relationships and our ability to get on with other people can make or break our success in all that we undertake. In the birth chart it is the planet Venus which gives us the vital information as to how we can improve the quality of our personal relationships. This is the planet which enables us to take a cool look at the way we really behave in close contacts rather than the way we would like to believe we do.

Learning to live peacefully with one another is possibly the greatest test we must meet in life, and each of us faces a specific challenge of our own to bring out the best of our relating potential. By studying the chart placement of our Venus we can familiarize ourselves with our own individual challenge, learning which attitudes and behaviour to emphasize and which to avoid.

The Sign Taurus
In accordance with its ruler Venus, the sign Taurus seeks to please the five senses, both for its own satisfaction and in order to bring enjoyment to others, and this will be most obviously the case when the Sun or Mars falls in Taurus. The realm of the senses is a vast one, and thus such diverse occupations as chef, couturier, interior designer, florist, gardener, builder, artist or musician, which commonly depend on an urge to appeal to one of the physical senses, all fall under the rulership of Taurus. Taurus is traditionally associated with money in that many sensual delights can be purchased, although in itself

cash is a crude and inadequate symbol of the true Taurean urge to express beauty.

As might be expected, this is a down-to-earth temperament, unlikely to be swayed by inexplicable highs and lows, and most noticeably so when the Moon falls in Taurus. The Taurus temperament is easily satisfied by the pleasure to be experienced in many facets of the material world and is therefore fairly placid.

But when Taurus is overplayed, the need for sensual satisfaction can turn to greed or unbridled sensuality. And this sign's dependency upon material security can render it highly vulnerable to fear of losing that security. This in turn may lead to inflexibility and unyielding resistance to any approach which is seen as a threat.

The Taurus intellect is keenly tuned to the five senses and especially when Mercury falls in Taurus is adept at converting sensation into reasoning and vice versa. The Taurus brain will naturally communicate ideas through the medium of the senses — that which is visible such as art, that which is audible such as music, or in a tangible, concrete form. On the other hand, in order to be acceptable to Taurus an idea must be able to be appreciated through one or several of the senses — it finds totally abstract concepts more difficult to assimilate. Mercury in Taurus often denotes artistic or practical skills, but when over-emphasized can be obstinate and excessively geared to mundane affairs.

Taurus relates in its characteristic fashion, i.e. through the five senses. In particular when Venus falls in Taurus, the aesthetic values will be highly developed and in any relationship there is a need to give pleasure and to share the experience of sensual enjoyment. Taurus is the sign most capable of perceiving the real beauty of the earth and of the human body. However, when over-emphasized it is also most likely to forget the other aspects of relationship and to see the loved one as a source of pleasure — yet another possession — rather than as an individual in their own right.

The Second House
The Second House may be considered to rule all matters connected with pleasure experienced through the senses. Traditionally this house has been associated with money and resources since it is a fact that hard cash is needed to acquire much that pleases the senses such as food, clothes, furnishings and *objets d'art*. But not everything that pleases the senses need carry a price ticket. The delights of nature, the joy of gardening and growing, the beauty of music, song and art can all be enjoyed for nothing and all come under the rulership of the Second House.

The Sign Libra

Libra is currently ruled by Venus and is considered to express the Venusian need for beauty not so much in the Taurean physical sense but at a mental level and in particular within the structure of one-to-one relationships, where it seeks to achieve and promote harmony and understanding.

The Libran desire to achieve harmony is pursued essentially at the level of intellect: there is the realization that peace on earth is ultimately dependent upon a state of *understanding* among the minds of human beings by their *coming to terms* with each other. War cannot end, conflict cannot cease, until respect for the other person's viewpoint has led to a compromise and a mutual stepping down from the position of attack. A vital function of Libra is to act as an agent of peace, not merely by patching up arguments and fights but by promoting harmony in a highly constructive way. After all, peace is not simply the cessation of conflict but a living and vital state of being which requires inspiration, creativity and application. Especially when the Sun or Mars falls in Libra, the urge will exist to work towards this end either within personal relationships or in careers such as counselling, public relations or the law.

Because of the strong need for harmony in contacts with others, especially at a one-to-one level, outbreaks of conflict are painful to Libra, especially when the Moon falls in this sign and in some cases the longing for peace takes precedence over all other considerations. Thus feelings of discontent may be camouflaged by a false smile and much suffered in silence to avoid angry words — with devastating effects on one's physical health.

Especially when Mercury falls in Libra, this sign produces cool detached thinking patterns which seek always to weigh and evaluate opposing ideas and principles with a view to finding the fair solution. It is a mind which works well in partnership with another capable of presenting a contrasting viewpoint. The objectivity of this placement is of great value in the legal profession, and ability to find the common ground amongst conflicting opinions gives skill in negotiating and mediating work. But when carried too far, Mercury in Libra can destroy all spontaneity and lead to indecision and procrastination.

In view of the fundamental link between the sign Libra and the issue of relationships, personal contacts, especially at a one-to-one level, will clearly be of the greatest importance to this sign, and particularly so when Venus falls in Libra. The ability to get along with another person on a regular day-to-day basis is dependent primarily upon compromise and it is here that Libra excels.

When the Libra function is over-emphasized, however, the motivation is often to seek peace at all costs, to have a quiet life, to back down or to remain silent even when one's principles dictate otherwise. At worst Libra is no more than a blatant coward who mistakes inertia for peace and fails to realize that real harmony must be actively worked for and established. For the true role of Libra is not to acquiesce but to *initiate* — hence its designation as a cardinal sign. In order to work actively for peace Libra may well have to live through some embarrassing or uncomfortable situations. By taking a leaf out of the book of its opposite number Aries, Libra must be prepared to confront its adversary when necessary in order to bring the dispute out into the open and intellectually thrash out its differences. Only then may it finally come to terms with the opponent.

The Seventh House

Just as Libra is the sign concerned with achieving peace, harmony and balance, especially within one-to-one relationships, the Seventh House is the house of partnerships and close friendships — the area of life where we must learn to come to terms with the other person if the contact is to be maintained on a happy basis. Note also that traditionally the Seventh House has symbolized enemies and lawsuits since it is only from the stance of dispute that we can practise coming to terms.

Mars — Aries — The First House — The Ascendant: The urge to assert oneself

Mars

Whilst Venus is the planet associated with female sexuality — the tendency to attract and give pleasure through the senses — so Mars is the traditional symbol of virility, although its influence is by no means confined to men. The individual portrayed in the birth chart is a soul which has variously incarnated in both male and female bodies, so that whatever the sex in this present incarnation the Martian drive is in-built into the psyche and will demand release in some form or other.

Given that Mars is the symbol of force and the urge to accomplish feats of strength, on the face of things Mars lends itself more easily to the strongly built masculine physique. However, especially since their 'liberation', the opportunity has existed for women to get in touch with their Mars function — to enjoy the exhilaration of bodily action, the satisfaction of releasing energy drive and the sheer thrill of physical accomplishment. Fast disappearing are the inhibiting social mores which forbade a woman to display any physical or sexual vigour and which must have been so frustrating to those females endowed with a larger than average proportion of male hormones.

Mars will delight in expressing itself through sex and indeed through any energetic bodily activity, but it can also manifest through many other channels and is best defined as any form of *self-assertion*. It is associated with how we get our will across, how we make an impact on the world around us, by whatever means we achieve this.

When expressed in balance, self-assertion is a natural and valuable asset since he who is afraid to stand up for himself and his ideas is simply a nonentity. In its finest form Mars represents *courage*, not violence. It is the willingness to stand up for ourselves and the refusal to allow others to push us around. It symbolizes the ability to take the action necessary for our own survival — a role played in the past by man on behalf of himself and his partner but which many women nowadays play for themselves.

Whereas a good Mars is bold but non-aggressive and provides for itself without treading on the toes of others, over-emphasis of the Mars principle is responsible for some extremely ugly human traits. The pushing forward of self to the detriment of others is a particularly odious form of egocentricity (although Sun, Moon, Mercury and Venus can all produce their own type of selfishness). Mars at its worst is the agent of war — the urge to destroy any thing or person which obstructs our goals. When there is over-emphasis on the power of physical might, life is reduced to an animalistic struggle which ensures the survival only of the fittest. Mars in its lowest form is a shallow brute force which seeks to prove its physical prowess on the battlefield or in the realm of sexual conquest.

Especially where sex is concerned, an over-emphasized Mars can produce a good deal of unhappiness — the raw masculine approach to sex is often no more than the urge to 'notch another score' and nowadays even women can be prone to this attitude.

The location of Mars in our birth chart is symbolic of the manner in which we assert ourselves and can help us to see more clearly the way in which we seek to win and to enforce our will. By studying the position of this planet we can learn to recognize any problems we face regarding our self-assertion, and to achieve a healthier and more effective release of our energy drive without detriment to others or to ourselves. Mars can also tell us a good deal about the nature of our sexual needs, and can help us to improve the quality of our sexual relationships.

The Sign Aries
In accordance with its ruler Mars, the essence of the sign Aries is self-assertion. Especially when the Sun or Mars falls in Aries, the energy drive of the ego pours forth in a glorious flood and there is the urge to express one's individuality in an active way. The need exists to assert one's will, to be thoroughly independent, untethered by consideration for any other being. Aries is motivated by a strong urge to take decisions for itself, to assume control and to take action rather than just stand about and hope for the best. The powerful energy drive of this sign demands adequate outlets either in energetic physical activities or sport, or at least in an independent self-determining job or lifestyle which allows it to act on its own initiative.

On the other hand, when over-emphasized, the desire to be recognized as strong and forceful can produce the belligerent bully, the 'macho' in both sexes, who is constantly on the attack and who can hope for no more than to be feared or shunned.

Aries symbolizes a passionate and volatile temperament, and most noticeably so when the Moon falls in this sign. The highly active emotions manifest as a spontaneity of reaction which at best can be delightfully incisive but when overplayed can result in foolish impulsiveness or downright offensiveness.

In particular when Mercury occupies Aries the brain operates at high speed rather in the same way as Gemini, but whereas Gemini is icy cool and calculating, Aries' patterns of reasoning are impassioned and instinctive. At best this produces a decisive mind and forthright speech backed up by the force and self-assurance of Mars, unafraid to go its own way and express its own ideas. But when intellectual conquest is paramount, Aries uses its mind and its tongue as a cruel weapon which can wield the power of the sharpest sword.

The tendency to assert oneself in relationships produces one who takes the initiative to get to know others. Especially when their Venus falls in Aries, men and women alike are quick to strike up a friendship or romance when they experience an attraction to another person — there is no question of shyness here. But the Aries tendency to act on impulse can sever relationships just as readily as it can instigate them; Aries passion is the source of as much jealousy and anger as it is of fun and excitement.

The First House
The First House represents our personality or how we assert ourselves — how we make impact on the world about us. The First House also rules our appearance and general demeanour by virtue of which we present ourselves to others and they receive their first impression of us.

The Ascendant

Technically the cusp or starting-point of the First House, the Ascendant represents the mask (persona) we adopt in order to make our presence felt and relate to the outside world. The sign on the Ascendant is of vital significance in that it indicates how we *put into practice* the drives symbolized by the planets and their placements and thus governs the mode of expression of the entire potential of the birth chart.

3.
JUPITER, FAITH AND UNIVERSAL LAW
Sagittarius and the Ninth House

Jupiter and Saturn — Guardians of Civilized Society

Throughout recorded history the life experience of man has followed a familiar pattern. On the one hand he has belonged to himself, delighting in his individuality which he has manifested through his Sun, Moon, Mercury, Venus and Mars. He has undergone personal experience in terms of his job or occupation, his family life, his love life, his friendships, his artistic and mental self-expression and his physical activities. But he has also belonged to his society and to his civilization, itself based on a specific philosophy or creed. Man is insufficient unto himself and needs to give some sort of meaning to his existence by joining together with others of like mind; linked to his fellows by a common philosophy of life he constructs and contributes to a social order based on the framework of his beliefs. It is this first short step beyond 'self' that constitutes the roots of all civilization.

Any philosophy involves the acceptance of certain laws. Depending upon its beliefs a society will impose a specific code of morality upon its members, decreeing which standards are acceptable and which are not. If we are to 'fit in' we must agree to live our life in accordance with the rules of the game or else suffer punishment from the guardians of the law.

The urge to give some meaning to our life, which has herded us into groups and is indeed the crux of all civilized existence, is astrologically associated with the planet Jupiter. Thus it is Jupiter which represents our *philosophy of life*. It is Jupiter which governs our code of morality and gives the need to formulate clearly defined *laws* of living. And finally it is Jupiter which demands that *justice* be seen to be done in accordance with those laws.

In contrast, the actual structuring of our society or civilization is ruled by the force of the planet Saturn. Saturn may be seen as the guardian of the law rather than the law itself, and is the planet which relates to our responsibilities and duties in living under the laws of our land — the outcome of our philosophy rather than the philosophy itself.

Faith: A Basic Human Need

The need to believe is inherent in every human being, and although many would protest that they have no beliefs, each of us places our faith in something. For some the faith is that of a religious sect or denomination, in which case the code of morality is clear-cut and predetermined. Political philosophies likewise impose their own code of morals which lay down what constitutes 'right' behaviour as opposed to 'wrong' behaviour. There is nevertheless a large body of us who have no religious or political conviction to speak of yet struggle on with life with a vague notion that there must be some point in it somehow. Or perhaps we simply have faith in the law of chance and believe that sooner or later our number must come up.

Whatever the belief, there is always a spoken or unspoken acceptance of its structural precepts. There is the notion of a 'system', of a set of immutable laws in which we can place our trust. To be able to depend on something outside of ourselves somehow brings an immense sense of relief, and this compensates for the penalties which inevitably ensue from such a system. The need for suitable punishment stems from the need to see the law in action, to know that the system is alive and well. We all have an overwhelming desire to see that justice is done. Each in his own way must be able to accept that life is fair, and to hold the conviction that eventually all wrongs will be righted.

Jupiter's Role in the New Age

Prior to 1781 which marked the start of the manifestation of the 'New Age' planets, the sum total of the experience of mankind was, by and large, represented by the seven 'discovered' planets, which effectively ruled out the possibility of unified consciousness. Thus in the past, faith has mostly been of a sectarian nature — be it Christian, Muslim, Buddhist, Fascist, Communist, etc. Religious and philosophical beliefs and their accompanying moral codes have been based in the main on the teachings of individuals leaders and in many cases have totally denied the validity of other belief systems. One may well reflect on the sorrow and strife which has resulted from this separatist attitude to faith and morality. The bloodiest of wars and the bitterest of feuds have been and still are conducted in the name of belief, and saddest of all it is the name of God which is often emblazoned on the banners.

The faith of the Old Age has been a blind faith, an unquestioning acceptance of the rewards promised by spiritual or political leaders, however illogical. It has been a faith which has often resulted in bigotry, a faith prompted not by reasoning but by the fundamental gut instincts of the emotionally orientated Piscean Age.

For the New Age of Aquarius, Jupiter must represent a *holistic* rather than a sectarian faith, one which is rational rather than purely instinctive. In accordance with the unifying planetary energies of Uranus, Neptune and Pluto, whose function is to draw mankind towards at-oneness, this will be a belief which can be commonly accepted by all men, a belief based on the clearly defined and soundly reasoned precepts of universal law. The need now is not so much for man-made laws which are subject to all the limitations and inadequacies of man, nor for separatists laws which set brother against brother. The New Age must be founded upon the spiritual precepts of an all-encompassing universal law, the justice of which is unquestionable.

When we speak of universal law we refer in effect to the notion of *karma* or cause and effect, fundamental to most religions of the East, which decrees that every thought, emotion and action will result in a *reaction* precisely in accordance with itself. At the most obvious level 'he who kills with the sword must be killed by the sword' but negative thoughts and feelings are equally powerful in terms of their implications and will likewise rebound upon us during the course of our lives on earth. The old maxim of 'as ye sow, so shall ye reap' best sums up this law. The law of karma is also fundamentally linked to the notion of reincarnation since not all actions and thoughts, etc., will be able to bear their reaction during this self-same life and may have to be carried over into future lives in order to be met. The law of karma is non-sectarian in that it applies to every human being of whatever race, sex, age, religion, wealth or class system and is thus universal to all mankind.

With knowledge of the law of karma the basis of our spiritual beliefs and morality undergoes a drastic transformation. No longer is our behaviour governed by blind faith in ill-defined and uncertain rewards promised by the churches or other leaders. Now, with awareness of the true value of positive thoughts, feelings and actions, there is the clear understanding that our future good fortune in this life or the next rests solely in our own control, rather than that of some whimsical deity or other external entity. The law of karma not only makes good sense but is also profoundly fair, satisfying the deep-seated human desire for justice which is so rarely fulfilled by the laws of the land or by the laws of religion.

In addition to fulfilling our need to see fair play, acceptance of the law of cause and effect also instils us with a soundly based sense of confidence. The faith and hope which can be ours at this time of vast spiritual change is based on the understanding that it lies within our own power to transform our entire destiny and to create the future of our own choice. If we can approach life with this assurance, we will experience the fruits of true optimism and we will share those fruits with others. Generosity becomes a natural quality based on the immutable law that whatever we give to others will be repaid to us. In the long run generosity can never result in loss.

Acceptance of and compliance with the law of karma is an essential forerunner to any form of self-healing under the guidance of the outer planets, for it is not until we can perceive the law of cause and effect at work in our lives that we can take any real responsibility for ourselves and begin the work of self-change. There can be no question of attuning ourselves to universal energies until we have first come to terms with the precepts of universal law.

Lack of Attunement to Jupiter

At whatever level we consider Jupiter, this planet basically represents the ability to take a first essential step beyond self by developing belief in a system of rule and order to which we commit ourselves. Whether that system is universal or mundane, the point is that the faith is in the system rather than the self. Therefore total lack of attunement to the Jupiter principle is reflected in a refusal to acknowledge 'the system' and to simply adhere to a blind faith in oneself, in one's ability to go it alone, to get by under one's own steam.

Others of us express the Jupiter principle by placing our faith in luck, a 'system' of sorts based on the laws of chance, which holds out false promises and diverts us from coming to terms with the realities of life. Whilst we cling to the subconscious assumption that our fortune lies 'in the lap of the gods' or in the stars, we deny ourselves the chance to begin to control our destiny and thus to bring about positive change in ourselves. Astrology has played no small part in reinforcing our obsession with the notion of luck since for so long it has been little more than a system of fortune-telling. The philosophy of karma goes beyond the notions of 'good luck' and 'bad luck' and allows us to accept everything that befalls us without bitterness and with a sense of constructive purpose, inasmuch as any situation represents not only the reaping of the fruits of the past but the sowing of seeds for the future.

For many, however, Jupiter is additionally or alternatively expressed by belief in a specific religious, philosophical or political creed, often with little logical basis, nearly always divisive and occasionally fanatical to the point of violence.

Lack of attunement to Jupiter not only distracts us from adopting a spiritually creative approach to life but is also responsible for the sense of resentment we feel as a result of seemingly unfair experiences. Once we learn to recognize and accept the workings of universal justice in our daily lives we are less likely to waste time uttering that well-worn phrase 'it's not fair' and instead can begin to learn from our mistakes rather than blaming our misfortunes on outside sources. We begin to laugh at the ups and downs in life and to appreciate the subtle humour inherent in the workings of the law of cause and effect. The greatest achievement is that of being able to laugh at ourselves, since it is much easier to see the effects of karma in other people's lives than it is in our own.

Judgement is a faculty which is vitally linked to our understanding of the law of karma since it represents our ability to assess the future outcome of our present actions. If we are unable to accept the idea of cause and effect we are likely to possess poor judgement in every sphere of life. Belief only in ourselves or in luck as opposed to a cosmic structure of law and order leads to the subconscious assumption that our potential is unbounded by any form of limitation and that it is fundamentally possible to 'beat the system' and thus to get what we want in life without paying the price. This in turn can cause us to overreach ourselves, to become involved in bad gambles or foolish risks, to promise too much or to expect too much from others. Religions and philosophies which hold out future rewards in return for blind faith in their respective figureheads rather than on the basis of our own efforts can also lead to bad judgement in that they instil us with unrealistic expectations.

Jupiter has been traditionally associated with extravagance and this too derives from a sense of lack of limitation and expectations in excess of what one can reasonably hope to deserve. Here an over-inflated sense of entitlement is accompanied by false optimism that eventually we will land on our feet. The great lesson of Jupiter is to teach us that this is not necessarily so: the spiritual rules of the game of life demand that we become conscious of the process of reaping and sowing.

Acceptance of karma can do much to overcome the characteristic restlessness which often results from lack of attunement to Jupiter. The lure of the 'lucky break' which awaits us round every corner often produces an inability to settle in any ordinary form of life and is associated with the Sagittarian urge to move ever on, looking for the gold at the end of the rainbow. In the school of Jupiter we come to learn that it is unnecessary to travel far and wide in search of bounty, for it is only by means of our actions and thoughts in the here and now that we can truly create our own good fortune.

We have seen that through the ages the key principles of Jupiter have consisted of the urge to have *faith*, the acceptance of *laws* and related codes of morality, and the desire to see *justice* done in accordance with those laws. Before the New Age, that faith has been a blind faith — in oneself, in 'Lady Luck' or in sectarian creeds — inevitably giving rise to division; those laws and the related codes of morality were likewise ill-defined and separatist; and inevitably the justice seen or hoped to be done was uselessly inadequate in itself.

For the future the trend will be towards a reasoned holistic faith and code of morality which unite man with his brothers and can be commonly held by all. When we believe only in ourselves we are isolated from others by the assumption that we are a law unto ourselves. Even when we place our faith in sectarian religions or philosophies we are still isolated from one another by separatist laws and codes of morality. But when we place our faith in the universal law of karma, we are united with others by the knowledge that we are all subject to a common system of law and order.

Jupiter in the Birth Chart
The chart placing of Jupiter points to the areas of life which will challenge our understanding of the universal law of karma and our ability to work in accordance with this law. On the one hand its placement by sign, house and aspect incidates where we are likely to reap the benefits of past 'good' karma in the form of opportunities and abundance. On the other hand it indicates where we are challenged to create our future good fortune by present generosity and positivity in terms of our thoughts, emotions and deeds — on the basis of our faith in the law of cause and effect. However, its position also points to where we may tend to flout cosmic law by believing only in ourselves, in luck or in a sectarian system of belief imposed upon us, and as a result may suffer the penalties incurred by poor judgement.

For a fuller interpretation of Jupiter by sign, house and aspect see Chapter 10, 'The School of Jupiter'.

The Sign Sagittarius
In accordance with its ruler Jupiter, Sagittarius expresses itself in a need to develop a *philosophy* of life by travel or by study, with a strong sense of *morality*, with respect for *laws* of fair play and with a need to see *justice* done.

Sagittarius is the sign concerned with the ability to develop a philosophical outlook, to be capable of riding over the ups and downs of life with a good-humoured shrug of the shoulders or the ability to laugh at one's troubles. Especially when the Sun or Mars fall in Sagittarius, the sign channels its drive with great enthusiasm into all activities which allow it to expand its horizons — thus it is often motivated by the urge to travel, whether at home or abroad, involving contact with individuals from different types of background. Often the 'travel' is conducted from the armchair in the form of study of religion and philosophy.

Inherent in the Sagittarian outlook is the need to stick to a code of ethics, and therefore there is a very strong urge to abide by principle and fair play, albeit in accordance with self-made standards! There is often the pull to work for some form of 'system', be this of a religious/civil/gambling nature, based on a clearly defined structure of justly implemented laws, so that this sign often finds itself working or in some way active in the field of the Church (priest or lay worker), the civil law (barrister, solicitor, clerk) or betting (bookie, croupier or punter). The energy drive is also often channelled into sport and games on account of the Jupiterian attraction to rules, laws and fair play.

When operating imperfectly, the Jupiter principle is expressed in Sagittarius as an unabashed confidence in oneself. Indeed, the self-assurance may be such as to result in many ill-fated wagers and errors of judgement. When misfunctioning, Sagittarius displays a marked need to 'beat the system' rather than to comply with it — often observed in a disposition towards gambling and a burning desire to come up with that 'big one' against all the odds. Nearly always there is a preoccupation with 'luck' — but not until there is understanding of the laws on which fortune is based can there be any true fulfilment for this fortune-seeking sign.

The most obvious characteristic of the Sagittarian temperament — and most noticeably so when the Moon falls in Sagittarius — is a marked need for freedom, which can manifest either as a definite wanderlust or simply as a resistance to emotional ties. The desire to be free exists in order to further the search to find a meaning to life, which inevitably involves travel of the physical or at least the mental variety. The 'philosophical' outlook can generate a glorious sense of humour and ability to raise the spirits of others — often by playing the fool — although Sagittarian horseplay can sometimes display insensitivity to the feelings of more delicate Zodiac signs. Sagittarius can also be irritating by virtue of its smug self-satisfaction or sanctimonious approach to others and where the beliefs are of a religious nature there is a tendency towards bigotry.

Linked as it is to the notions of philosophy, fair play and justice, the Sagittarian intellect will always strive to see meaning behind every situation. In particular when Mercury occupies Sagittarius, this is a deep thinker which demands a broader understanding of the world about it than does its opposite sign Gemini which is content to process more immediate facts and figures. This desire for truth will manifest in the speech as the well-known Sagittarian bluntness which, when overplayed, is famous for 'putting its foot in it' in the form of embarrassingly plain talking. This unwelcome directness usually occurs when Sagittarius feels the need to take justice into its own hands rather than allow the forces of cosmic law and order to take effect.

As the role of Sagittarius is to develop a faith or a philosophy, the purpose of its relationships will be to engender new ideas or a different outlook on life. Noticeably when Venus falls in Sagittarius, friends and lovers are often of a different race, religion or cultural background and can thus broaden one's philosophical or spiritual horizons. In any case, relationships are conducted in accordance with strict principles as this sign is strongly committed to playing fair. Problems can arise, however, when relationships are seen as little more than a game and although the 'rules' aren't effectively broken, feelings are disregarded.

The Ninth House
The Ninth House rules activities which serve to develop our philosophy of life, hence foreign travel and 'higher' education which involves the study of belief systems. Indeed the moral or religious philosophy of a person will be represented by the Ninth House. The Ninth House also stands for institutions which are based on the observance of religious or moral laws — thus the Church and the civil legal system.

4.
SATURN AND COSMIC RESPONSIBILITY
Capricorn, the Tenth House and the Midheaven

The Mainstay of Civilization

Jupiter and Saturn represent two planetary principles which co-operate as a team and which throughout the ages have together represented the structure of civilized society. Jupiter has instilled man with a sense of meaning to life; Saturn has provided the concrete means by which that philosophy may be put to work. If we consider Jupiter as the law itself, Saturn is the agent of the law which puts it into practice. This is easily understood by considering that Jupiter rules the fiery sign of Sagittarius and is thus concerned with belief, passion or enthusiasm, whereas Saturn is associated with down-to-earth Capricorn which always seeks to manifest in tangible form. Saturn is not so much related to the acquisition or experience of faith, but rather with the concrete outcome of that faith and the sort of lifestyle and social behaviour in which it results.

Since civilization began, Saturn has ruled the urge to prove by actions that one is committed to a certain philosophy of life — generally speaking, a political or religious belief. It has governed our willingness to fulfil our obligations as a member of that religious or political institution. For the great majority of us it has represented the urge to conduct ourselves in a responsible manner towards our fellow citizens — our need to 'fit in' to the system.

Part and parcel of the Saturn principle has been the urge towards respectability since the respect of society is seen as confirmation that we have fulfilled our duty towards 'the system'. Consequently this planet is strongly drawn to that which attracts respect whilst it has positively no time for anything which might detract from our 'standing'. Here *status* is all-important in every sense of the word. It is a Saturnian maxim that respect is given to he who respects the law, whatever that law might consist of. There is no room here for originality or experimentation, merely for self-control, hard work and results.

The kind of results sought by Saturn are not to be gained in five minutes and neither would this planetary principle desire the distinctly solar glory of the overnight star. The sort of respect which motivates Saturn can only be gained when we have proved our reliablity over a period of time. After all 'status' is not commonly ascribed to a young person, but rather is something earned by many years of toil and effort. For this reason *patience* is an essential prerequisite of the Saturn function. The link between time, patience and the Saturn energy is clearly demonstrated by the association of this planet with the Greek god Chronos who was the ruler of time cycles and from whom we acquire the word 'chronological'. It is widely recognized that Saturn becomes easier to handle during our old age.

The notion of *limitation* must also be understood in the context of the urge we refer to as Saturn, since to be truly responsible is to know our limitations. Structure, as represented by Saturn, must always be governed by *boundaries* and similarly any concrete action which we desire to put into effect must itself be defined by certain limits. Concrete achievement is a question of concentration on the matter in hand and a refusal to be side-tracked down non-productive alleys. In addition we must be very clear about the limitations of our responsibilities and duties: to feel that we are responsible for everything and everybody is actually highly irresponsible since it is impossible to spread oneself in all directions at once, and invariably we end up by achieving nothing.

In this way the Saturn principle can be seen to have stood for the main driving force towards a civilized organization of society based on our philosophy of life. Without our sense of responsibility towards our king and country, law and order would have broken down into a free-for-all shambles. Without our desire for status to gain the respect of our fellow citizens there would have been little achievement at a practical level. And without the ability to concentrate on the job in hand, the wheels of civilization would have ground to a halt.

Nowadays, of course, the most popular philosophy of the West is that of materialism, so that the sense of duty is directed primarily towards consumerism — we feel obliged to 'keep up with the Jones's' and to buy, buy, buy. The need for material status is so very obvious that it scarcely requires commenting on. And the characteristic Saturnian concentration is firmly riveted upon 'getting for oneself' to the exclusion of all distractions.

Saturn's Role in the New Age
However, as we enter the Age of Aquarius gradually the energy of Saturn is acquiring a new and far more meaningful outlet. In line

with the fundamental significance of the New Age, Saturn is no longer to be considered merely in a sectarian sense but rather in terms of the whole. Until very recently it has been enough to believe in the religious or moral philosophy of one's own isolated environment and to do one's duty thereby, for the main part without question or objection. But now, with the advent of the new consciousness, there is the realization of the horror that sectarian faith and duty can produce. A blind sense of responsibility to king, country or faith has been the root cause of every vicious war and conflict. The urge to 'do one's bit' for one's flag may well prove one's patriotism but it in no way takes into account one's responsibility towards the *whole* of mankind, nor one's responsibility to oneself as a component of that whole. At long last we are awakening to the fact that first and foremost we are citizens of the cosmos and this must come before any duty to our state.

This newly born sense of responsibility towards the cosmos as a whole has manifested along many interesting lines. The ecological and anti-nuclear movements are each affirming in their own way that their sense of duty towards the planet earth exceeds their obligation to prevailing governmental policies. We are starting to reject the notion of 'my society is all right Jack' in concern for the well-being of the world in its entirety.

In a spiritual sense also, there is an awakening to the realization that we are all basically responsible to cosmic law rather than merely to the civil law of our country. Just as universal law goes beyond the laws of our land or religion, so also our universal responsibilities supersede any duties we owe to Church or State. Acceptance that we are ultimately answerable to a universal rather than a separatist system actually means that we also take a far greater responsibility for *ourselves*.

This is a truth brought home with a bang by the cosmic law of cause and effect to which all men are subject regardless of their faith, race or status. That which we meet with now in terms of events, emotions or thoughts is almost without exception of our own making. From the New Age standpoint, whereas Jupiter represents the actual doctrine of the universal law of karma, Saturn may be considered as the agent thereof, a sort of cosmic police force whose function is to implement the law and who teaches us the hard way.

The idea of karma is unpopular with those who still need a scapegoat to blame for their woes, since it certainly does away with buck-passing, whether to the Government, the immigrants, the 'stars' or to the Creator. But from another standpoint, understanding of karma is a great relief to those of us who could never accept that

God was responsible for the pain in our life.

Whether we like it or not, we are all obliged to co-operate with the law of karma. And whether we are aware of the fact or not, we are collectively paying our debts where these have been incurred. To take the step of consciously accepting responsibility for our own karma may not in itself absolve us from the strong arm of the law since we must still face our destiny — but it does bring home the importance of carefully examining our every action, thought and feeling. And it is this desire to clean the slate and adopt a more conscientious approach to our behaviour as a whole which can lead us to seek to co-operate with the transformatory energies of the three outer planets in order to initiate self-change.

The desire to put right past wrongs by dedicated effort and hard work — to cancel out our debts by hard-won credits — represents a new outlet for Saturn in accordance with New Age consciousness. Now the Saturnian concepts of responsibility, effort, patience, concentration and achievement acquire a vitally new significance. For the New Age, Saturn allows us firstly to accept responsibility for ourselves in co-operation with cosmic rather than sectarian law. Secondly it provides us with the impetus to work towards spiritual rather than material goals by putting concentrated effort into the challenge at hand. Finally the famous Saturnian patience can now be channelled towards our spiritual rather than our material progress.

Lack of Attunement to Saturn

At the most basic level, to ignore the Saturn principle is to neglect our responsibility to ourselves in a physical sense. Before we start to think of anything else, the duty of every human being is to care for his or her own body and material needs, to ensure his or her own survival. But even here there are those of us who expect others to look after us, who will allow others to take responsibility for us if at all possible. Of course, there are situations in which a person is physically or mentally incapable of caring for himself for a specific karmic purpose, in which case the abandoning of responsibility for oneself is involuntary.

At the next level there may well be a willingness to care for ourselves, but as yet there is a refusal to act with responsibility towards others or to carry out our duties towards them. This consists of an attitude of 'I'm all right Jack' and implies a willingness to look after our own needs but a refusal to help anyone else. Often there is something of a compromise in that we will take on token responsibility if we are beginning to feel the need to do 'the right thing' in the eyes of our peers. At a superficial level we can be seen to be taking our part in society, but in actual fact we are putting in very little effort.

Ultimately this approach can only culminate in loneliness, frustration and depression. In fact this cut-off state of being is the direct prelude to rediscovering our links with the rest of creation under the guidance of Uranus, Neptune and Pluto — perhaps why Saturn precedes these three planets in the sequence of the solar system. But before we can attempt to work with the outer planets we must co-operate with Saturn: we must accept that we are responsible to the whole before we can actually start functioning as a part of that whole.

The Status Trap

The commonest level of expression of Saturn is where there is a feeling of responsibility towards our peer group, society, culture, king and country, etc., but as yet a sense of responsibility towards the whole and for our own role within the whole is absent. This is the level which is most representative of the Old Age expression of Saturn, by which we are all governed to some extent at the present time.

A sense of responsibility towards a sectarian group often exerts enormous pressure on us to prove ourselves within the system. In almost every aspect of present-day society — although the position is starting to change gradually — the respect of the establishment is dependent firstly on attainment and secondly on maintenance of convention. Failure or impropriety cannot be countenanced since these indicate that we have rejected the principles of the system. Those of us motivated by a sense of responsibility towards a sectarian group will often drive ourselves mercilessly in pursuit of this or that status symbol. Worldly achievement can become our god, so that our whole lifestyle revolves around 'getting on' and obsession with work becomes a likely pitfall.

Not only may we ourselves labour ceaselessly within the system, but we may also demand from others the same austere diligence, the same respect for conventional status that we ourselves display. Here we have the makings of the strict disciplinarian, the narrow-minded authoritarian who makes life a misery for those around him and ultimately for himself.

The need for social acceptance is often such that there is a sense of permanent apprehension that we may fall flat on our face or become a laughing stock, which tends to freeze us to the point of curtailing our self-expression in every sphere. Always there is the consideration as to how this or that will affect our standing. What the neighbours — or the world in general — may think becomes our self-restricting yardstick. As a result, this level of Saturn expression is dominantly governed by a whole series of inhibitions which limit and repress our actions, speech and feelings. The need for acceptance amongst our peers leads to a pronounced yet usually unadmitted state of self-consciousness in which we become adept at 'keeping a stiff upper lip' and shunning all behaviour which we feel is 'not done'.

The problem with this sort of self-repression is that it involves a continuous inner build-up of tension which tends to wreak havoc with our physical and mental health. And although we may strive valiantly to give the outer impression of being entirely 'normal', our true state of mind is inevitably disturbed.

Depression is the most common by-product of incomplete expression of the Saturn principle — depression in all its various forms which are commonly based on a prolonged accumulation of frustrated energy which we have been unable to discharge in the normal way due to our inhibitions. The true anti-depressant is never a drug or medicine but a genuine determination to seek the root of these inhibitions and a willingness to change our outlook on life.

Saturn lies behind a vast number of stress-related health problems which cause so much suffering in life. The most degenerative or consumptive diseases seem to result from an over-active will (Pluto), but Saturn is probably responsible for those ailments which are recognized as resulting from anxiety, such as insomnia, allergies, skin problems and digestive disorders.

Incomplete expression of the Saturn principle is also the root of snobbery in all its equally unattractive forms — social, intellectual, artistic, etc. The snob is one who attaches importance only to status, to the exclusion of any other merit. Thus it is achievement within the establishment and the ability to comply with the establishment which form the criteria behind all judgement — as yet there is no acceptance of holism, of the equal value of all parts within the whole.

The Question of Cosmic Responsibility

The problems described above are almost entirely due to overdependence on the approval of some sector or other of society and thus it is an inability to break free of our social conditioning which chains us to the prison of our inhibitions — although we seldom realize this to be true.

In contrast, full attunement to Saturn involves the understanding that it is our duty to assume responsibility for our *own* beliefs and attitudes rather than to lean on those of others. There is the acceptance that the well-being of humanity as a whole is governed by the willingness of each of us to stand on our own two feet and our ability

to make independent decisions, decisions which take into account
the interests of all our fellow beings rather than simply our own
interests or the interests of one small sector of society.

Now there is true self-reliance in that we are no longer seeking
to please others and so we are immune to their criticism or disapproval.
Inhibitions and worries of all sorts disappear and the temperament
becomes much steadier and more serene. Indeed, this serene self-
containment represents one of the most important of the *true*
qualities of Saturn. Now the serenity is natural and innate rather
than a 'face' presented to the outside world in order to gain
acceptance. There is no longer any question of repression of emotion
since there is no build-up of tension in the first place.

A sense of cosmic responsibility serves to break down the barriers
which isolate us from one another and which derive from a limited
sense of responsibility, limited either to ourselves or to one or another
social group.

Saturn's Position in the Birth Chart
Saturn's position in the birth chart will primarily indicate where our
notions of *responsibility* need development. In the designated areas
of life we must first ask ourselves whether we have any sense of
responsibility for ourselves. If so, is this a sense of responsibility to
the universe as a whole rather than to one small sector of society?
To the extent that our sense of duty is limited to some sectarian group
we will be liable to a feeling of obligation to live up to the associated
standards, leading either to a driving ambition and achievement
mania, or conversely to inhibitions or inertia due to the fear of failure.
By way of contrast, when we release ourselves from the burden of
social responsibility in the areas in question, we likewise release
ourselves from the pressure and stress which result from the struggle
to maintain the status quo. And when we accept *spiritual* responsibility for ourselves and the problems that face us in life, we have
the opportunity finally to clear our karmic debts and to pave the
way for a whole new positive approach to life. For a full interpretation
of Saturn by sign, house and aspect, see Chapter 11, 'The School
of Saturn'.

The Sign Capricorn
In accordance with its ruler Saturn, the function of Capricorn is to
learn to cope with the notion of *responsibility*. At the highest level
Capricorn is one who is capable of accurately defining and fulfilling
his responsibilities to the rest of the cosmos. At the lowest level,
Capricorn is totally unwilling to shoulder any burdens — it 'passes'

on life. Somewhere in between lies a range of Capricorn expression which involves a certain sense of duty but always of a limited nature. That is, it may look after itself but be oblivious to others' needs. Or it may feel obligated to its country but be unable to look beyond the borders of its homeland. Always Saturn is associated with limitation and boundaries which gradually and progressively extend until one reaches the total absence of barriers associated with Uranus, the next planetary energy in the solar system. At each stage of this process Capricorn must grapple with problems of adjustment to a *balanced* sense of responsibility.

Part and parcel of the urge to take on responsibility — and the most obvious Capricornian characteristic, in particular when the Sun or Mars falls in Capricorn — is the need for concrete achievement: Capricorn has no time for big talk without follow-up either in itself or in others. This sign takes great pride in its self-discipline and its ability to concentrate exclusively on the task in hand. Generally it will wish to be acknowledged as a solid pillar of the social milieu which it inhabits. Above all it desires respect, but not so much for its self-expressive talents, as with the sign Leo, as for its quality of steadfast conscientiousness and its capacity to fulfil its duties well. It is desirous of a 'good reputation' but will willingly wait for this until the end of the day. When over-emphasized, the unquenchable thirst for respect gives rise to a burning and unattractive ambition and also makes this sign highly vulnerable to any threat or blow to its standing.

The prime motivation of Capricorn ambition is not so much money as status amongst its peers. Within a materialistic society status may well be symbolized by material assets, but it is possible to measure status in a spiritual sense also. We may generalize by saying that Capricorn energy drive is channelled into living life with a sense of responsibility towards its philosophy and into living up to its principles, whatever they might be. Especially when Mars falls in Capricorn adrenalin is dispensed in carefully measured quantities, the sense of structure allowing a carefully planned and patiently executed assault on any target. Self-discipline is likely to be excellent, but when overplayed can turn Capricorn into a slave-driver, to itself and to others.

Emotionally this sign is well-known for its reserve, which is usually considered to be a fault rather than a potential virtue. Especially when the Moon falls in Capricorn the feelings will tend to be well-disciplined and the temperament self-contained, although the motivation towards that self-containment may well vary. At the highest level there is an admirable ability to take responsibility for its own emotions rather than to unburden them onto all and sundry. But where the respect of its peers is more important to Capricorn than its own self-respect or its sense of duty towards the 'whole', fear of offending convention can lead to extreme self-consciousness and embarrassment about even the most trivial show of feeling. Repression of this kind can often result in depression and sickness.

Capricorn produces a practical mentality which is more concerned with end-results than with concepts. In particular when Mercury is in Capricorn, the mind is a serious one which needs to think things through carefully before making a pronouncement. It feels a good deal of responsibility for its decisions and its speech which obviously leads towards caution and perhaps to taciturnity. At best this results in a high degree of integrity and excellent mental discipline with accompanying success in many fields of study. At worst there can be an excessive concern about upsetting propriety which reasons 'if in doubt say nowt' and which can manifest as a boring and annoying reluctance to communicate. Capricorn is famed for its sense of structure which produces a mind capable of analysing any problem in a systematic and orderly manner. The capacity for limitation produces good concentration, but if overplayed can give rise to narrow-mindedness and an inability to see beyond the prevailing opinions of the day.

Capricorn may not be the most romantic of lovers but it certainly has the capacity to be the most loyal, faithful and dutiful. Especially when Venus falls in Capricorn, relationships are approached with a firm sense of responsibility. Personal contacts are entered into primarily with a need for achievement — perhaps why Capricorn has acquired the reputation of being a social climber. Indeed, when social approval is of paramount importance to this sign, relationships are likely to be conducted with a sense of propriety that does not offend convention. In general it is the long-term success of a relationship which is important rather than short-term excitement — a conscientious approach which makes it hard for Capricorn to react spontaneously to others and can inhibit the success which it desires so much. Fear of failure continuously haunts it and can sometimes lead to a total 'passing' on close associations or the tendency to go for an 'easy number' where success is relatively assured. On the other hand it can often result in Capricorn working long and hard at seemingly exasperating alliances with almost inexhaustible patience.

The Tenth House
The Tenth House rules activities which are based on the acceptance

of responsibility, the fulfilment of duty, the attainment of achievement and status within society. Therefore in practice the Tenth House may be considered to represent the career — in the sense that it is through the career that status is gained. In a more general sense the Tenth House represents our public standing, existent whether we pursue a career as such or not, and in particular our attitude towards status.

The Midheaven
The Midheaven, technically the cusp or starting-point of the Tenth House, likewise represents our public status, our career and our responsibilities to society.

5.
THE OUTER PLANETS: GATEWAYS TO UNIVERSAL ENERGY

It is widely accepted that the outer planets symbolize collective rather than personal energy drives, but it is often claimed for this reason that they are meaningless to us as individuals and merely serve to sway humanity *en masse*. This attitude assumes that we have no control over these energies and once again denies the notion of man's free will.

The view presented in this book is that it is the outer planets which in fact provide the greatest challenge to man as regards the use of his free will. Co-operation with the true nature of these powerful New Age energies can help bring about positive change in the world through the establishment of a new at-oneness, whereas a refusal to have any part in the new consciousness which they represent can only lead to frustration.

Uranus, Neptune and Pluto together stand for the next step beyond the group awareness which we have seen to be ruled by Jupiter and Saturn. However, the holistic outlook which they symbolize is a comparatively new phenomenon whose first dawn occurred somewhere around 1781, that period of socialist stirrings marked by the discovery of Uranus. Prior to that time, group consciousness was the accepted order of the day. By and large it was entirely accepted that one's beliefs and duties would align with the political or religious system of which one was part — not so much because we rejected opposing ideas or philosophies, but simply in that most of us knew of nothing outside of our immediate environment. Possibilities of communication were virtually zero. Travel and book learning, the only means of expanding one's horizon, were the prerogative of the privileged few. For the ordinary man there was really no alternative but to be narrow-minded.

Inasmuch as the root cause of separatist attitudes and behaviour was an inevitable lack of communication, it was fitting that the first step in the New Age drive towards unification should be the manifestation of the planet Uranus, whose function was to bring us closer to one another by promoting communication in every shape and form, but particularly through the discovery of telecommunications.

Mutual understanding paves the way towards a Utopian state of peace on earth since it dissolves fear, which is the enemy of love. Without first understanding one another and establishing a sense of rapport there can be no hope of overcoming discord. So it was that Uranus was the first new energy to make itself felt, followed at a relatively short interval by the discovery of Neptune in 1846, marked by the influx of another new energy whose function was to bring us closer to one another at the level of our feelings rather than simply that of our minds.

Uranus and Neptune, although each important in their own way, are forerunners to that most dynamic New Age energy which is concerned with the transformation of power both at an individual and a world level and which we refer to as Pluto. So whereas Uranus serves to break down the barriers which divide us in terms of our *thinking* and Neptune to break down those barriers which divide us in terms of our *feelings*, it is Pluto which serves to unite mankind in terms of the expression of its *will* and its energy drive.

It is the privilege of each one of us to avail ourselves of these New Age energies in order to effect profound self-change at the levels of the intellect, the emotions and the will. Far from representing impersonal cosmic energies somehow divorced from our real-life activities, or forces of fate over which we have no control, Uranus, Neptune and Pluto positively insist on incorporation into our psyche. If we freely admit them, in understanding and acceptance of the task they are to accomplish, the benefits to our well-being are enormous. If we refuse them entry, they will nevertheless not be denied and will demand recognition in ways which can be intensely painful. Together these three planets represent the birth pangs of the New Era, and just as the first contractions must inevitably build up to a peak prior to the actual delivery, so the 'labour' of the New Age is already under way and the manifestations of Uranus, Neptune and Pluto must increase in intensity in order to fulfil the function which they have initiated.*

---

* This increase in intensity may well correlate with the discovery of Chiron in 1977, a visiting 'planet' to our solar system which is located inside the orbit of Uranus, thus forming a bridge between Saturn and the outer planets, and one of the possible associations of which is with birth and the process of adjustment thereto.

Coming to Terms with Spiritual Energy

Many people find it difficult to understand the significance of the outer planets, and it is quite true that at the physical level the notions of holism or unification are meaningless. In terms of the physical there is no unity, neither is there any equality in a world in which so much seems totally unfair. To appreciate the meaning of the outer planets it is necessary to tune into a spiritual awareness, and this is precisely what these three planets are concerned with.

Thinking in spiritual terms means to be aware of the existence of the soul over and above that of the physical body. It is to be conscious of that part of man which is eternal, which successively assumes many different bodies, and which may be defined as a tiny radiant point of light. To be soul-conscious is no longer to be ego-conscious since the ego is only a temporary personality which has been assumed for the purpose of this one life. To be soul-conscious is to experience a profound sense of unity with all other beings whether alive or so-called dead, since the barriers of race, sex, age and status — and even the obstacles of the three dimensions — are swept away. To be soul-conscious is also to accept that all souls commonly derive from the divine source of spirit energy. We are truly brothers in a spiritual sense in that we share a common origin.

As planets which function at the spiritual level, Uranus, Neptune and Pluto serve to raise the level of expression of their physical energy counterparts, Mercury, Venus and Mars. Thus Uranus, as the higher vibration of Mercury, is concerned primarily with holistic *thinking*; Neptune, as the higher vibration of Venus, focuses mainly on *relating* in a holistic sense; and finally Pluto, as the higher vibration of Mars, is concerned with directing our *energy drive* towards the good of the whole rather than simply the self.

A Question of Terminology

There are many different labels we can use for the outer planets. If we refer to these planets as 'collective energies' it is important to see them as actively rather than passively collective; in other words to consider them not merely as abstract but as having a definite purpose as regards unifying human beings. On the other hand we might speak of them as spiritual mind (Uranus), spiritual love (Neptune), and spiritual force (Pluto), suggesting that they are to be applied at a soul level rather than a physical level. (The term 'psychic' (Greek *psyche* = soul) is also occasionally used.)

We can also describe these planets as *universal mind* (Uranus), *universal emotion* (Neptune) and *universal force* (Pluto), implying the unifying function of these energies and the fact that when they are operating harmoniously they do indeed provide access to wisdom (Uranus), inspiration (Neptune), and force (Pluto) of a universal and thus of an all-powerful nature.

A universal energy comprises within itself the sum content of every part of the whole and therefore is almost incomprehensibly mighty in terms of its potential. It may be contrasted with a personal planetary energy in that whereas the latter is basically self-orientated and participates in every situation purely from a subjective standpoint, a universal planetary energy provides an overview which is capable of analysing every component part of the whole.

Similarly a universal energy goes beyond the world of matter and provides the realization that all levels of experience — thinking, communication, emotion, action — can take place not only within these three dimensions but also beyond.

The Outer Planets and the Quest for Grace
The outer planets have yet another significance in terms of their ability to promote world change. We have seen that in helping us to moderate the demands of the ego they can contribute towards the establishment of peace and unity. But just as they may be considered the builders of the new, so also they can act as the destroyers of the old. For a major function of Uranus, Neptune and Pluto is to release us from much of the negative karma which we have accumulated during past lives.

Prior to the discovery of the 'big three', Jupiter and Saturn symbolized the limits of our spiritual potential; ignorance and limited awareness prevented us from releasing ourselves from our negative karma. Now, however, through the medium of Uranus, Neptune and Pluto, there is the possibility of mitigating our karmic debit balance by transforming our state of awareness. If we are willing to place the ego on one side by working with the energies represented by the three outer planets, it lies within our power to free ourselves from the karmic suffering which derives from self-absorption and isolation from others.

If we pursue the path of 'grace'* by co-operating with the principles of Uranus, Neptune and Pluto, we engage in the process of self-transformation from three standpoints:

1. Through Uranus we come to acknowledge where our *thinking* is self-opinionated, intolerant and cruel and where we need to become more acceptant of others.

* Here 'grace' is to be understood as the process whereby we release ourselves from karmic suffering by spiritual regeneration.

2.   Through Neptune we come to acknowledge where our *emotions* are self-centred, self-pitying and heartless to the suffering of others and where we need to become more attuned to the way others are feeling.

3.   Through Pluto we come to acknowledge where our *will* is directed towards self-gain and where we are challenged to surrender ourselves to universal will.

The outer planets are therefore energies which serve to adjust the functioning of mind, heart and will and may be seen as sources of *healing power* which can help us to overcome the inner dis-ease which lies at the root of all our physical illness. For in accordance with New Age medical philosophy,* it is when we fall out of step with universal consciousness that we become prone to sickness. In rekindling within us a sense of concern for the whole, the outer planets restore us as individuals to a wholeness and soundness of body.

To be accurate, the outer planets do not in themselves constitute universal qualities but may be considered as *gateways* to these qualities. Thus by virtue of the learning processes they generate in our lives they promote our attunement to universal consciousness. The three outer planets may be seen as a common gateway to the New Age brotherhood of man in which all souls experience a sense of kinship and express that harmony in their relationship with each other.

---

* See Dr Edward Bach, *Heal Thyself* (C. W. Daniel, 1931).

6.
URANUS: GATEWAY TO UNIVERSAL MIND
Aquarius and the Eleventh House

Uranus, the higher vibration of Mercury, is concerned with raising our level of intellectual awareness so as to give *understanding* of the notion of at-oneness, and thus by implication the relative insignificance of the ego. Uranus demands a soul-conscious outlook since the at-oneness of all life can be understood only in terms of the spiritual as opposed to the material. Uranus is referred to as *universal mind* since it is based on holistic rather than subjective reasoning and since it can provide access to the source of universal knowledge by breaking down the barriers of personal prejudice.

We may contrast Uranus with Mercury by remembering that whereas Mercury represents the reasoning faculties of the ego, Uranus symbolizes the reasoning faculties of the soul. Whereas Mercury can effect only a limited mental analysis, Uranus is capable of breaking through the boundaries of subjective thinking and drawing on the stupendous wisdom represented by universal mind.

Like its physical counterpart, Uranus is concerned not merely with reasoning but also with communication since the natural follow-up to formulating an idea is to pass it on to others. But just as Uranian *thinking* differs totally from that of Mercury, so equally Uranus *communicates* along quite different lines. In the same way that Uranus is a reasoning function which goes beyond the three dimensions and indeed may be described as a psychic function, so also at its highest level it stimulates a method of communication which depends not on physical but on psychic expression. Uranus transfers thought without the need for speech: it symbolizes telepathy or the ability to convey and pick up thoughts over any distance without the use of the spoken or written word.

Individuality/Equality: a Uranian Paradox
The function of Uranus is to develop our mental appreciation of the at-oneness of the universe, of its constituent parts, and of our

own role within it. This process is twofold and consists firstly in accepting the unique and vital part played by each element of the cosmos, and secondly in realizing the equal value of each of these elements since they are all, without exception, essential to the efficient functioning of the whole.

In order to accept the unity or interdependency of all humanity it is necessary to realize that the individual is not spiritually self-sufficient. When we think only in terms of the ego we tend to feel cut off, we are unaware of our interdependency one upon another. But Uranus brings the realization that the world cannot function without each individual playing his or her part and teaches us to view life rather like a drama in which each actor's role is different and yet equally important. With this realization comes the understanding that not only is each human being unique but also of equal value to every other. The message of Uranus is stark and clear-cut: no one person, no one constituent part is of greater or lesser importance within the whole.

Uranus is associated with the concept of brotherhood since it helps us to accept each person as an individual and as our brother — under the influence of this planet all barriers are broken down. It is representative of socialism in the non-political sense (Latin *socius* = friend). This is an influence which eliminates prejudice and snobbery, allowing us to mix freely with all conditions of man. Through Uranus we come to see the value and worth of that which is *different*. Thus we come to realize that we are all individuals yet at one with each other.

The acceptance of others associated with Uranus is nevertheless void of emotion. This is the higher vibration of Mercury and relates purely to intellectual understanding. We accept the concept of at-oneness at a reasoning level, but the heart and feelings remain untouched. There is friendly (social) and unprejudiced interaction with others, but in a totally detached way.

Freedom and Free Will

A principle closely bound up with the energy of Uranus is that of freedom. At its highest level freedom can be understood as the ability to shift at will from one's own standpoint to that of others. It represents independence from all ties and attachments — whether material, emotional or intellectual — which may impede our mobility and capacity to absorb understanding of the world about us. As such, freedom allows us to follow up our intellectual acceptance of the manifold constituent parts of the universe by actually participating in experiences and outlooks which differ from our own. In so doing we do not lose our own individual viewpoint but simply learn to approach any situation from a plurality of different angles — the secret of true intelligence.

A refined expression of freedom never allows the urge for personal liberty to bring suffering to those to whom we owe commitment or to infringe on others' rights. If we accept that all individuals are equally necessary to the functioning of the whole, then it should follow that each be accorded equal rights and an equal degree of freedom to play their role unhindered. This in turn implies that none of us is entitled to a greater degree of personal liberty than the next person. If we reject the idea of hierarchy in terms of our personal worth, then we must also reject the idea of graded privilege.

Neither can there be any question of superiority or inferiority. Given our inherent equality, no one individual is beholden to any other in the sense that he or she should feel subservient or answerable to the other person. Each role is valuable in its own right. Anarchy need not necessarily result, for true Uranian awareness could give birth to a society in which there is no call or need for the imposition of authority nor for government as we know it. If the notions of class and hierarchy were extinct we would cease to witness the struggle for rights and freedom reflected in present-day politics. If the principle of equality was inborn in men, external imbalance and injustice would disappear of their own accord.

Like the notion of equality, the question of liberty can only be fully understood when viewed in a spiritual light. The true liberty of man is that enjoyed by his soul, a liberty which cannot be crushed by persecutors or oppressors of our body or mind. Although we may well be subject to multiple limitations in the physical sense which give us a feeling of restriction or restlessness, the nature of the soul is such that it enjoys absolute freedom over its destiny. For just as we have created our present reality by virtue of past choices, so we are right now creating our future reality on the basis of our current thoughts, emotions and actions.

The finest definition we may give to Uranus is that of free will — a quality available to every soul which permits us to choose between the different options open to us. Free will is the great unknown factor in astrology since the birth chart can only indicate the choices available to an individual, not the decision that the individual will take.

In order to make a totally objective decision we must be detached from all factors which might hold us back from making the choice which is in our true interest. And for this reason we cannot really exert free will until we have released ourselves from all attachments whether of a material, physical, emotional or intellectual nature.

Only then can we consider ourselves free agents who can move on at will from one situation to another as becomes necessary for our growth without casting a look of regret behind us.

The detachment and adaptability which form the basis of true free will may be contrasted with the mock independence which we often imagine to represent freedom but which in reality is no more than a frantic fear of commitment and responsibility.

The Mark of Genius

The ultimate in Uranian attunement consists of an extraordinary clarity of vision which can manifest as flashes of intuition, inventiveness, 'brain waves' and heightened ESP — in other words access to universal mind and stimulation of universal communication.

In essence Uranus represents the quest for the 'multi-faceted jewel of truth'* wherein true understanding can be gained only by studying and appreciating each of those facets. Uranus impresses upon us that there is no one path to truth and that there exist many different ways of looking at any one thing. It is this ability to detach self from any given situation and approach it from many varying angles which is the mark of true genius and the secret behind all advances in understanding. Also essential to this sort of achievement is the ability to admit the existence of that which is not immediately or materially obvious. Thus Uranus brings the possibility of grasping abstract ideas — clearly why it is so prominent in the charts of mathematicians and scientists. It is here that the importance of developing greater tolerance and adaptability becomes apparent. For it is only when we are able to respect standpoints which differ from our own and to move away from our own standpoint to view things temporarily from a different angle that breakthroughs in knowledge can occur.

The outstanding leaps in scientific insight which date from the discovery of Uranus are directly related to the manifestations of this planet's vibrations.

At its highest level Uranus brings comprehension of the interrelatedness of all matter and spirit. A mind which is sufficiently attuned to the concept of universality is unlimited in its scope since it is able to grasp the unity behind the multiple facets of truth. The boundaries which impede our capacity for total understanding reflect our inability or refusal to accept the notion of at-oneness. When Uranus has completely broken down the barriers of prejudice and fear, then also may total awareness be ours.

When the mind becomes adept at breaking through barriers it

* Term used in White and Swainson, *Gildas Communicates*.

is able to move beyond three-dimensional consciousness in order to tap a vast store of information not immediately available to our physical minds. It thus becomes able to pick up information from the source of universal knowledge.

Uranus and ESP

As we have seen, receptivity to universal mind gives the potential for psychic communication, so that Uranus is the governing force behind all ESP. Extra-sensory perception is a means of 'seeing' which is independent of our five physical senses — an accurate definition of the non-physical understanding and communication which we are striving towards with Uranus.

It is given in many sources that telepathy was one of the original attributes of man which has gradually been lost in accordance with our 'fall'. It is also widely believed that ESP will tend to redevelop as one of the manifestations of the New Age. As we work on ourselves to clear out the dross which we have collected over a period of many lives, we gradually uncover abilities we scarcely believed possible. The phenomenon of telepathy is one such ability and there seems to be plenty of evidence that it is indeed on the increase.

Astrology as a Tool of Uranus

Our most powerful tool in breaking down the barriers that limit our vision and deny us access to universal knowledge and universal communication is *humility*. All studies which engender a sense of humility by stressing the interrelatedness of the various components of the universe express the principle of Uranus. But astrology, based on the concept of 'as above, so below' and concerned as it is with demonstrating the connection between the macrocosm and the microcosm, is undoubtedly one of the most characteristically Uranian disciplines. Not only does astrology throw light on the repetition of basic themes through every stratum of the universe, but by highlighting the common struggle of all human beings to come to terms with various spiritual forces — the focal points of which are the planets — it stresses the fundamental unity of mankind. Above all things, astrology is the great leveller.

Furthermore, through astrology we come to appreciate the worth and significance of each of the basic modes of human expression, as represented by the planets and their associated signs and houses. In this way we develop our tolerance and respect for all outlooks and approaches even where these differ vastly from our own. Through the study of astrology we can begin to break down the barriers of prejudice.

Lack of Attunement to Uranus

Where there is lack of attunement to Uranus the notions of uniqueness and freedom are entirely or mainly directed towards self rather than applied to others. In other words we are more concerned with our own individuality rather than that of other people; similarly we are preoccupied with our personal rights over and above those of others.

We have seen that the true expression of Uranus is to break down the barriers which inhibit our understanding of the universe, since this is a universal energy. In contrast, where we are lacking in attunement to Uranus, our understanding is likely to be limited by blind spots which divide and isolate us from others.

Self-Importance, Arrogance and Prejudice

If we accept that the perfect expression of the Uranus principle involves respect for the uniqueness of each entity within the cosmos and the importance of its contribution to the whole, then the antithesis of that awareness must consist of respect only for the uniqueness of self. Here we are in our own eyes the most significant person in the world and a feeling of *self-importance* is fundamental to our state of being. We have a strongly developed sense of our own individuality and a marked need to 'do our own thing', but as yet there is insufficient appreciation of the individuality of others. We are so dazzled by our own uniqueness that we fail to notice that others are special too.

This state of awareness is usually accompanied by *arrogance* — literally meaning refusal to ask — in that our preoccupation with our own way of going about things leads us to ignore or disdain the qualities and talents of others. Self-orientated Uranus produces the big-head, the know-all who would never ask anything of anyone and can never be told anything. For although we are keenly aware of our speciality, as yet we cannot see that there is much we do not know.

Not only is there arrogance, but there is also an inability to understand the ways of others where they differ from our own. Just as true expression of Uranus results in perfect understanding of all mankind, so lack of attunement to Uranus results in failure to understand others. The measure of our mastery of Uranus is our ability to tolerate and accept every variety of expression within the cosmos — even where this is totally opposed to our own. Without this tolerance we are apt to criticize or mock whatever is alien to us. When we react in this way we are always right and the others of course are always wrong! 'Everyone's odd except thee and me and even thee's a bit strange!' By expecting others to act, feel, think and speak as we ourselves do we are demonstrating our lack of awareness of the multiple facets of the whole. We have not fully appreciated how dull the world would be if we were all alike.

We have failed to understand the essential concept of variety which invalidates the notions of 'good' and 'bad' or those of 'right' and 'wrong'. For it is only when we no longer judge others and express total tolerance — even of those who are themeselves intolerant — that we are completely in tune with the principle of Uranus and that we have fully broken down our intellectual barriers.

Personal Freedom and Personal Rights

A fundamental principle of Uranus consists in refining our understanding and expression of freedom. We learn to respect the equal rights of every cosmic entity based on the equally important part played by each component of the whole. Therefore failure to observe this principle will result in preoccupation with our own freedom regardless of the rights of others.

It goes without saying that when we view life only from our own standpoint, our behaviour will be totally governed by the way we look at things. This can manifest as stubbornness, a refusal to adapt to suggestions, and rebellion against attempts to divert us from our course. In itself this does not imply a desire to convert others to our ways (as is the case with Pluto) but simply an insistence on following our own mind. Frequently we might refer to this type of independence as a need for freedom, but in reality it is a stunted freedom which chains us to a narrow field of experience and which fails to result in any growth. Certainly it can never lead to inspiration or universal understanding since it prevents us from further expanding our vision of the 'multi-faceted jewel of truth'.

Total absorption with our own rights can also mean that we trample on others whose rights must of necessity take a back seat to our own. Within a family unit, for example, one partner's excessive insistence on personal freedom may curtail the freedom of the other partner who may have to take on additional responsibilities as a result. It is one thing to exert our liberty to be true to ourselves; it is another thing entirely to respect the liberty of others to do likewise.

The non-conformist who indulges in offensive or violent behaviour which is calculated to shock is out of touch with the rights of others to exist in their own fashion. When our rebellion makes life supremely difficult for those with whom we are in contact, we are failing to allow others to play their own part without harassment. Uranus demands that we respect the validity of every role, however different it may be to our own. And it teaches us that if we wish to avoid being harassed, we must first cease to harass others.

Problems of Adjustment to Uranus

In adjusting to Uranus we must learn to cope with a multi-faceted outlook and the problems arising therefrom. Awakening to the exciting realization that life offers so many different experiences, each unique and fascinating in its own right, can lead to a strong urge to widespread experimentation so as to achieve maximum assimilation in the shortest time possible. This can result in a dizzy whirl of diffuse activity by which we effectively achieve nothing and succeed merely in confusing ourselves.

But it is not simply dizzy exhilaration which is responsible for the erratic fluctuation in behaviour which is characteristic of attunement to Uranus. The ego can be remarkably reluctant to move beyond its own stance, so that although we may well desire to look on the other side of the fence, there is a fear of stopping long enough to begin to identify with different outlooks and to jeopardize our own clear-cut approach. The outcome can be a marked pull towards experimentation coupled with a tendency to change course unpredictably whenever any form of commitment is required. We develop a stop–go pattern which eventually leads to a spasmodic energy flow and problems with consistency and continuity. Such general lack of stability can place stress on the nervous system, hence the close association of nervous problems — and in some cases nervous breakdowns — with Uranus.

Problems of inconsistency and fluctuation are less likely to occur when we are motivated by a sincere desire for truth. We are thereby drawn towards those activities which will prove most fulfilling and enlightening instead of catapulting ourselves into a multitude of purposeless and disassociated experiences which do nothing to widen our horizons.

As long as we do not fully appreciate the worth of that which lies outside ourself, our experimentation will inevitably demonstrate our lack of concern for others. Thus in pursuing the path of freedom we are likely to neglect the needs of those close to us and our responsibilities to those to whom we owe commitments. As yet we have failed to grasp the essence of Uranus, which demands recognition of the equal importance of all parts of the whole. The final outcome of this unbalanced approach to freedom is likely to be isolation and loneliness as we alienate others through our independence. In working with the energy of Uranus it is important to bear in mind that freedom can — and indeed must — operate in unison with responsibility.

Another difficulty in adjusting to Uranus occurs when we seek to express its principles at a group level. In its perfect expression Uranus brings a sense of universal brotherhood, but this is often preceded by a group awareness in which personal liberty is subjugated to the welfare of a sect. The Uranian disgust with oppression and persecution and strong desire to bring about equal opportunity may be present, but as yet it is limited. All those who represent sectarian interests may well experience a strong sense of brotherhood within their group but all too often the needs of the group are placed before the needs of the planet as a whole. The fact is that Uranus is not a group-orientated principle but a universal energy and that which is truly universal must always take into account the well-being of the whole rather than any one section thereof.

Uranus and Politics
The wave of revolution which made itself felt shortly after the 'discovery' of Uranus in 1781 may be considered merely as the birth pangs of true Uranian consciousness, for the fact is that physical revolution is *not* the essence of Uranus. Because Uranus is fundamentally an attitude of mind, those who inflict harm upon others by taking violent action in the name of 'liberty, fraternity or equality' are actually traitors to their cause. All three of the outer planets represent *psychic* rather than physical energies so that it is inappropriate that they should be expressed purely in a physical sense. The New Age planets are each concerned with bringing about spiritual changes which go beyond material changes or more correctly must always precede material changes. And so the function of Uranus is to generate an *inner* revolution in terms of our thinking which will break down the barriers of prejudice at the mental level.

If we can accept the two principles of Uranus inasmuch as men are not merely equal but also individuals in their own right, we may acknowledge that equality must coexist together with diversity. It is interesting that the two main political philosophies of the present time each reflect one facet of Uranus, Capitalism standing for 'liberty' and Communism representing 'equality'. It is not until the twain finally come to meet that the essence of Uranus will have been fully assimilated at a reasoning level. Acceptance solely of equality can lead to a faceless anonymity or to cloning, whereas support for the concept of individual liberty to the exclusion of that of equality is responsible for the unacceptable selfishness of the Western lifestyle.

Uranus in the Birth Chart
The sign placing of Uranus is common to all those born within a

span of seven years or so and therefore it is the *house* placing of this planet and the aspects it forms with other planets which will relate more closely to our personal life challenge. The study of mass karma or generation karma as indicated by the sign placings of the outer planets is a subject in its own right which is worthy of separate consideration elsewhere.

In the birth chart the function of Uranus is to develop our universal understanding by providing opportunities for us to witness various aspects of the 'multi-faceted jewel of truth' alongside of our own individual self-expression. In the area of life in question we are challenged to overcome a sense of self-importance and develop an appreciation of others' standpoints. In so doing we begin to break down the barriers which isolate us from others at the mental level and develop our potential for intellectual insights and ESP.

Similarly we are challenged to move away from blind independence and resentment of restriction towards a position of positive flexibility where we recognize the need to experience life from many different angles yet with consideration for the impact our actions will have on others. This is the area of life in which we must learn to distinguish between valuable experimentation which allows us to expand our understanding through our experiences, and erratic experimentation and inconsistency which simply prevent us from absorbing anything of worth.

For a fuller description of the meaning of Uranus in each of the houses and in aspect with other planets, see Chapter 12, 'The School of Uranus'.

The Sign Aquarius

In accordance with its ruler Uranus, the sign Aquarius expresses itself in a need to understand the fundamental at-oneness of the universe in terms of the unique role played by every constituent part of the cosmos, and the equally valuable role played by each of those constituent parts. This is the sign concerned with the exploration of alternatives, which represents a basic theme of the Age of Aquarius.

Especially when the Sun or Mars fall in Aquarius, the motivation behind the activities of this sign is to create an equal society in which every sector or individual is recognized for its own worth. At its best this sign will be aware of the significance of every component of the universe and will be working for the well-being of the whole rather than any one section thereof. There will be a strong need to be seen as one who is truly universal in outlook, having an equal respect for man, nature and the entire cosmos.

At the other end of the scale, Aquarius can be self-important and prejudiced against those who differ from itself. Equally it can be concerned with its own freedom to the disregard of the rights of others and to the extent of angry and often violent rebellion against those who seem to threaten its personal liberty.

Somewhere in between we find the partisan Aquarius which will often concern itself with campaigning to establish the rights of a minority group but is as yet unable to grasp the concept of at-oneness and take into account the interests of the whole. At this group-orientated stage, politics — and especially socialism — is often a fervent interest, as is social work in any shape or form. Aquarius is attracted to any type of group endeavour which gives the opportunity for mutual co-operation and democratic administration.

Aquarius's reactions will usually be based on a cool analysis of the situation, but of a considerably wider scope than that effected by its counterpart Gemini (Mercury, the lower vibration of Uranus, rules Gemini). At its best this sign has the quality of objective judgement, being able to perceive many different facets of the truth rather than adopting a personally biased attitude. Especially when the Moon falls in Aquarius there is the capacity for understanding and acceptance of all the various conditions of man — an inability to condemn which makes for a sense of ease in every social environment and within a vast circle of acquaintance. But at worst there is arrogance and intolerance of all emotions which are unacceptable to its own detached approach.

Potentially this is a superbly functioning intellect — and noticeably so when Mercury falls in Aquarius — with the inherent capacity to tap the universal source of knowledge, thereby coming up with 'new' ideas or inventions. At the very least there is the possibility of rapidly tuning into new ideas both in the realm of science and the occult. At the root of this gift lies the capacity to understand the interrelationship between every component of the universe or to see in the mind's eye the at-oneness of the whole. But until this stage is reached the intellect will still be struggling against the barriers which impede its vision and which stem from an inability to see the value of ideas which differ from its own. Aquarius at this level will pour scorn on such ideas. It is certainly in touch with its own freedom of speech but as yet is denying the same to others.

This is the sign ultimately capable of true brotherly love — non-emotional, equal affection for all its fellow men and women. In order to extend itself in so many directions Aquarius must of necessity remain detached since strong feelings of involvement would inhibit the Aquarius urge towards liberal fraternizing. But the big challenge of this sign — and especially when Venus falls in Aquarius — is to arrive at a state of balance between its own freedom and that of others. Its active defence of its right to associate with whoever it likes, whenever it likes may well be at the expense of others. In any partnership or group setting the freedom of each member must be equal — otherwise there can be no true freedom.

The Eleventh House

The Eleventh House relates to all pursuits which serve to promote universal understanding. It stands for those activities which help us to see others as our brothers and sisters, each unique yet of equal standing with ourselves and with each other.

These will be basically group activities (clubs, societies, social gatherings) which bring us into contact with large numbers of different people and which tend to be run along democratic, egalitarian lines. Communes or co-operative enterprises would also fulfil this purpose. The same activities can also develop a more balanced approach to freedom, since their successful functioning is dependent upon mutual respect for the equal rights and liberties of all the members.

The Eleventh House may also be considered to represent social work of all descriptions since through these activities we develop understanding for all types and classes of individuals and through that understanding build up a sense of fraternity (Latin *socius* = friend). Equally, those drawn towards social work generally feel a strong urge to help others to assert their rights and to bring into being fairer conditions within society. Note that the type of 'social work' connected with the Eleventh House differs from that of the Twelfth House in that the emotions are not involved. The function of the Eleventh House is simply to develop a detached intellectual awareness.

Politics figure strongly amongst Eleventh House affairs since the purported function of political organizations is to represent the rights of their supporters and to secure improved social conditions for them.

7.

NEPTUNE: GATEWAY TO UNIVERSAL BEAUTY AND UNIVERSAL LOVE
Pisces and the Twelfth House

Neptune has become known as the higher vibration of Venus, since whereas Venus is concerned with the experience of beauty and love from a personal standpoint, Neptune's function is to uplift our experience of beauty and love to a level which supersedes the needs of the ego. Neptune is the second of the three New Age energies which appeal to the spiritual rather than the physical nature of mankind and urge us to set aside the self for the greater purpose of universality.

We have seen in the preceding chapter that the foundations of cosmic unity are laid by Uranus which promotes mutual understanding in that it breaks down the barriers of *intellectual* intolerance and thus paves the way for a state of loving co-operation. It is this next stage of overcoming the barriers which separate us from others at the *emotional* level and of experiencing love for every aspect of the universe which is ruled by the planet Neptune.

Neptune relates to a state of feeling rather than simply understanding, as was the case with Uranus. Now we undergo the challenge not merely of comprehending but of actually experiencing the concept of at-oneness. Whereas Uranus is an intellectually based function like its lower octave Mercury, the purpose of Neptune is to engender an emotional response. With Neptune we do not simply *understand* others — we *feel* for them too. The feeling function of Neptune is more complex than the reasoning function of Uranus, and just as it offers greater rewards, when misapplied it is likely to result in more problems.

Universal Beauty

In contrast to its counterpart Venus, Neptune symbolizes a joy which is not linked to matter or the physical senses, but which is spiritual in nature. Whereas Venus finds its fulfilment in the delights of nature, matter and the human form, the beauty sought by Neptune lies beyond the three dimensions. Because it is a universal energy, Neptune represents the quest for unlimited beauty, which clearly is not to be found within the realms of the consciousness we call earth. If Venus is the search for joy of the ego, then Neptune symbolizes the yearnings of the soul to experience ecstasy. From the earthbound viewpoint, Neptune may be considered the search for an *ideal*, or that which is seemingly impossible to achieve.

The appreciation of universal beauty implies a potential to see goodness and loveliness in the *whole* rather than any one part of it. On the one hand, as we have seen, it is necessary to look beyond matter for our deep satisfaction, and at the same time it is necessary to look beyond the ego and its immediate surroundings. While we are preoccupied with ourselves we cannot appreciate the goodness in others.

Idealization, Visualization, Imagination

In order to respond to Neptune it is necessary to move towards some level of spiritual awareness since very often the physical condition of the world about us leaves much to be desired. Neptune teaches us that beauty is in the eye of the beholder and urges us to focus on the full potential of an entity over and above its existing form. All beings have an inherent beauty which we can keep in mind over and above their physical manifestation.

It is here that the *imagination* has an important role to play by conjuring up images and pictures of our ideals which when kept in mind move closer towards fulfilment. It is not a question of remaining blind to negativity or of behaving as gullible fools who allow the unscrupulous to take advantage of us. The rose-tinted spectacles of Neptune must naturally take into account the hard facts before any actions or decisions are made and here Neptune cannot function safely without the discrimination of Virgo, the sign which opposes Pisces. But then, through a conscious effort of the mind, negativity can be placed on one side and replaced by uplifting images.

The mind is all-powerful in its influence and that which today is a product of the imagination will in the future become our reality. Where the mind dwells on beauty, beauty will be met, but where it is preoccupied with ugliness, then, too, so will be the reaping.

If we come to appreciate the beauty of the whole, this need not mean that we no longer see the good in ourselves — that we become self-critical or self-defacing — any more than Uranus demands that we disregard our vital role within the whole. But just as Uranus teaches us to get our sense of importance into perspective, so Neptune can help us to take a more proportionate view of our own virtues. If, when working with Neptune, we lose track of our self-worth we have invariably failed to grasp the message of Uranus: each spoke in the wheel is essential to the functioning of the whole.

Whereas Venusian appreciation of beauty is purely subjective, restricted as it is by the limitations of the ego, Neptune can open us up to the experience of an all-embracing joy which comprises within itself the sum content of every part of the whole, and which thus is universal. To those finely attuned to its energy, Neptune provides access to the source of universal beauty from whence all musical and artistic *inspiration* is derived. The key to this source is gained by the ability to see beauty in all things and the ability to express selfless love. This may be compared with Uranus's function as guardian of the source of universal knowledge, the key to which is acceptance of all the component parts of the cosmos and a sense of personal humility.

Universal Love

Whereas Venus is a comparatively simple energy, Neptune is undeniably complicated, considered by some to be downright confusing, standing as it does for the urge to experience that which is intangible or in fact spiritual in essence. The ego-orientated Venus drive simply seeks love in the form of human relationship, generally at a one-to-one level, and is based for the main part on the concept of give and take. In the case of Venus, only reciprocated love can bring fulfilment, whereas unrequited love cannot.

By way of comparison, Neptunian love is selfless in nature — the factor of personal gain is eliminated from the issue. The notion of selfless love was exemplified by Jesus the Christ, the great spiritual teacher of the Age of Pisces, the sign ruled by Neptune, and although practised by few is nevertheless still held as an ideal by many.

It is a hard but unavoidable fact that as far as Neptune is concerned, any relationship pursued with a view of self-gain will eventually prove to be disappointing. Neptune is an exacting taskmaster and in order to teach us the concept of univeral love demands that we love even when we ourselves are unloved. And it is for this reason that it is often associated with one-sided or unreturned love.

Universal love is necessarily selfless since it extends beyond the 'self'. It is a quality not of the temporary ego but of the soul, the infinite component of man which by its very nature is interlinked with all other souls.

Unlimited Relationship

The difficulties involved in attunement to universal love have earned

Neptune a notorious reputation as far as earthly happiness is concerned. Nevertheless, happiness *is* to be found through Neptune if we know where to look for it. A self-motivated relationship is bound to be ultimately sorrowful since our happiness is directly dependent on what the other person can give to us. And however much love we receive from the loved one, under the influence of Neptune we are still likely to experience a sense of dissatisfaction. For the fact is that no one relationship, nor even several, can prove totally fulfilling. The whole point about Neptunian love is that it does not limit itself in any way. It is equally distributed amongst the whole.

Venus may well be content to enjoy a restricted experience of love, restricted firstly in quantity and secondly in quality. But the goal of Neptune is *unlimited relationship* and the experience of *unlimited love* — seemingly impossible by earthly standards, but then Neptune is by no means earthbound. Universal love of this kind cannot possibly be found with one person or even within the scope of several relationships. Rather it implies relationship with all humanity or with the entire universe, and is experienced in a sense of at-oneness with the whole.

Universal Compassion

Part and parcel of universal love is the quality of compassion, literally the ability to 'suffer with' others, to put ourselves in their place and sympathize with their feelings. When we experience universal compassion we are able to empathize with others to the point where our own feelings are no longer foremost. At its highest level Neptune demands that personal sensitivity be channelled outwards and that self-pity be transmuted into compassion for others. Here again, although the self is placed on one side, it is not annihilated. It is simply a question of developing a sense of perspective about our own significance in relation to the whole.

Through the experience of compassion we develop the quality of mercy — we learn to forgive the blows which others deal us. Not until we can express this quality of Neptune are we in a position to attune fully to the highly demanding energy of Pluto. For it is when we are lacking in mercy that we run into the greatest difficulties in learning to handle the power represented by Pluto.

Neptune and Mediumship

Mediumship is a talent possessed by those who have come some way towards relating to others in a universal or limitless sense. It implies the ability to break beyond the bounds of relationship in the physical form, so that emotional contact is possible with souls not currently incarnate. In a more general sense Neptune also governs our ability to 'pick up' others' feelings at long range.

There is a subtle difference between the psychic faculties assigned to Neptune and those referred to in connection with Uranus, in that Neptunian psychic awareness functions at an emotional level in contrast to the purely factual range of Uranus.

Mediumship can be dangerous unless it is strictly controlled and trained.

Mysticism — the Vital Outlet for Neptune

There would seem to be little doubt that mystical practices are by far the most rewarding outlet for the expression of Neptune. Through the experience of meditation and yoga (yoga = 'union'), we develop a feeling of spiritual unity with all other beings and with all creation.

Meditation is the ideal Neptunian activity since it meets the two basic needs which stem from that planet. On the one hand, by allowing us to establish a link with the Source it is the only truly effective way of enjoying the level of limitless relationship we long for. Secondly it opens us up to the experience of ecstasy which goes beyond the senses — the *ideal* — the only form of happiness which can satisfy the soul in the way demanded by Neptune. Through the experience of at-oneness during our meditation periods we may come to experience greater universal beauty and love in our everyday life. We may also become less dependent on personal love and thus less subject to sorrow in our relationships.

Neptune and the Arts

Meditation may well be the mainstay of Neptune, but there are other methods of developing a sense of universal beauty and love. For example, artistic activities open us up to the world of universal beauty, whether we ourselves are creative or are simply spectators of the creative work of others.

The Neptunian approach to art and music is quite different to that of Venus. In the case of Venus our appreciation is linked to the rhythm and tune of a song to which we specifically respond. The Neptunian response is more diffuse but can likewise be more profound. Now we associate ourselves with the *feeling* behind the work of art, with which we can experience a sense of at-oneness.

Music and the arts bring us very close to the experience of unlimited joy and emotion, firstly since they reflect inspiration from the source of universal beauty and secondly since they express feelings which are common to all mankind. The arts, and especially music, can represent a unifying force in which all can 'lose themselves' and feel temporarily part of a greater whole.

Drama comes very much under the rulership of Neptune since, for actor and spectator alike, it affords the chance to step out of our own shoes and identify with another personality. Let us here differentiate between the Neptunian approach to drama and that of the Sun/Leo/Fifth House. Whereas the latter is attracted to theatre on account of the opportunity it provides for self-expression, it is precisely in order to *transcend* self that Neptune mounts the boards. Fundamentally the Sun performer always remains himself, whilst the Neptunian delights in becoming somebody different. For Neptune, theatre and films are an important means of participating in universal emotion. Every tear shed in identification with some 'role' is an expression of sympathy for the common sorrows of the human race.

The mediums of dance and of opera deserve a special mention since they allow us to lose ourselves not only in the experiences of the characters but in the beauty of the music also.

The Role of Service

For others, involvement in various forms of institutional life provides wide-scale contact with human sorrow and gives an outlet for the expression of unselfish love. Under the influence of Neptune we may choose to work in prisons, asylums or hospitals, etc., whereas others of us may find ourselves involuntarily spending time in these places. But whether we serve or suffer in such places, the purpose is the same: to come face to face with universal suffering and to develop universal compassion.

Cut off from material diversions, nurse and patient alike are immersed in the world of feelings as they attempt to come to terms with the question of pain. Suffering is a condition which spares no one and is common to all sentient beings. Very often a spell in an institution is needed to open our eyes to the feelings of others. In sharing the troubles of others we begin to experience a sense of at-oneness with them — we are developing the capacity for selfless love. A stay in an institution of any description is also an opportunity to rest the mind from material concerns and explore the world within.

Lack of Attunement to Neptune
Limited Beauty

When we lack attunement to Neptune our appreciation of beauty is limited to the ego and we are thus unable to see good in anything other than that which directly relates to ourselves. This is equivalent to a Uranian absorption with our own self-importance, where we disregard the value of others. In the case of Neptune it is not so much the importance of others as their goodness which is disregarded. The outlook is cynical (literally meaning 'incredulous of human goodness') and only the failings of others are noticed and drawn attention to. As opposed to the true Neptunian idealism where we see the best in others, here we can only think the worst of them.

Sometimes there is a *self-righteous* attitude which often extends to those directly in our entourage — 'I and mine can think no wrong and do no wrong'. This sense of personal virtue can occasionally manifest as a saviour complex where we believe that we have been divinely appointed to accomplish a mission of great spiritual importance.

In other cases it can lead to a sense of persecution where we believe that all are against us but fail to question our own integrity. As in the case of a positive expression of Neptune, here too the imagination is at work but serves to paint only ugly and sorrowful pictures. The mind becomes obsessed with morbid fears and worries which we often live out as vividly as if they had actually materialized. What we fail to realize when we allow ourselves to become caught up in negative thinking patterns of this kind is that our mental images of today will to some degree become our reality tomorrow — good reason to take care in directing the colourful wanderings of the Neptunian mind.

Limited Love

Whereas universal love embraces every component of the whole, lack of attunement to Neptune restricts us to limited love — a love which is limited to the demands of the ego. Not only is there an inability to love others unless our feelings are at least partly returned, but in addition all the sensitivity that we could be expressing towards others turns inwards and focuses on our own reactions: '*I'm* so hurt', etc. Here, often due to difficulties in understanding what the other person is going through, there is an inability to make allowances for behaviour which is aggressive or hurtful towards us. Instead everything is taken personally, even in situations where no offence was intended. Imagined or deliberate slights prey on our mind to such an extent that we become full of *self-pity* and totally preoccupied with our own emotional pain.

Problems of Adjustment to Neptune
Adjustment to Universal Beauty
As we become attuned to the concept of universal beauty, we may notice that sensual pleasures are increasingly disappointing and a growing disillusionment with matter begins. Spurred on by Neptunian

yearnings, we may indulge in ever larger and more spectacular bouts of sense-gratification, but these can only deepen our disillusionment.

At the point where we are discontented with the material world but have not yet found the answer to our desires, the question of escapism becomes a serious problem. The desire to experience the ultimate 'high' can lead to over-indulgence in alcohol and sex or to experimentation with drugs which stimulate our psychic faculties and produce a temporary state of euphoria but which, through their addictive effects, may finally reduce us to further despair. Escapist fantasy — not to be confused with positive visualization — can also have grave consequences. When our would-be world begins to encroach on the territory of the here and now it becomes increasingly difficult for us to distinguish between fact and fiction, which in extreme cases can result in mental illness.

It is not only the world about us which causes us disappointment but also ourselves as individuals, and it is this self-disillusionment which can be the hardest of all to cope with. As we begin to realize our own failings and weaknesses we can become engulfed by a sense of worthlessness which deals a severe blow to our self-confidence and draws us further into escapist activities. The feeling that we are 'no good' can be counteracted by a healthy Uranian respect for our self-worth.

As our idealism begins to develop we may now become hopeful of finding goodness in others but as yet we are unable to bridge the chasm between our ideals and harsh reality. Now we may have high hopes of others and may initially acknowledge their good qualities, but this is likely to give way rapidly to a profound sense of let-down as our illusions are dispelled. Once again escapism is a possible outcome.

Adjustment to Universal Love

In working with Neptune we need to move from a position in which we focus only on our own feelings to the complete disregard of those of others towards a position in which we can tune in to the feelings of others whilst still remaining in touch with our own. Problems inevitably arise during the process of adjustment, the most common of which is that of *projection*. At the stage at which our powers of perception as yet lack the necessary refinement, we may believe that we are aware of the other person's emotions and motives whereas in reality we have completely misunderstood them. We fall into the pattern of assuming that another person is reacting to a situation in a certain way simply because that is how we ourselves would react. When we unwittingly project our own responses onto others we are not only liable to incur misunderstandings and confusion but can also torture ourselves unnecessarily through misplaced compassion.

In other cases we may assess the other person's feelings with reasonable accuracy but over-empathize with them to the point of losing track of our own identity. At the worst extreme, this gives rise to the risk that we may be 'taken over' by extraneous emotions leading in some cases to psychological disturbances. More likely, however, over-identification with the problems of others will manifest as a tendency towards *martyrdom* and irrational feelings of *guilt*. Increased sensitivity to the suffering we perceive around us and difficulty in defining the limits of our personal involvement can lead us to feel responsible for the pain experienced by others and an irrepressible urge to run to their assistance.

In many cases it is the notion that pain seems to occur without rhyme or reason that leads to an obsession with human suffering and the inability to shake off the sense of personal guilt. Here acceptance of the Jupiterian law of cause and effect and the understanding that life always follows clearly defined laws can sometimes help. Also helpful is the Saturnian concept that each of us is personally responsible for ourselves. We cannot shield others from their own karma nor can we live their lives for them.

Uranian detachment is needed to prevent us from becoming totally immersed in the feelings of others. Although apparently contradictory, we cannot really love others until we have become detached from them, for universal love is equally distributed amongst the whole. Uranian appreciation of our own self-worth also helps to prevent us from martyring ourselves. A characteristic common amongst martyrs is a lack of awareness of their personal value; due to feelings of worthlessness they tend to give themselves away for nothing. Where our sense of personal identity is strong we are less likely to fall into the trap of making doormats of ourselves.

Deception, perhaps the most notorious of the traits associated with Neptune, represents another by-product of the process of attunement to this planet. In any contact with others the situation will no longer be considered purely from our own standpoint, but we will additionally take into account what the other person's attitude may be. By prejudging the likely reaction of others in response to what we say or do we may find ourselves (usually subconsciously) adapting or modifying our instinctive inclinations accordingly. Sometimes there is an altruistic motive behind the 'deception' in that we would not express our truthful opinion out of genuine concern for the other person's well-being, but in most cases we are motivated by a desire to protect ourselves. Here we are exploiting our growing ability to identify with others purely and simply for our own benefit.

A closely linked behaviour pattern is that of *treachery*. Here our empathy for others is such that there is the ability and willingness to share their feelings and experiences, often to the extent of drawing out personal secrets. But this sharing of confidence may be exploited if that trust is betrayed at a later point for purposes of self-gain. We have not yet sympathized with others sufficiently to ensure that we protect their well-being at all costs.

In many cases, however, we may be unfairly accused of deception when we are simply suffering from Neptunian absent-mindedness. As our intuitive faculties develop and we become increasingly attuned to relating to others at the psychic level, we may no longer be able to recall clearly what has actually taken place on the material plane. As a result it is common to reach a state of total muddle as to what was actually the outcome of any situation. Here we may be unfairly charged with deliberately misleading others whereas in reality we are simply experiencing confusion.

Neptune in the Birth Chart

As with the other two outer planets, we look to the aspects of Neptune and its house placing for indication of its challenge to us as individuals. The sign placing of Neptune relates more to the general karmic challenge of the generation born within fourteen years or so of us.

The areas of life highlighted by Neptune in our chart are where we are challenged to break down the barriers which separate us from others at the level of feelings. In so doing we allow ourselves access to the source of universal love and universal beauty and thus to the source of all artistic and musical inspiration.

It is here that we may begin to feel at-one with others and ultimately with the entire universe. It is here also that we may begin to sense the insignificance of the ego as we learn to relate to the greater whole and consequently may struggle with feelings of worthlessness. Here we will be given the opportunity to sympathize with the feelings of others — although we must guard against over-identifying with them. Here too we may be tested by self-pity (self-love as opposed to universal love).

In the areas in question we will seek a very high level of fulfilment and our expectations will be extremely high. As a result we may be liable to disappointment, disillusionment and to generally feeling sorry for ourselves when we fail to experience the euphoria we crave.

Our idealism in the areas of life designated by Neptune exists for a definite purpose. Its function is to help us to define our goals, to determine what we want and where we are going. The reality of the situation we find ourselves in may well cause us to despair but it is only by contrast that any notion can exist and we must confront the banal before we can reach out towards the superb. The dissatisfaction which most of us must live with in the areas ruled by the placing of Neptune in our chart can be relieved by the practice of meditation which can help us to see greater beauty in that which surrounds us. In addition, involvement in the arts or in selfless service can help to fulfil the urgent cravings which are associated with the placing of Neptune and which, if ignored, can lead to dependency and escapism.

For fuller details of the placement of Neptune in the birth chart see Chapter 13, 'The School of Neptune'.

The Sign Pisces

In accordance with its ruler Neptune, the function of Pisces is to work towards the experience of universal beauty and universal love. In so doing it is challenged to move beyond *self-love* and the commonest problems which confront Pisces consist in overcoming self-centred emotions and the psychological suffering which they engender.

Especially when the Sun or Mars falls in Pisces there can be a marked pull towards activities which stimulate the experience of universal love and beauty either in the form of the career or by way of a hobby. Thus the three main spheres of Neptunian expression — mysticism, the arts (music, painting, drama and literature) and service — will hold a particular fascination. The basis of all Pisces motivation is a yearning for emotional kicks, for a state of euphoria which cannot be satisfied by material goals. However, unless a fulfilling role in life can be found, Pisces may seek its 'highs' through the medium of drugs, sex, excessive fantasizing or dishonesty in a way that can be detrimental to its well-being.

Piscean idealism is often misconstrued and considered as a failing rather than the fine quality which it can represent. Difficulties occur only when reality proves too much of a let-down and Pisces is unable to rise above its personal disappointment. Especially when the Moon falls in Pisces it is necessary to consider very carefully the extent to which we are indulging in *self-pity* since the function of this sign is to develop compassion for others rather than remain totally absorbed with personal emotions. In learning to empathize with others it faces further challenges, however, as it must avoid projecting its own feelings onto other people or becoming over-involved with others' problems.

The imagination is potentially both the greatest asset and the greatest test for this sign — and especially when Mercury falls in Pisces. At its highest level Pisces allows access to the source of universal beauty and therefore is capable of producing inspired works of art and music. At a more general level Pisces is challenged to exercise its imagination by momentarily stepping into others' shoes, for example through books, films or caring work. But as soon as the imagination turns in on itself it runs the danger of becoming morbidly self-destructive even to the point of developing a persecution complex. The Piscean intellect must face many challenges as it learns to sympathize with others' feelings whilst remaining true to its own standpoint. Small wonder that it suffers so frequently from confusion.

The most demanding challenge for Pisces is the expression of selfless love and this is especially true when the planet Venus falls in Pisces. In learning to put its own needs on one side, Pisces can be prone to martyrdom in relationships, a sure sign that it is not in touch with its own self-worth. One of the greatest sources of sorrow for this sign is the lack of happiness attainable in contacts with others — whether romantic or otherwise. Yet its clearest path to fulfilment is to strive towards a level of consciousness where it feels at-one with creation as a whole and where personal relationships are no longer of paramount importance. The practice of meditation and yoga can help Pisces towards this goal.

The Twelfth House

The Twelfth House rules all activities which relate to the breaking down of barriers between ourselves and the rest of creation at the emotional level. These include:

— meditation, yoga, prayer and spiritual practices, whereby we develop a sense of at-oneness with the universe as a whole;
— work in hospitals, mental homes, institutions, charity organizations, prisons, etc, whereby we come into contact with the suffering of all living beings and thereby develop compassion;
— enforced confinement in the above-mentioned establishments, where again we are obliged to confront the suffering of others which helps us to get our own problems into perspective, and, free of distractions, we often have our only chance for spiritual reflection;
— personal seclusion, our quiet time on our own where we can 'lose ourselves' to the exclusion of all material concerns but equally where we can indulge in self-pity;
— that which goes on in secret, including deception, acts of

treachery, etc., resulting from exploitation of an awakening ability to sympathize with others' feelings and a betrayal of confidences they entrust us with;

— all forms of escapism, especially drugs and alcohol, potentially self-destructive forms of 'getting high' in pursuit of that euphoric state of at-oneness with the universe which motivates all Twelfth House activities.

The Twelfth House also rules the hidden world of our imagination (1) through which we can receive inspiration for creative work, (2) through which we can practise positive visualization techniques and (3) through which we can indulge in morbid, escapist or guilt-ridden thought-patterns.

The Twelfth House is a difficult field of expression for those whose feet are firmly planted on the earth. Not one of the activities listed are linked to material goals and all are cut off from the mainstream of life. Consequently many of us with planets in the Twelfth House may fail to provide these bodies with any sort of expression, perhaps other than through an over-active imagination — resulting in a build-up of frustrated energy at a subconscious level. Therefore the Twelfth House deserves special attention in any chart analysis and careful investigation as to how far it is being put to work.

8.
PLUTO: GATEWAY TO UNIVERSAL FORCE
Scorpio and the Eighth House

Pluto undoubtedly represents the most powerful energy available to mankind for the purpose of its advance and betterment. As the third in the trilogy of the outer planets it constitutes the final aspect of our transformation to universal consciousness. In the school of Uranus there is the mental awareness of being part of a greater whole; in the school of Neptune there is the emotional awareness of being part of a greater whole; through work with Pluto we begin to use our very life force with the awareness that we are part of a greater whole.

Pluto may be defined as the gateway to *universal force*, literally meaning power derived from the sum content of the universe and therefore inconceivably mighty in its potential. For in accordance with the notion of synergy, the whole is not merely equal to but *greater* than the sum parts thereof, and thus the tapping of universal force provides access to energy more powerful than that which is actually contributed by each individual.

The role of Pluto is to provide us with access to universal force, by transforming the energy drive which we have hitherto used merely for self-orientated goals. In this way it follows the pattern of Uranus and Neptune, which release us from limited thinking and limited feeling functions and allow us access to unlimited knowledge and emotion.

Some might explain the function of Pluto as that of stimulating the manifestation of 'holy spirit', literally meaning soul power (spirit) used for the good of the whole and therefore in the name of the Creator (holy).

We can also refer to Pluto as the gateway to *universal will* as it is the will which concentrates, focuses and motivates our energy drive. Force and will are irrevocably intertwined since the power of our adrenalin flow is dependent upon our determination to succeed: when our desire to win is strong enough we draw on seemingly inexhaustible energy reserves, but when the will to live disappears the life force deserts the body. Before we can release our energy drive our will must thus be stimulated along the appropriate lines. When we are attuned to universal will we have the potential to channel power of a universal nature.

The Wrath of Mars Spiritualized
In the same way that Uranus and Neptune represent higher vibrations of Mercury and Venus respectively, so Pluto is considered to be a higher octave of Mars. As a personal planet, Mars governs our ability to fight for our own survival by the assertion of our personal will and the use, where necessary, of physical force. In contrast, Pluto governs our ability to surrender our personal will for the good of the whole of mankind. For in aligning ourselves with universal will we dedicate ourselves to that which is beneficial to all. Whereas Mars is linked to our sex drive and the use of sexual energy for the purpose of conquest, Pluto may be described as the spiritualization of sexual energy: it challenges us to use our life force to improve the lot of others rather than only ourselves.

Release from Ego Pain
The surrender of personal desires to universal will can result in a personality change which can greatly benefit our everyday state of mind. The anxiety and exhaustion involved in struggling to run our life *our* way are replaced by a sense of relief that we will be automatically guided along the right path for us.

The relinquishing of obsessive personal goals releases us from ego pain since the ego is no longer vulnerable to sorrow. The bitterness which results from the thwarting of our cherished dreams gives way to a feeling of assurance that we will be directed to our rightful and unique role, and that all we require to fulfil that role in a universally beneficial way will be provided. By surrendering our 'wants' we guarantee the granting of our 'needs'.

It is the acquisition of true happiness as a result of far-reaching self-change which represents one of our greatest gains from working with the planetary energy of Pluto. And it is this internal revitalization leading in turn to a revitalized form of outer expression which can represent the basis of our entry into the New Age.

Pluto and Healing Power
The concept of universal force implies a power which is mysteriously limitless in its capacity and its potential. The nearest analogy at a physical level may well be that of atomic energy, whose magnitude

is so great that we can hardly come to terms with it. But the fact remains that universal force is in no way bonded to the physical — the power of Pluto is psychic in essence, pertaining to spirit rather than matter. As such it may appear to be a diffuse concept of little practical use to mankind, yet because of its very calibre its potential to bring benefit to the earth is undoubtedly without measure.

There is something of the miraculous about Pluto in that it provides access to a magic power of which present-day man has not seen the like. Cosmic energy could well provide the key to all the seemingly insoluble problems with which mankind is currently faced: since it follows that there is nothing that limitless force could not accomplish, no difficulty or deadlock need remain beyond us if we could but tether the power of Pluto.

Already there is ample evidence that miracles are on the increase as spiritual healing is practised by an ever-growing number of individuals and groups. Psychic healers who have developed an ability to tap universal power are effecting cures which are beyond the understanding of orthodox medicine but which bring to the suffering a well-being of both body and mind. For universal power has the potential to eliminate disease in every shape and form where this mars the healthy functioning of the earth and the human race.

In the same way that astrology and meditation represent the manifestation of Uranus and Neptune respectively, the spread of spiritual healing reflects the influx of Pluto energy the world is experiencing right now, and represents the third of the three New Age activities which are triggering such profound changes in man.

In drawing on universal force — or holy spirit as some might call it — the healer surrenders his or her own will in order to act as a focal point for a higher healing power. In some cases he may be aware of the presence of spirit guides — entities operating in other dimensions who act as intermediaries, relaying the power to earth in stepped-down form to enable it to be assimilated at the human level. In others he may be aware of a direct link with a source of healing energy. But in all cases it is the desire and ability to place the ego on one side to serve for the universal good which marks the psychic healer or one who has assimilated the planetary energy of Pluto. Thus it is only by aligning ourselves with universal will that we begin to gain access to the healing power of universal force. Indeed many healers have been called upon to surrender a cherished personal attachment before entering fully into their vocation.

Each of the outer planets is linked to psychic phenomena in that they point the way to the source of a universal energy and allow us to 'pick up' that which is not commonly available to man. In the case of Uranus it is factual information — the solutions to all those unanswered questions. Neptune is responsible for the channelling of emotion and may be considered the key to inspiration. In contrast, Pluto relates not to ideas or feelings but to *force* and fosters the ability to attract and utilize unseen energy from beyond the three dimensions. For this reason it is associated not so much with clairvoyance as with psychic feats. Those who have felt the heat emanating from healing hands or even glimpsed encircling smoke can be in no doubt that this is indeed a fiery energy of the same essence as Mars yet applied in a totally different consciousness.

The Law of Manifestation

When we are attuned to the energy of Pluto we may discover the ability to 'make things happen' in our lives. As a follow-up to the visualization technique of Neptune we may find it possible to translate into reality the images we have conceived in our imagination. For in accordance with the law of manifestation, when we are aligned with universal will and are thus able to tap universal power, we have the potential to bring into being on the physical plane that which we have already created on the spiritual plane.

The Key to Universal Force

In order to tap universal force for purposes of healing we must fulfil two basic conditions. On the one hand, as we have seen, we must align ourselves with universal will in the awareness that we are part of a greater whole. Where self-will predominates, the life force is tapped from the lower centres (or endocrine glands) to be channelled into the fulfilment of physical and material desires. But when self-will is brought into alignment with universal will, during the act of healing the life force is permitted to continue its path of flow to the head centres where it may attract universal force, that all-powerful magic energy which not only serves to regenerate the individual himself or herself but is likewise radiated out into the atmosphere in the form of golden healing light.

   In addition, however, in order to tap universal energy or the energy of the whole, it is necessary that we ourselves should become whole and recognize those aspects of ourselves which we fear to express. Thus we are challenged to release the subconscious emotions and drives whose existence we deny but which feed greedily on our life force. Since the process of healing derives its momentum from our life force, if the life force is sapped by frustrated and non-productive energy, our healing power will be diminished. As we begin to acknowledge and release such emotions and drives, we allow ourselves ever-increasing access to universal force and thus magnify our power to heal ourselves — and others.

The Role of 'Negativity'

Our subconscious is home to many different kinds and qualities of feelings. In particular, each of us is the unwitting host to a multitude of deep-seated 'negative' emotions, such as fear and anger, which we have pushed into the recesses of our mind where they increase in power over the course of time.

In attuning ourselves to Pluto we are challenged to confront and discharge such emotions, perhaps with the assistance of therapeutic counselling. Then, by offering up our discharged 'negativity' to the forces of light for transmutation, we each make our own contribution to the creation of healing power.

A major theme of Pluto consists in the important role to be played by 'negativity' in terms of the generation of 'light', based on the notion that negativity is actively creative in its own right. To quote from 'The Seamy Side of Aquarius' by Gildas, channelled by Ruth White, published in *Light** in March 1973: '. . . it is the jewel brought forth from darkness which is the eventual strength of the individual or nation. Out of the darkness — the horror — the violence — shall be born love, light and joy.' Thus 'negative' emotions and drives are to be respected rather than despised or denied and are to be recognized as having their own part to play in bringing the New Age into being.

The transformation of 'darkness' to 'light' represents a continuously ongoing process within the context of the new consciousness ruled by Pluto. This process forms the basis of the 'transformation' which is often spoken of in association with Pluto, and each of us is challenged to *confront*, *discharge* and *transmute* our own 'darkness'.

The Moral of the Phoenix

The process of Pluto has been described by the myth of the Phoenix, a bird which having lived for five or six centuries burnt itself on a funeral pyre and rose from the ashes with renewed youth to live through another cycle.

Similarly, mankind has reached a point in its history at which it is in need of renewal. Each of us has the opportunity to undergo symbolic death as we prepare for entry into a new era of existence. The 'death' in question represents the realignment of our will and

* *Light* is the quarterly journal of the College of Psychic Studies, London.

the transmutation of our 'darkness' into 'light'. Although our revitalization is dependent on death by fire, the pain we endure as we 'burn away' that which is outworn and useless is more than compensated for by the new lease of life we acquire.

Pluto has strong links with the notion of death but only inasmuch as death represents the beginning of a new life just as much as the ending of an old one. It is a human weakness to dwell unnecessarily on the notion of destruction without giving due consideration to the complementary notion of creation. Thus we fear death and treat it as a taboo because we focus only on its destructive rather than its creative nature.

Pain, too, has become a similar taboo which we fear and seek to camouflage by the over-liberal use of tranquillizers. In the attempt to counteract every unpleasant emotion we have forgotten the value of suffering as a cleansing agent of the psyche. Let us remember that the Phoenix *burns* prior to its renewal: pain can, in its final outcome, redirect us into a new pattern of existence which is ultimately to our benefit.

It can also be helpful to consider the Pluto experience in relation to the notion of purgatory, generally understood as a state of being cleansed from sins, often by fire, and traditionally considered to follow death. However, the influence of Pluto as a tool of New Age transformation makes possible the concept of 'death' whilst remaining in the body in the sense of an abandoning of outworn habit patterns and 'rebirth' as a new entity.

Lack of Attunement to Pluto
Whereas attunement to Pluto allows us access to universal healing power, when we are lacking in attunement to Pluto we deny ourselves access to this power by erecting barriers which isolate us from the universe as a whole. On the one hand, we cut ourselves off from others through insistence on self-will and an obsession with personal power. On the other hand, we isolate ourselves through lack of trust and self-defensive behaviour patterns.

The Exercise of Self-Will
At the beginning of a soul's experience it seems that all activities and associations are selected on the basis of its ability to exercise absolute freedom of choice. But over the course of many lifetimes, the perpetual exercise of self-will leads to deeply engrained attachments. We thus become dependent on that which at one time we could simply take or leave and our wants develop into compulsions. The exercise of self-will — once the joyful symbol of the soul's sense

of individuality — in the long run actually robs us of every ounce
of personal freedom. We become slaves to the maintenance and
defence of that which we feel is necessary to us.

Where our self-will has developed to this extent, the need to remain
in control at all costs is an overriding concern, whether in business,
in relationships or in intellectual confrontation. Domination and
manipulation of 'opponents' becomes second nature to us and often
there is no limit to the ruthlessness we will indulge in to safeguard
that which is ours. At the same time there is a marked reluctance,
even inability, to give in, to step down, or to admit that we are wrong.
Our attitude is likely to be that of inflexibility — an unwillingness
to budge from a given stance in order to avoid being driven back
and finally defeated.

The challenge of achieving control over individuals or situations
may become a crucial test for the strength of our will-power and
we may find ourselves involved in power games of all kinds, reflected
at an international level in world power politics. The need to wield
power can be especially marked in sexual areas where we may harbour
the notion that sexual conquest will somehow provide us with total
control over another individual.

The notions of possessing and belonging come to represent a major
theme in our activities and relationships, and we run the risk of
developing into voracious vampires who suck the blood of those close
to us in a compulsive urge to 'consume' them.

The desire for victory now becomes obsessive and endows us with
tremendous persistence in achieving our goals, no matter how long
this may take us: the impatience of Mars hardens into a relentlessness
which is far more dangerous. Furthermore, the obsessive need to
remain in control inevitably gives rise to a fear of losing control, which
in turn results in the need for a sophisticated defence system.

The Price of Self-Defence

The fear which we now experience is based on the dread that our
will may be overpowered and our security snatched from us. At the
deepest level this is a fear of personal annihilation and thus of death,
inasmuch as we view death as a threat to our continued existence.
However, it is also a fear of suffering *any* type of loss which might
threaten our existence as we know it, and thus a fear of losing anything
or anybody without which we believe we could not live.

Our fear is likely to be expressed largely at the sexual level: just
as we seek to gain power over others through sexual conquest, so,
too, we fear the sexual power they may hold over us.

The close link between our feelings of vulnerability in respect of death and sex explains why the life-threatening, sexually transmitted disease AIDS represents the perfect hook for mass fears of mankind as we struggle to come to terms with the challenge of Pluto.

The fear linked to Pluto may be contrasted with that linked to Saturn in that in the case of Saturn it is simply social disgrace that we fear whereas in the case of Pluto it is utter destruction.

In defending our security we are likely to keep a check on any behaviour which might render us vulnerable to annihilation or loss. We will tend to repress all emotions and drives which, if expressed, might pose a threat to the stability of our current pattern of life and lead to unwelcome change. We are liable to intense secrecy, keeping to ourselves anything which might at some point be used against us. In particular we are careful to conceal our deepest feelings and 'weaknesses' which others might use to gain power over us.

We are beset by a lack of trust and suspicion and our relationships are constantly marred by nagging doubts as to the motives of others. Although we closely guard our own secrets, we feel the need to be kept fully informed of our 'opponents'' movements. This is reflected internationally in the practice of political and industrial espionage.

But however great our insecurity we would never admit to it, since we believe that the open expression of fear renders us even more vulnerable. And however great our need, we would hesitate to ask for help for fear of revealing ourselves to be incompletely in control.

Finally we find ourselves incarcerated in a veritable prison of self-imposed isolation whereby we deny ourselves true closeness with others. In order to safeguard our ego we construct a massive wall of protection which effectively condemns us to an innate loneliness. Our individual defensiveness has reached mammoth proportions, reflected at a world level in our huge arms arsenals. The planet earth channels more of its resources into defence than it does into any other single factor.

Pluto, God of the Underworld

Our tendency to 'hold back' due to a sense of vulnerability is intensified by subconscious memories of situations from earlier in our life or from past lives when our will has been overpowered or we have suffered the pain of loss. Fear of repeating the same behaviour patterns which culminated in loss can lead us to repress those emotions and drives which we have unwittingly come to associate with pain. The unrecognized assumption that open expression of these emotions and drives will inevitably lead to further suffering can cause us to keep them under tight lock and key and thus to frustrate their expression.

However, we are likely to repress not only the emotions and drives which we fear will give rise to loss but also the deep-seated, powerful feelings which we have experienced in the past in *response* to such losses:

When retaining control and holding on to the existing structure are all-important to us, we will inevitably suffer pain if our security is snatched from us. But because it is often impossible for us to express our pain openly at the time it is actually experienced, it may be repressed. Thus feelings of sorrow, resentment, jealousy or hatred which result from karmic losses or blows to our will, particularly those suffered during childhood, may be pushed down into the depths of our subconscious where they increase in intensity with each subsequent blow to our will which reawakens memories of our earliest frustrations. Subconscious emotions of this kind also date back to karmic experiences undergone in past lives.

The planet Pluto is closely associated with that which is hidden away, and it is no mere coincidence that the Roman God Pluto, also known as Hades, was the ruler of the Underworld.

Repression of emotions and urges leads to a build-up of frustrated energy which will inevitably erupt or boil over whenever it has the chance. Thus quite trivial situations may occasionally strike a chord which will activate the subconscious emotions and lead to a reaction which is totally out of proportion to the event. Frustrated emotions are often responsible for uncontrollable and irrational behaviour, such as fits of rage or violence.

The continuous build-up of frustrated energy becomes increasingly difficult for us to acknowledge and discharge. Our basic fear of losing control now manifests as a fear of losing control over repressed emotions and drives which we have successfully kept the lid on for so long. Our basic fear of annihilation now manifests as a fear that, if released, our subconscious may somehow destroy us or at least destroy our existence as we know it.

The fear we have of confronting subconscious urges within ourselves is also likely to be mirrored in our attitude towards the same urges in the world about us. Sometimes we will shun individuals or situations which represent that which we fear; at other times we will attack them. As a rule the behaviour which we condemn most strongly in others is that which we most fear to face in ourselves. When we fail to recognize our own behaviour patterns but criticize these in others, we are guilty of *projection*.

The final outcome of our fear is a liability to physical and mental sickness. Increasingly there is the realization that much psychological and physical illness, particularly that which long remains hidden whilst mercilessly eating away at our minds and bodies, is the inevitable outcome of suppression. And an important aspect of this state of being is our inability to confront our own malady.

Problems of Adjustment to Pluto
The Urge for Confrontation

The need to confront forms an intrinsic part of the Pluto challenge and often manifests in our behaviour when we are working with this planet as a compulsive urge to face people and situations square on and a tendency towards blunt and often crude straight talking. There is often the desire to force others to confront the truth about themselves yet difficulty in seeing ourselves clearly. Nevertheless, Pluto is basically concerned with *self*-confrontation and the urge to root out the source of our own emotional pain. The stimulus to self-change can come only from ourselves rather than any outside source — the Phoenix hurls *itself* upon the transformatory furnace rather than being flung in by others.

However, many of us may never even begin to instigate self-change because we are unable to recognize that our problems lie within ourselves. Thus whatever the nature of our pain, we tend to lay the blame on an outside source, be this our spouse, the Government, the immigrants, God, to name but a few. Such unwillingness to take responsibility for oneself indicates the need for work with Saturn; otherwise the sense of bitterness may continue unchecked for a lifetime, surfacing at intervals which coincide with Pluto transits but unable to lead to any worthwhile self-change and serving merely to strengthen our inherent negativity.

The Pluto process is frequently compared to the formation and bursting of a boil: the pain is most intense when the poison remains beneath the skin but as it is drawn slowly to the surface so our discomfort reduces. And it is only when the ugly head of pus is clearly visible to us that it can be discharged and the healing process can begin. Occasionally a boils fails to come properly to a head; equally we are sometimes unable to clear the venom from our system, in which case it remains trapped to resurface later in some other shape or form.

Facing up to our own 'negativity' can present problems where we look on emotions such as jealousy or hatred as 'wrong' or immoral. Here it is helpful to bear in mind the Uranian concept of the equal worth of each and every cosmic factor and to accept that negativity is valuable in its own right in terms of its function in the creation of light. Indeed, no healing can take place without the transmutation of negativity.

Where we feel ashamed of our powerful 'negative' emotions and drives, the business of seeing the truth about ourselves can involve the experience of self-hatred. A certain amount of self-disgust can be a necessary forerunner to self-change since it is not until we experience distaste for the way we are now that we can gain the impetus to be any different. It is effective to call ourselves degrading names — as is the practice in certain self-transformation techniques — provided we have the ability to move on from this stage and not become entrenched in the mire of self-loathing.

The themes of confrontation and research are repeated throughout the many levels of Pluto expression. Fundamental to Pluto is an interest in getting to the bottom of a mystery or discovering the truth. Psychology clearly represents an important Pluto activity, linked as it is to plumbing the depths of the human mind and the confrontation and discharge of subconscious pain. Scientific research of all kinds also falls under Pluto. Pluto is the planetary detective supreme, but its most valuable tracking-down activities are those which pertain to our own psyche.

The Importance of Discharge

We have already noted the importance of discharging subconscious emotions in the context of the conversion of 'darkness' into 'light', which forms the essence of the Pluto process of transformation.

Discharge also represents a fundamental aspect of self-healing since it allows us to free ourselves of repressed negative energy which saps our life force and can ultimately lead to the destruction of our minds and bodies.

Pluto karma generally involves the loss of people or things to which we are deeply attached, and it is our reaction to such losses — whether at the hands of other individuals or simply as a result of circumstances — which represents the source of our pain.

The wounds we suffer as a result of Pluto karma require healing in order to prevent them from festering and poisoning our emotional outlook. It is essential that we give ourselves the opportunity to discharge the grief and fury which represent a normal response to loss, either at the time of the karma itself or if this is not possible at a later point. Psychotherapy in a safe environment forms the ideal means of achieving this discharge, perhaps accompanied by physical or spiritual healing therapies to help restore us fully to a state of balance.

Discharge, however, should always be accompanied by transmutation. It is not enough simply to let go of our negative emotions — we must convert them into a new form. Given that psychic energy is indestructible (and compare this with the problems faced by mankind in disposing of that very Plutonic force, atomic power), negative emotions dispersed into the ether may be attracted to others in order to continue their sinister work elsewhere. The theme to bear in mind is that of 'acknowledge — discharge — transmute'.

Sexual activity is also closely linked with the process of self-healing. Sexual release can promote the expulsion of pent-up frustrations which in time can develop into detrimental forces within us, and thus represents an important system of discharge.

The ability to throw off unwanted energy is of importance not only in terms of our ability to heal ourselves but also in terms of our ability to heal others, since having identified with a patient's disease, a healer must be able to discard the negative energy he may have drawn towards him.

The process of discharge is also vital in helping us to lower the defensive barriers which isolate us from others. Through the process of discharge we begin to rid ourselves of those subconscious fears which cause us to hold back from giving of ourselves fully to others, and thus we begin to achieve greater unity with creation as a whole.

Learning to Trust
In order to overcome the defensive behaviour patterns which cut us off from the rest of humanity it is essential that we learn to trust. Not until we begin to have trust can we gain the courage to open ourselves completely to others and surrender ourselves at the deepest level. Suspiciousness and lack of trust can also inhibit us from initiating the necessary healing therapy in order to confront our subconscious.

The challenge of learning to trust is fundamental to Pluto and is most commonly played out at the sexual level where the depth of our attachment and consequent sense of insecurity can place us in a position where trusting can be difficult. Nevertheless, the degree to which we are willing to trust our partner and surrender ourselves fully can make or break the success of sexual relationships, where 'holding back' can inhibit complete union.

The sexual act actually mirrors what takes place in the practice of spiritual healing. In the act of healing, we lay aside our own will in order that universal energy may flow through us; in the act of sex we likewise surrender ourselves to unite with our partner's energy flow.

The question of trust becomes easier to deal with as we attune ourselves to universal consciousness. As the need to remain constantly in personal control lessens, we become more prepared to open

ourselves to others and to take a chance as to the possible outcome.
We come to see others less as threats to our security and more as
instruments of divine will.

The Trauma of Self-Surrender

The challenge of aligning our own will with that which we term
'universal will' is immeasurably deep. Self-preservation, the most
primitive expression of the life force, is such a strongly developed
human instinct that it is difficult for us to think in terms of
relinquishing personal will. Indeed our whole way of life — both
at the individual and national level — is geared to resistance to
submission, since the laws of men dictate that one person's gain must
involve another person's loss. Yet as far as universal will is concerned,
we supersede the whole question of gain and loss. That which is
universal must of its very nature take into account the well-being
of all parties concerned, so that ultimately all must gain and none
can lose out. For this reason the idea of relinquishing control to
universal will need not involve fear.

The relinquishing of self-will need not imply that we should bow
down to individuals, groups or nations which seek to impose their
own will upon us in order to gain power for themselves. The challenge
is not that of learning to give way to other human beings, since there
is no assurance at all that their narrow-sighted view of things will
be any better than our own. Rather, it is a question of developing
attunement to universal will, for it is only by this means that a
beneficial solution to ALL those involved may be found.*

Our greatest problem can be to remain content to fulfil that which
is asked of us without necessarily seeing the final result. This represents
a particular challenge to those involved in healing work who, in spite
of their strong desire to see the sick restored to health, must submit
to universal will in that healing can only be accomplished at the
given time and in the given way regardless of their own personal
wishes.

The tricky question emerges as to what extent we can sit back and
allow universal will to manifest through us and to what extent we
must continue to devise goals for ourselves. The answer may lie in
remaining willing to initiate developments in our lives, yet retaining
the flexibility to modify our aims if we find that these are consistently
blocked. It is not a question of weakness or passivity but of checking

---

* *The Magic of Findhorn* by Paul Hawken describes how this philosophy is put into practice
at Findhorn New Age Community, where the conflicts of will which inevitably arise in everyday
communal living are resolved in this way.

the excessive assertion of our personal will. The key to the dilemma
may be the degree of push that we must exert in order to fulfil our
goal. For that which is in accordance with universal will may well
call for hard work on our part, but never for the ferocious pitting
of our will against that of others. The pieces of the universal jigsaw
should fall easily into place.

A Question of Identity

As far as Pluto is concerned, the notion of self-surrender gives rise
to particularly marked fears of self-annihilation. There is often the
anxiety that if we relinquish our will-power we will become puppets,
void of a mind of our own, stripped of all personality or individuality.
Where this fear is marked there is generally a lack of understanding
of the principle of Uranus which emphasizes the unique part to be
played by every individual within the whole. The challenge of Pluto
is not to destroy that part — since it is indeed indestructible — but
to make a commitment to enact it under the guidance of divine
direction. It is Saturn rather than Pluto which threatens to mould
us into puppets or zombies, for it is in blind duty to sect, state or
nation that we really relinquish our identity.

The fear of losing our identity is present in all situations in life
where we are asked to leave behind that which is familiar and safe
to plunge headlong into the unknown. Our fear is that we may no
longer exist if we are stripped of that which constitutes our reality.
Wherever such painful change takes place in our lives we can be sure
that the challenge is of a Plutonic nature (rather than Uranian where
change is an expression of freedom rather than of letting go). Death
can be seen as the supreme example of a Plutonic identity crisis where
we must leave behind everything with which we currently identify.
Equally the loss of a partner or a long-standing job can produce the
sense that we are no longer 'whole' people, that we have suddenly
ceased to exist in some way. The phase of reassessing who or what
we are, or of feeling in a void, is an important aspect of the Pluto
process which occurs at a point where we have confronted but have
not yet transformed our old modes of thinking, feeling or acting.

The function of Pluto is not to annihilate our identity but to
enhance our individuality. For the energy released by the breaking
of attachments which have hitherto consumed our very life force may
now be channelled into new, more fulfilling directions. Often we
will emerge from a trauma with the consciousness of being much
more of a whole person and of having discovered resources which
we did not know were there.

Pluto in the Birth Chart

Although the sign placing of Pluto represents an important challenge to the generation of those born every twenty years or so, our attention should firstly focus on the house placing of this planet and its aspects to the inner planets. These will indicate the specific areas of life in which we as individuals are challenged to break down the barriers which isolate us from others in terms of the expression of our will. Here we are challenged to overcome self-will by developing our attunement to universal will. Here, too, we are challenged to overcome the feelings of personal vulnerability which make it hard for us to express trust and to reveal ourselves fully to others. As we work with Pluto along these lines we begin to gain access to universal force, the power whereby we heal ourselves and the planet as a whole.

In the areas of life ruled by the placing of Pluto we will inevitably have to cope with strong attachments and compulsions, leading to a sense of insecurity and fear of loss. Here we may be prone to dominating and manipulative tendencies, and also to those defensive behaviour patterns whereby we cut ourselves off from others and suffer a sense of isolation.

In these areas we will be liable to powerful feelings of grief, resentment and rage in response to defeats, losses or threats to our security. However, difficulty in openly expressing such feelings, especially during childhood, may mean that they remain repressed and increase in intensity, resulting in extreme tension in the areas in question.

Consequently it is in the areas of life ruled by the position of Pluto that we are challenged to overcome fear and to acknowledge and release all blocked emotions and behaviour patterns which we are reluctant to confront.

Not only will we be capable of self-analysis and self-change in the areas in question, but we are also likely to possess a talent for research and/or diagnosis and the potential to induce positive change in our environment.

For a fuller interpretation of the placements of Pluto, see Chapter 14, 'The School of Pluto'.

The Sign Scorpio

In accordance with its ruler Pluto, the function of Scorpio is to develop alignment to universal will, thereby gaining access to universal force, the source of healing power through which we cleanse ourselves and are ultimately able to bring help to others also. In order to achieve this high goal, Scorpio must face the challenge of overcoming self-will, thus the compulsive need to get its own way, to win at all costs and to remain in perpetual control.

Especially when the Sun or Mars fall in Scorpio, the motivation centres around the pursuit of power and in particular the power to effect change. Generally this expresses itself as an urge to remould others in accordance with its own desires by the use of will-power and pressure. The desire for conquest is likely to be exceptionally strong, particularly in sexual areas, and ruthless measures may be adopted in order to achieve victory. Elaborate defence tactics including compulsive secrecy are also likely to form part of the strategy, yet may contribute to feelings of personal isolation.

However, at the highest level the urge to bring about change in others is expressed through healing work, especially in psychic healing, in which case self-will is aligned with universal will. This inevitably calls for a deep level of self-transformation, frequently induced by traumatic experiences through which Scorpio is compelled to let go of that to which it is attached.

Scorpio represents the urge to root out that which is hidden, manifesting in everyday life as a keen interest in research, especially that of a scientific nature, a marked pull towards psychology and a fascination with investigative work of all kinds. However, at the highest level Scorpio will experience the urge for *self*-analysis, whereby it may confront those repressed drives and emotions which are buried in its subconscious and which sap the life force. In so doing, it accomplishes its own self-healing and also makes a contribution to the creation of cosmic 'light'.

In particular when the Moon falls in Scorpio, emotions are strongly felt yet may be consistently blocked. Thus they are allowed to fester inside, developing slowly but surely in intensity — a particular problem where 'negative' feelings such as jealousy and hate are concerned. But such feelings must occasionally rise to the surface like a persistent boil which comes periodically to a head yet fails to burst, at which times Scorpio suffers inescapable inner torment. This pattern remains unavoidable — and leads to an increasing sense of personal isolation — until Scorpio learns to discharge and transform 'negative' feelings at the times of their upsurgence and to free itself from the attachments which produce such feelings in the first place.

In order to achieve such self-change Scorpio must learn to cope with the fear of having to let go — of things, people, emotions — and to develop sufficient *trust* to reveal itself fully to others. It must also be prepared to tolerate periods of self-hate and self-absorption as it unearths and comes face to face with its innermost feelings.

Scorpio is associated with the type of mind and communication capable of great swaying power. Especially when Mercury falls in

Scorpio, an extraordinary degree of force is wielded by the pen and speech, which have potential transformatory power. In general, however, the 'power' will manifest as nothing greater than a desire to win all intellectual arguments for the gratification of its own ego. This is likely to lead to ruthless intellectual struggles and verbal warfare of a defensive rather than an impulsive bent.

The Pluto capacity for confrontation is recognizable in the characteristically penetrating Scorpio intellect, which is capable of pin-pointing the crux of an issue, and in the succinct and often crude Scorpio mode of speech which is adept at unmasking the weaknesses of others. But the true power of this mind is not released until it first turns its analytical clear-sightedness to its own psyche.

Strongly present in Scorpio, and especially when Venus falls in this sign, is a fear of losing control in relationships, manifesting as an urge to keep the upper hand at all costs. This motive is pursued by a strong line of defence, leading to a tendency to keep its distance and avoid self-surrender rather than place itself in a vulnerable position where it is at the mercy of its feelings for others. At the same time, a subtle and persistent form of possessive manipulation is likely to be employed and in some cases Scorpio can conduct its relationships as a perpetual exercise of will, culminating in hatred and an undying need for revenge when its desires are thwarted. However at the highest level Scorpio relationships can serve as a transformatory medium in that they challenge us to develop trust and to open ourselves fully to our partner.

The Eighth House
The themes ruled by the Eighth House all stem from the planetary energy of Pluto and thus relate to the exercise of the will at every level of expression and to the process of transformation of the will from its lowest to its highest form. These themes include:

— the challenge we face in the expression of will-power in everyday life;
— plutocracy or big business and large-scale power politics;
— our sexuality, and in particular sexual relationships where the urge to possess is strong but the ability to surrender is often absent; sex is also an important means of emotional discharge;
— healing of all forms, e.g. medicine and surgery, which aim to eliminate the 'disease' in the body, but especially psychic healing which calls upon universal force to effect the necessary transformation at a psychic (spiritual) level and which thus deals with the root of the problem;

— all forms of psychoanalysis and self-awareness therapies which
   bring us face to face with our true emotions and motives and
   allow for their discharge;
— investigative, diagnostic and research work of all kinds, especially
   that of a scientific nature.

Death represents a traditional meaning of the Eighth House since
it constitutes the ultimate 'letting go' whereby we relinquish all our
attachments in order to face an unknown future; those with particular
Eighth House influence may find themselves in close contact during
their lives with death and all its trappings.

Traditionally this house also relates to joint finances, legacies, wills,
etc., possibly because such matters are commonly the root of struggles
for power, a fundamental theme of the Eighth House and of Pluto.

PART TWO

9.
THE INTERPRETATION OF THE BIRTH CHART

Deciphering Our Spiritual Curriculum
The interpretation presented by this book suggests how we can uplift our personal drives so as to become more in tune with universal consciousness. It is of course important that we should be aware of ourselves as individuals, but only in so far as we can simultaneously experience an at-oneness with others and with creation as a whole. For, as given in the Edgar Cayce Readings, the '. . . birthright given each soul [is] that it may know itself to be itself and by choice become one with the Creator'. (Reading No. 2571-1)

Our scheme of interpretation will consist of finding and analysing the chart features which indicate how we can link the various facets of our individuality with principles of universal consciousness. We shall be considering specifically the links between on the one hand the five personal planetary energies (Sun, Moon, Mercury, Venus and Mars and associated signs and houses) and on the other hand both the law and order planets (Jupiter and Saturn and associated signs and houses) and the outer planets (Uranus, Neptune, Pluto and associated signs and houses). Links of this kind represent the major karmic challenges of our life. These links are to be understood primarily as:

1. A personal planet forming an aspect with Jupiter, Saturn, Uranus, Neptune or Pluto;
2. Jupiter, Saturn, Uranus, Neptune or Pluto falling in a house or sign ruled by a personal planet;
3. A personal planet falling in a sign or house ruled by Jupiter, Saturn, Uranus, Neptune or Pluto (of major significance only when one or more of the above-mentioned links is additionally present).

Where such a link is expressed in more than one way simultaneously we can be sure this represents an important karmic lesson. For example, if we have Venus opposition Neptune, Venus in Pisces and Venus in the Twelfth House, our chart is stating in three separate ways that we need to perfect our expression of universal love in personal relationships.

In addition, we shall be looking at mutual contacts between the non-personal planetary energies — thus between Jupiter, Saturn, Uranus, Neptune and Pluto (and associated signs and houses) one with another. Due to their inherent power, the non-personal planets exert a two-way effect on each other, so that in the example of a Jupiter–Pluto aspect, on the one hand the individual is challenged to express the true principle of Jupiter in his approach to the Pluto urge, but on the other hand to express the true principle of Pluto in his approach to the Jupiter urge. For this reason, inter-aspects between non-personal planets have been analysed in two separate sections, both of which should be read for interpretation of such an aspect.

Aspects have traditionally been considered individually in accordance with varying shades of 'good' and 'bad' so that the trine aspect has been thought of as most fortunate whereas the square was reputed to entail the greatest difficulties.

Although it is undoubtedly true to say that traditionally 'good' aspects will be linked mainly to positive karma and traditionally 'bad' aspects mainly to negative karma, *any* contact between a personal and a non-personal planet indicates the need for further work in combating the excessive demands of the ego. So for general purposes it is most effective to treat all aspects between the same two bodies as representative of the same basic challenge.

The important point to understand is that no one aspect can bring us all good or all bad, since each and every one of us must have achieved some degree of attunement to universal consciousness but equally we must all have something still to learn. Just how much difficult karma a particular aspect will involve depends not only on the label it bears but also on the extent to which we have mastered the principles involved through past efforts. And it is this very factor, which we might term the quality of the soul, which cannot be gleaned from the birth chart.

Opinions differ as to the amount of play with which an aspect can be considered valid. I would advise 1° for the quintile series and septile series, 2° for the quincunx, semi-square, sesquiquadrate and semi-sextile, 4° for the sextile, 8° for the trine and up to 10° for the conjunction, square and opposition. However, it is most essential to judge the importance of an aspect in accordance with the degree of its exactness. Thus a precise quincunx may be of much greater significance than a 10° square. The rule is that the more exactly an aspect is formed, the more we need to listen to it. The strength of an aspect is additionally influenced by whether it is applying or separating.

The analysis of our birth chart, which we may glean from the following pages, will in effect provide us with our own 'spiritual curriculum', reflected by the zodiacal positions of the planets at our birth, which in turn throw light on our past-life behaviour. We shall be looking in particular at what the birth chart tells us about our karma, both in terms of the general nature of the deeds, thoughts and words we have committed during previous lives on earth and also in terms of the resultant consequences we may be called upon to face during this present incarnation. This karmic analysis is based upon the notion that the arrangement of the planets in our birth chart indicates the spiritual lessons we have studied between lives prior to taking this birth, and that these lessons in turn reflect the attitudes we have held and the actions we have committed during previous lives.

A Definition of Karma

Since our interpretation will focus specifically on karma, it is well that we should fully consider what is meant by this term. Karma is simply a Sanskrit word meaning 'action' which has come to symbolize the law of cause and effect inasmuch as every action results in a reaction precisely in accordance with itself, so that 'good' actions bring benefit to the soul whilst 'bad' actions result in difficulties. Rather than use the words 'good' and 'bad' it is more meaningful, however, to speak of selflessness and selfishness since — as given by Cayce amongst others — the greatest challenge faced by all of us at this time is that of putting the ego in its place.

The whole purpose of karma is to teach us the worth of selflessness and the worthlessness of selfishness by the most effective lesson of all — undergoing ourselves the experience of precisely the behaviour we bestow upon others. For it is only when we understand the pain an action causes that we can resolve to reject it. For this reason it is preferable to view negative karma not in terms of retribution or punishment but simply as an educative experience.

Although we may well 'sow and reap' within one and the same life, generally our karmic account will carry over from one life to another, for this is the account of the soul rather than the incarnating individual. And because of the complexities involved in setting the scene for the karmic repayment, karma may often be carried over for a period of several lifetimes before it is finally met.

Although universal law dictates that we are basically obliged to meet our karma at some point, the view presented in this book is that it is possible to obviate the need to meet karma — or at any rate to mitigate its severity — if we can prove that we no longer need to undergo the particular lesson in question. This 'grace' is possible since karma is only ever met as a means of understanding, and if the understanding has already been gained by some other channel, logically there is reason to suppose that the lesson may no longer be necessary.

The greatest difficulty faced by most of us relates to discovering the nature of our karmic debts, since we remain obstinately blind to the 'dark' side of our character. It is here that astrology can prove of assistance since it represents an objective record of our karmic account. It allows us to cut through to the root causes of our present-life situation and also provides us with guidelines as to how we can create a better future, since karma is to be understood not merely as relating to the past but also as the seeds we are sowing now for our forthcoming lives.

The extent to which we will meet with positive or with negative karma of actions, thoughts and emotions depends on our present level of attunement to universal consciousness and the work which still remains to be done. Whereas each of the following interpretative descriptions includes a section on favourable karma and a section on challenging karma, it is unlikely that any of us will experience all of the one or all of the other. But by attempting to identify honestly with the various experiences described, we can gauge for ourselves how much effort we need to put in at this particular time in attuning ourselves to a specific planetary energy.

The Parents as Vehicles of our Karma

Much of our karma will of necessity need to be paid during our childhood since this is the time in life when we are least able to resist or escape — we are prisoners of our parents or guardians who are frequently the vehicles whereby we meet the karma of our own past actions and attitudes. Given that our mother and father so often serve to implement our karma, it is important to remember that the quality of care we receive from our parents is a reflection of the sort of person we ourselves have been in the past. Unless we can come to terms with our childhood trauma, which so many of us undergo in some shape or form, it can be difficult to achieve positive self-change. But if we can hate the deed, not the do-er, we may learn from our parents' mistakes rather than carry with us a sense of bitterness and hatred which can only perpetuate our own negative patterns and might even introduce additional ones.

Although we must understand our karma, it's important not to become obsessed with it, but to realize that through our 'planetary sojourns' we have gained the necessary knowledge whereby it can be successfully overcome or mitigated. Thus it is helpful to see a planetary placing not simply in terms of karma but equally in terms of *challenge*.

The Challenge Reflected in the Birth Chart

In respect of each 'link' in our chart between a personal factor and a non-personal factor, we must therefore consider the following points:

1. The past-life actions/thoughts/emotions which led to our present state of being. To some extent these have been of an unselfish (positive) nature but in other cases they have been excessively self-centred (negative).
2. The purpose of the 'planetary sojourns' which resulted from this past-life behaviour and which have given us the opportunity to gain knowledge between lives in order to help us meet our karma during this incarnation.
3. The sort of karma — on the physical, mental and emotional planes — which we may meet with during our present life as a result of our past-life behaviour. To some extent this will represent positive karma resulting from qualities already acquired, but we may also meet with problems resulting from insufficient development of such qualities. Not all such karma — if any — may be 'paid off' during this life (it may be carried over to a more appropriate setting).

By taking a frank look at ourselves, we can consider whether we are simply repeating negative past-life patterns or whether we are benefiting from what we have learned between lives to adopt a less self-centred attitude and to accept and utilize our hard karmic experiences as opportunities to stimulate self-change.

In most cases there will be a mixture of these two responses since the behaviour patterns we have repeatedly enacted on the earth over a period of many lives are deeply ingrained in our psyche and are difficult to throw off; but equally our between-life learning will have 'programmed' us to the extent that we can draw upon a vast reservoir of wisdom if we so choose.

Astrology, Meditation and Healing — the Vital Link

Astrology in itself can do no more than present us with choices — as the mainstay of Uranus, it is concerned principally with intellectual awareness rather than active transformation as such. But if we are keen to adopt a means of putting self-change into practice, we can combine our astrological studies with a programme of meditation and healing.

We can gain the motivation for self-change by the practice of meditation which encourages us to step beyond ego-consciousness and to define and visualize the ideals on which our self-transformation is to be based.

An important feature of meditation is that it activates the flow of kundalini through the endocrine glands which represent the transmitters/receivers of planetary energies. In this way it stimulates the function of these glands in 'picking up' spiritual energy at times of transits — thus allowing us to achieve greater attunement to the principles which we are attempting to develop at such times. This will help us to refresh the planetary wisdom which we have already gained between lives and will enable us to meet our karma more ably at the times of such transits.

Suggested meditations for the planetary placements have been listed in Appendix II.

Healing techniques fall mainly under the umbrella of Pluto and comprise all forms of therapy which encourage us to look penetratingly at ourselves in order to discover our weaknesses and to draw upon divine healing power in order to bring about positive change in ourselves and our environment.

A special healing therapy which has been suggested in the second half of the book consists of the *The Bach Flower Remedies*. These natural healing agents were discovered by Dr Edward Bach MB, BS, MRCS, LRCP, DPH (1886–1936) and are based upon the recognition that all disease stems from disharmony between the soul and the ego. Thus each of the flower remedies serves to realign the individual with a greater sense of universal consciousness by correcting a specific attitude of mind which is excessively self-absorbed and therefore detrimental to his/her well-being.

Not only do the remedies represent a source of nature's own healing, but also involve our *recognition* of the negative attitude which is causing our mental or physical dis-ease. For it is necessary for us to select the suitable remedy which most closely matches our own state of mind, a process which obliges a keen self-awareness.

Appropriate Bach flower remedies have been suggested in association with the various planetary combinations. The remedies are absolutely free of side-effects and may be safely taken by all. For information as to where to obtain the remedies, see the end of Appendix III.

10.
THE SCHOOL OF JUPITER

The essence of Jupiter consists of learning to understand the influence of universal law, i.e. the law of karma, within our daily lives, and working in accordance with this law. In effect this involves acceptance of a universal system of spiritual justice to which we are all subject, and the necessity to move away from the stage where our faith lies only in ourselves, in luck, or in limited sectarian beliefs. Attunement to Jupiter requires an integrated study of many branches of philosophy and religion, possibly including travel to foreign lands.

The general karma of Jupiter consists in meeting with the outcome of a *past-life pattern* which has been composed *on the positive side* of:

— understanding of the workings of the law of cause and effect, i.e. that we reap as we sow and that success and happiness must be earned by personal generosity;
— in this way, understanding that we cannot achieve that which we haven't worked for, and that there is no such thing as 'luck';
— generosity and positivity in terms of our thoughts, emotions and deeds in the awareness that whatever we give out to others will eventually return to us;

but *on the negative side* has been composed of:

— blind belief in ourselves, in luck or in sectarian religions and philosophies;
— extravagance, ostentation, boastfulness and smugness on the basis of such beliefs.

In the case of a positive past-life pattern the result of past acceptance of the law of cause and effect is likely to be that:

— We have an inborn philosophical outlook on life which helps us to understand why we don't always succeed and provides us with a sense of humour about our own misfortunes.

— We are likely to possess good judgement — which often equips us for work in the legal profession and in other fields where this quality is called for. In particular we may possess good judgement as to our own capabilities which helps us to avoid taking on too much, promising too much, or becoming involved in foolish risks and bad gambles.

— As a result of having given generously of ourselves in the past we may enjoy opportunities for success and self-fulfilment. These are likely to include opportunities to further develop our philosophy and understanding of life — often by way of travel.

— Our contacts with others, especially our parents, are likely to be based on generosity, optimism and a sense of humour.

In the case of a negative past-life pattern the result of past lack of acceptance of the law of cause and effect is likely to be that:

— We are unable to learn from our mistakes in life and although we may well tend to laugh at others' misfortunes, we may consider our own difficulties to occur unfairly.

— We may be over-confident, careless and slapdash.

— Our judgement is likely to be poor, leading to errors of all types. In particular we may possess poor judgement as regards our own capabilities and expectations so that we take on or promise others too much or expect others to give us more than they are capable of.

— We may be liable to compulsive gambling and risk-taking — a subconscious urge to 'beat the system'.

— Restlessness may be a problem, urging us to continually move on in the belief that the 'big break' awaits us around the next corner, although in reality satisfaction persistently eludes us.

— A past pattern of ostentation may result in lack of control and involuntary excess in all areas of our life, which can alienate others and cause us to quickly exhaust our resources.

— The 'Jupiter' types we encounter, and in particular our parents, are likely to encourage us beyond our capabilities, to teach us to trust excessively in luck or sectarian beliefs, and are themselves likely to be prone to extravagance, risk-taking or moral smugness.

The general challenge of Jupiter is:

— To adopt a spiritually creative approach to life in the awareness that we bring about our future good fortune by present generosity and positivity.

— To guard against excessive and unreasonable optimism which can result in unrealistic expectations and foolish extravagance.

Links of Jupiter to the Sun Principle,
to Leo and to the Fifth House
(See Appendix I)

In past lives
On the positive side, in the knowledge that everything given freely
to others returns manifold to us, we have been generous in giving
of ourselves in accordance with the sign or house placing of the Sun
or Jupiter, even where no immediate recognition was to be gained.

On the negative side, blind and unreasonable belief in ourselves
and our talents has manifested as boastful and ostentatious behaviour
and the tendency to hog the limelight to the detriment of others'
rights of self-expression.

Between lives we have had the opportunity to gain understanding
of the workings of the law of cause and effect as regards the
achievement of recognition of our talents.

The karma:
1. To the extent that our self-expression is in tune with the law
    of cause and effect:
— We will possess a philosophical outlook towards our successes
    and failures.
— We will possess good judgement as to our capabilities and
    prospects of success and thus avoid bad risks and gambles. We
    are also unlikely to alienate others by suggesting to them that
    our talent is greater than it really is.
— As a result of past generosity in the giving of our talents, we
    will gain opportunities for self-expression — in particular in the
    area represented by the sign or house placing of the Sun or Jupiter
    — or through giving birth to children who provide us with
    fulfilment — or through travel. Instinctively we understand when
    to take advantage of these opportunies and when not.
— Males in our life — and in particular our father or male partner
    — are likely to possess a philosophic/optimistic/generous nature,
    encourage us towards a positive self-image and help us to make
    the most of our talents.

2. To the extent that our self-expression is not yet fully attuned
    to the law of cause and effect:
— We will be unable to see the funny side to our own failures —
    although we may well laugh at other people's — and
    consequently will tend to continuously make the same mistakes

and to complain that life is unfair to us.
— Due to poor judgement, we are likely to over-estimate our talent and our chance of achieving success and consequently take on commitments beyond our capacity or make promises without due consideration, thus disappointing and alienating others.
— We may be generally prone to gambling, in particular in connection with our career, and may run into difficulties as a result.
— We may be prone to uncontrollable extravagance, especially on items which will bring us admiration and recognition, and may be liable to incur debts.
— The belief that each new opportunity may be the 'big break' which will bring us fame or recognition can be the source of restlessness and our inability to settle for long in any one job or way of life.
— Males in our life — and in particular our father or male partner — are likely to themselves possess an inflated self-image and expectation of success and encourage the same in us. They may believe excessively in luck, be prone to gambling, extravagance, poor judgement or restlessness, and may be of the type who never learn from their mistakes.

The challenge:
1. To consider how far we may be repeating the traits described in association with our negative past-life pattern.
2. To take personal responsibility for difficulties we may encounter arising from extravagance, over-commitment or foolish risks and gambles.
3. To ask ourselves whether we are using our talents with or without consciousness of the law of cause and effect.

Suggested meditation affirmations
See Appendix II: 1(a).

Bach Flower Remedies
See Appendix III: 1(b), 6(a)(f), 16(a)(l), 29(o), 34(a)(j).

Links of Jupiter to the Moon Principle,
to Cancer and to the Fourth House
(See Appendix I)

In past lives
On the positive side, with the understanding that emotional security

and a good home are earned by generosity on our part, we have given freely of ourselves in nurturing others and providing them with sound emotional and moral support and encouragement, and we have been dedicated home-makers and generous hosts, even where no immediate thanks or gain were to be had.

On the negative side, blind faith in our personal philosophy of life — often based on our belief in some sectarian religion — has manifested as ostentatious and inappropriate expressions of encouragement and cheerfulness or sanctimonious preaching and moral smugness. Here, too, we may have been lavish hosts and home-makers, but more due to exhibitionism than to magnanimity.

Between lives we have had the opportunity to gain understanding of the workings of the law of cause and effect as regards the attainment of emotional security and contentment and a happy home environment.

The karma:
1. To the extent that we are in tune with the law of cause and effect:
— We will possess a philosophical outlook on life or a strong faith, likely to see us through emotional ups and downs. In addition a highly developed sense of humour will help us to overcome disappointments.
— We will possess excellent judgement, both of other people's dispositions and of our own emotional capabilities. Therefore we are unlikely to expect too much of ourselves or of others, or to overstretch our emotional resources. We will possess an instinct as to when to take a chance and when not to, and thus be able to avoid bad risks and gambles.
— As a result of past generosity, we are likely to enjoy a good home both as a child and as an adult, to be surrounded by many people and to receive generosity and love from others. There may also be the opportunity to travel as a child or to live overseas when adult.
— Females in our life, and especially our mother or female partner, will possess and pass on to us a strong philosophy of life, religious faith, and/or sense of humour and will encourage us to give generously to others in a balanced and sensible way.

2. To the extent that we are not yet fully in tune with the law of cause and effect:
— We may be quick to criticize others' moral failings but unable to recognize our own. Therefore we are likely to be slow learners

in life, tending to consider that we have been treated unfairly when things go wrong.
— Due to poor judgement we will tend towards over-optimism and thus mistakes, risk-taking and bad gambles. In particular we may make rash promises of help and support which we are then unable to follow up.
— We may be liable to emotional excess, to over-commitment in the nurturing of others and to uncontrollable spending in our desire for home comforts, with the result that we quickly exhaust our emotional and financial resources.
— The belief that happiness lies around every corner may result in restlessness, making it hard for us to commit ourselves emotionally or to settle down to a steady home life.
— Females in our life, and especially our mother or female partner, may encourage us to believe excessively in 'luck', to over-extend ourselves, to gamble and take risks, or to develop moral smugness or religious bigotry.

The challenge:
1. To consider the extent to which we are repeating negative past-life patterns.
2. To take personal responsibility for difficulties arising from bad judgement; over-estimation of personal strengths; extravagance; restlessness.
3. To consider whether or not we are giving love and emotional support to others in consciousness of the law of cause and effect.

Suggested meditation affirmations
See Appendix II: 1(b).

Bach Flower Remedies
See Appendix III: 1(b), 6(a)(f), 16(a)(l), 29(o), 34(a)(j).

Links of Jupiter to the Mercury Principle,
to Gemini and to the Third House
(See Appendix I)

In past lives
On the positive side, with an awareness that intellectual success and communicative skills result from generosity in the giving out of knowledge to others and the willingness to speak openly to others, we have given freely of ourselves both intellectually and verbally.
    On the negative side, blind and ill-founded belief in our

intellectual ability and communicative skills has manifested as 'big ideas' and 'big talk' which effectively prevented others from airing their views.

Between lives we have had the opportunity to gain understanding of the workings of the law of cause and effect as regards intellectual ability and communicative skills.

The karma:

1. To the extent that we are in tune with the law of cause and effect:
— We will possess the ability to accept academic failures, together with successes, with understanding and a sense of humour. Our general mental attitude will be bright and cheerful.
— We will possess good general judgement, equipping us for professions calling for this quality. In particular we will possess good judgement as to our own intellectual capacity which helps us to avoid expecting too much from ourselves or pursuing blind alleys in our studies and career. We will know instinctively when to push ahead and when not to.
— As a result of past intellectual generosity we will now enjoy good schooling and opportunities to broaden our mental horizons, sometimes involving travel. We may be natural scholars and achieve good results. Opportunities to work in the field of communication, such as teaching, writing, journalism, etc., may arise.
— We are likely to be eloquent, with a good sense of humour, and consequently good company.

2. To the extent that we are not yet fully in tune with the law of cause and effect:
— We may be unable to see the errors in our thinking and speaking so that we constantly make the same mistakes and consider the difficulties that befall us to occur unfairly.
— Due to poor judgement we may over-rate our intellectual ability. Mental pride may lead to our trusting to luck in studies and exams in place of hard work, with failure and disappointment as a result. This same lack of judgement can cause us to be easily taken in by what others tell us, or to say the wrong thing at the wrong time, which does not make for popularity.
— Our mind is likely to be slapdash, give insufficient consideration to detail and be liable to error. We may be subject to an uncontrollable tendency to exaggerate and to talk too much.
— The hope that the next line of study will be the one to bring success can lead to intellectual dilettantism.

The challenge:
1. To consider the extent to which we are repeating negative past-life patterns.
2. To take personal responsibility for difficulties arising from errors of judgement; excessive trusting to luck; indiscretion; exaggeration; restlessness.
3. To consider whether or not we are using our powers of thought and communication in consciousness of the law of cause and effect.

Suggested meditation affirmations
See Appendix II: 1(c).

Bach Flower Remedies
See Appendix III: 1(b), 6(a)(f), 16(a)(l), 29(o), 34(a)(j).

Links of Jupiter to Virgo and the Sixth House
(See Appendix I)

In past lives
On the positive side, with the understanding that physical fitness and work satisfaction must be earned, we have striven to improve our own and others' health and have given generously of our labour and skills even when no immediate results were visible, in the assurance that such efforts eventually pay dividends.

On the negative side, blind and ill-founded belief in our physical fitness and working efficiency has manifested as ostentation and boastfulness in these areas.

Between lives we have had the opportunity to gain understanding of the workings of the law of cause and effect as regards the attainment of physical fitness and work satisfaction.

The karma:
1. To the extent that we are in tune with the law of cause and effect:
— We will possess a philosophical acceptance of ill health and frustration in our work, understanding the reason why this is experienced. Consequently we will be able to laugh at our own troubles.
— We will possess good judgement as to our physical capabilities, which avoids us overdoing or underdoing work, exercise or play. By maintaining the ideal daily regime for ourselves we ensure our fitness.

— As a result of past generosity, we may now enjoy opportunities to become involved in a fulfilling job of work — often in the health sector and sometimes involving travel — which serves to broaden our horizons and add to our understanding. Our good judgement ensures that we take advantage of the most beneficial of these opportunities.

2. To the extent that we are not yet fully in tune with the law of cause and effect:

— We will find it difficult to learn from the problems we experience in our work and health since we are unable to see the law of cause and effect in operation. Instead all difficulties are considered to be unfair.

— We may possess poor judgement as to our capabilities in terms of work and health, leading to problems arising from:
    - taking gambles with our health in the belief that we will avoid paying the price,
    - taking risks at work in the form of laziness or cutting corners.

— We may tend to overstretch ourselves at work and adopt an over-enthusiastic approach to diets, exercise and health cures, causing a rapid exhaustion of our physical resources. We may be prone to compulsive perfectionism and a tendency to be over-critical of our colleagues.

— The belief that total satisfaction awaits around the next corner may lead to restlessness in our work, in some cases causing us to be continuously on the move.

The challenge:
1. To consider the extent to which we are repeating negative past-life patterns.
2. To take personal responsibility for difficulties arising from overwork; the overdoing of health regimes; over-indulgence; perfectionism; restlessness.
3. To consider whether or not we are approaching the area of physical fitness and work satisfaction in consciousness of the law of cause and effect.

Suggested meditation affirmations
See Appendix II: 1(d).

Bach Flower Remedies
See Appendix III: 1(b), 6(a)(f), 16(a)(l), 29(o), 34(a)(j).

Links of Jupiter to the Venus Principle, to Libra and to the Seventh House
(See Appendix I)

In past lives
On the positive side, with the awareness that good relationships must be earned, we have given generously of ourselves to others, especially at the one-to-one level, even where there were no obvious or immediate results, in the knowledge that as we sow, so shall we reap.

On the negative side, blind and unreasonable belief in our ability to win people over and to be successful in the area of personal relationships has manifested as ostentation and boastfulness in our social life and/or love life.

Between lives we have had the opportunity to gain understanding of the workings of the law of cause and effect in our partnerships and friendships.

The karma:
1. To the extent that we are in tune with the law of cause and effect:
— We will possess a philosophical attitude towards relationships which allows us to accept disappointments with understanding and a sense of humour.
— We will possess good judgement about people (equipping us for the legal profession, etc.) and be capable of correctly assessing relationship prospects. We are unlikely to promise that which we cannot fulfil nor to expect our partner or close friends to give more than they are capable of giving.
— As a result of past generosity to friends and partners we will now enjoy popularity and gain many opportunities to form fulfilling friendships and/or romantic partnerships, often involving travel, or with people from different countries or philosophical backgrounds. This provides us with the chance to further widen our horizons and to develop our philosophy of life.
— Females, especially our mother or female partner, will be of a generous, optimistic or philosophical bent, possess a good sense of humour and good judgement, and encourage us in our social life.

2. To the extent that we are not yet fully in tune with the law of cause and effect:
— We are liable repeatedly to make the same mistakes in our love life and social life in that we are unable to see where our own faults have contributed to our difficulties.

— Due to poor judgement we may make promises to friends and partners which we cannot fulfil and which therefore lead to difficulties. We are likely to expect too much from our partner or friends or to take them for granted.
— We may be subject to uncontrollable extravagance in our social life to the detriment of our health and our finances. Involuntary affectation may cause us to appear insincere and thus to incur dislike.
— The belief that total satisfaction may lie around every corner can lead to restlessness in personal relationships.
— Females in our life, especially our mother or female partner, may themselves be a poor judge of character and/or prone to extravagance, gambling or restlessness, or may encourage us in our social life to take on more than we can fulfil or afford.

The challenge:
1. To consider the extent to which we are repeating negative past-life patterns.
2. To take personal responsibility for difficulties arising from poor judgement; over-commitment in relationships; taking others for granted; extravagance in social life; restlessness.
3. To consider whether or not we are conducting our personal relationships in consciousness of the law of cause and effect.

Suggested meditation affirmations
See Appendix II: 1(e).

Bach Flower Remedies
See Appendix III: 1(b), 6(a)(f), 16(a)(l), 29(o), 34(a)(j).

Links of Jupiter to the Venus Principle, to Taurus and to the Second House (See Appendix I)

In past lives
On the positive side, with the awareness that material prosperity is the result of giving generously of our assets to others, we have given freely of our material goods even where others were unable to repay us. In addition we have brought pleasure to others through the medium of the senses, such as through music, art, food and the fruits of the earth, without asking for anything in return.

On the negative side blind and ill-founded belief in our ability to achieve material success and prosperity has manifested as extravagance, wastefulness and boastfulness in respect of our material resources.

Between lives we have had the opportunity to gain understanding of the influence of the law of cause and effect upon our capacity for material prosperity.

The karma:
1. To the extent that we are already in tune with the law of cause and effect:
— We will possess the ability to accept ups and downs in our material assets with understanding and with a sense of humour.
— Our financial judgement and business ability will be good, enabling us to push ahead at the right time and to avoid risks, gambles and bad buys.
— As a result of past generosity we will now enjoy material prosperity, sometimes by being born into a wealthy home, sometimes by wealth gained in adulthood. Wealth may also be gained through travel and/or through females in our life, especially our mother or female partner.
— We may possess keen senses — of rhythm, harmony, colour — good taste and a general sense of style, leading to talents in the sphere of music, art, design, cooking, gardening, etc.

2. To the extent that we are not yet in tune with the law of cause and effect:
— We may continuously run into the same money problems as we never learn from our mistakes. Instead we consider our financial problems to befall us unfairly.
— Due to poor financial judgement we will tend towards bad buys, unnecessary risks and the possibility of compulsive gambling in the belief that the big break is just around the corner.
— We may experience an uncontrollable urge to over-indulge in food and luxuries, which leads us to spend money as soon as we acquire it and to borrow when we run out, with the possibility of debts and bankruptcy.
— Females in our life, especially our mother or female partner, may be wasteful of money, liable to run up debts and to gamble and/or may encourage us to do so.

The challenge:
1. To consider the extent to which we are repeating negative past-life patterns.
2. To take personal responsibility for difficulties arising from a lack

of funds; gambling; extravagance and debts.
3. To consider whether or not we are approaching our material assets in consciousness of the law of cause and effect.

Suggested meditation affirmations
See Appendix II: 1(f).

Bach Flower Remedies
See Appendix III: 1(b), 6(a)(f), 16(a)(l), 29(o), 34(a)(j).

Links of Jupiter to the Mars Principle, to Aries, to the First House and to the Ascendant (See Appendix I)

In past lives
On the positive side, with the awareness that physical strength and stamina must be earned, we have given of our physical resources for the benefit of others, often for no obvious reward but in the understanding that everything given eventually returns to us.

On the negative side, due to a blind and ill-founded belief that there were no limits to our physical resources we are likely to have been boastful and ostentatious about our strength, stamina and personal assertiveness.

Between lives we have had the opportunity to gain understanding of the influence of the law of cause and effect upon our physical strength and powers of self-assertion.

The karma:
1. To the extent that we are in tune with the law of cause and effect:
— We will be capable of philosophically accepting why our attempts to assert ourselves are sometimes unsuccessful and why our physical strength sometimes gives out. We thus have the ability to laugh at our own failures.
— We will possess good judgement as to our physical strength, which allows us to sense instinctively when to push ahead and take advantage of opportunities and when to avoid overstrain.
— As a result of past generous use of our vitality, we are likely to possess an extroverted, self-confident personality which attracts others towards us. We will be blessed with plenty of energy and physical strength, self-assertiveness, self-initiative and qualities of leadership. We will enjoy opportunities to excel in sport or outdoor activities and chances for adventure or travel.

— Males in our life, and especially our father or male partner, will
encourage us to build our physical vitality, whilst not over-
reaching ourselves, and to travel. They themselves are likely to
be generous with the use of their time and energy, optimistic,
philosophical and possess good judgement and a sense of
humour.

2. To the extent that we are not yet in tune with the law of cause
and effect:
— We may be unable to learn from situations where we have over-
asserted ourselves, and although we may well derive amusement
from others' mishaps — and in some cases may tend towards
practical jokes and horse-play — we may find it difficult to laugh
at our own mistakes since we cannot see our own foolishness.
— Due to poor judgement we may over-rate our physical strength,
leading us to promise too much to others or over-commit
ourselves to tasks which we are unable to carry through. Over-
impulsiveness and rashness may lead us to become involved in
fights we will inevitably lose. There may be a tendency towards
gambling and risk-taking, particularly in feats which test our
physical strength.
— We may be liable to carelessness and an uncontrollable urge to
show off our physical prowess, leading to over-adventurousness,
accidents and physical strain.
— We may be subject to restlessness, due to the idea that the 'big'
adventure awaits around the next corner.
— Males in our life, especially our father or male partner, may place
too much emphasis on the importance of physical strength,
initiative and self-assertion, encouraging us to over-reach
ourselves and to be impulsive. They themselves may be over-
ambitious, ostentatious or restless.

The challenge:
1. To consider the extent to which we are repeating negative past-
life patterns.
2. To take personal responsibility for difficulties and accidents arising
from over-exertion; rashness; over-adventurousness; carelessness;
showing off; risks and gambles.
3. To consider whether or not we are using our energy drive and
powers of self-assertion in consciousness of the law of cause and
effect.

Suggested meditation affirmations
See Appendix II: 1(g).

THE SCHOOL OF JUPITER

Bach Flower Remedies
See Appendix III: 1(b), 6(a)(f), 16(a)(l), 29(o), 34(a)(j).

Links of Jupiter to Sagittarius and the Ninth House
(See Appendix I)

In past lives
On the positive side, with the understanding that whatever we give out to others through sheer generosity returns to us many times multiplied, we have given freely of our philosophical knowledge to others, in particular through work for the Church, in teaching (especially in higher education), in writing or in the civil law.

On the negative side, a blind and unreasonable belief that our existing philosophy of life was the right one is likely to have manifested as excessive moral self-confidence, self-righteousness or bigotry, and in some cases we may have involved ourselves in religious crusading for self-glory.

Between lives we have had the opportunity to gain understanding of the influence of the law of cause and effect upon the level of our philosophical knowledge and wisdom.

The karma:
1. To the extent that we are in tune with the law of cause and effect:
—   We will possess a strongly developed faith which allows us to ride over ups and downs in our life, to remain optimistic and to possess a sense of humour.
—   We will possess good judgement which allows us to sense when to take advantage of opportunities and when to avoid risks and gambles.
—   As a result of past sharing of knowledge we will now gain opportunities to acquire higher education, to travel and/or meet individuals from other cultures, thus further expanding our philosophy of life. There may also be chances to work in the field of religion, higher education, publishing or civil law.

2. To the extent that we are not yet in tune with the law of cause and effect:
—   We may be unable to learn from our mistakes in life since we do not fully understand the origin of our problems. We may well laugh at others' foolishness but not at our own, seeing our troubles as occurring unfairly.
—   The notion that our wisdom is unlimited may lead us to over-

estimate our spiritual strengths and thus to make serious errors of judgement.
— We may be prone to an involuntary and uncontrollable tendency to 'preach', thereby alienating others.
— We may be subject to general restlessness and wanderlust.

The challenge:
1. To consider the extent to which we are repeating negative past-life patterns.
2. To take personal responsibility for difficulties arising from errors of judgement; alienation of others due to self-righteousness or preaching; restlessness.
3. To consider whether or not we are approaching the search for wisdom in consciousness of the law of cause and effect.

Suggested meditation affirmations
See Appendix II: 1(h).

Bach Flower Remedies
See Appendix III: 1(b), 6(a)(f), 16(a)(l), 29(o), 34(a)(j).

Links of Jupiter to the Saturn Principle, to Capricorn, to the Tenth House and to the Midheaven (See Appendix I)

In past lives
On the positive side, with the awareness that no effort goes unheeded and will eventually pay off, we have willingly shouldered our responsibilities in society and in particular in our career, even where no immediate gain in status was to be achieved.

On the negative side, due to a blind and ill-founded belief that there were no limits to the status we could reach, we may have been boastful and ostentatious about our career prospects and public standing.

Between lives we have had the opportunity to gain understanding of the influence of the law of cause and effect upon our career, status or public reputation.

The karma:
1. To the extent that we are in tune with the law of cause and effect:
— We will possess a philosophical approach to ups and downs in our career which helps us to accept disappointments with a sense of humour.

— Due to good judgement we will possess the ability to plan and organize our career shrewdly, allowing us to seize those opportunities most beneficial to our advancement. Since we know our limitations, it is improbable that we will over-stretch ourselves or take foolish risks.

— As the karmic reaping of past fulfilment of responsibilities, we are likely to achieve status, authority and possibly wealth in our career, and in some cases our career will involve travel, giving us the chance to further widen our horizons.

2. To the extent that we are not yet in tune with the law of cause and effect:

— When we encounter career difficulties we may feel that life is treating us unfairly and be unable to learn from our mistakes.

— We may exhibit poor judgement in the planning and pursuit of our career, leading us to try to assume responsibilities we are incapable of fulfilling, to over-commit ourselves or to make wrong choices and take foolish risks. There may be a tendency to be slap-dash and make errors.

— We are liable to expend an excessive proportion of our time and energy in pursuit of our career or public duties, thus leading to the depletion of our physical resources and alienation of friends and family.

— The belief that every new opportunity will be the 'big break' may result in restlessness in our career and the inability to settle for long in any one situation.

The challenge:
1. To consider the extent to which we are repeating negative past-life patterns.
2. To take personal responsibility for difficulties arising from poor judgement; carelessness and career errors; restlessness; excessive involvement in duties outside the home.
3. To consider whether or not we are approaching our career and/or social responsibilities in consciousness of the law of cause and effect.

Suggested meditation affirmations
See Appendix II: 1(i).

Bach Flower Remedies
See Appendix III: 1(b), 6(a)(f). 16(a)(l), 29(o), 34(a)(j).

Links of Jupiter to the Uranus Principle, to Aquarius and to the Eleventh House
(See Appendix I)

In past lives
On the positive side, with the willingness to be true to ourselves as individuals whilst playing our part within our group, we have been generous in unselfconsciously sharing our talents, assets and insights with others and thus contributing to the community to which we belonged, even when recognition and results were not readily attained.

On the negative side, arrogance and ill-founded self-confidence in our rights of self-expression and our importance in our group or community may have manifested as ostentatious non-conformism, exhibitionism and boastfulness, and as a tendency to pursue our own freedom at the expense of other group members.

Between lives we have had the opportunity to gain understanding of the influence of the law of cause and effect upon the degree of recognition of our personal talents and the level of our influence within the group or community to which we belong.

The karma:
1. To the extent that we are in tune with the law of cause and effect:
— We have the ability to accept philosophically restrictions and disappointments and ride over difficulties in our social or group relations. In general we will possess a sense of humour about ourselves and our relationships with others.
— We will possess good judgement as to when and where to do our own thing, go our own way, or try out original ideas. We will also possess good judgement in our dealings with others in group situations.
— As a result of past generosity, we will possess originality, inventiveness and opportunities to do exciting things in life, in particular to travel. We will have the chance to make many friends and acquaintances and to enjoy good social and community relations. We are likely to feel at ease in group situations and to receive benefits and good turns from friends.

2. To the extent that we are not yet in tune with the law of cause and effect:
— We may be unable to learn from problems caused by our excessive independence and non-conformism, or by our mistreatment of friends and neighbours. Unable to see the origin of our

difficulties, we are likely to consider others to have treated us unfairly.

— We may possess bad judgement as to when and where to be different, to go our own way, or to try out original ideas, resulting in the failure of projects and initiatives. Our judgement may be poor in dealing with other people, giving us the tendency to promise them too much, expect too much, or take too much for granted.

— We may be prone to involuntary affectation and a strong urge to shock, or to uncontrollable extravagance in our social life and thus to debts and other difficulties.

— The notion that the big break awaits us around every corner can give rise to restlessness and boredom with conventional life.

The challenge:
1. To consider the extent to which we are repeating negative past-life patterns.
2. To take personal responsibility for relationship problems caused by our excessive independence and non-conformism or by taking other people for granted, and for difficulties arising from our mis-timing of ventures, restlessness and extravagance.
3. To consider how far we are aware that the attainment of recognition and influence within our community and harmonious group relations is governed by the law of cause and effect.

Suggested meditation affirmations
See Appendix II: 1(j).

Bach Flower Remedies
See Appendix III: 1(b), 6(a)(f), 16(a)(l), 29(o), 34(a)(j).

Links of Jupiter to the Neptune Principle,
to Pisces and to the Twelfth House
(See Appendix I)

In past lives
On the positive side, with the understanding that spirituality, psychic ability, creative imagination and artistic inspiration must be earned by attunement to the source of universal beauty and love, we have attempted to hold on to our ideals and look for the best in life even in the midst of despair, and have attempted to love others even when they showed no affection in return.

On the negative side, due to ill-founded and unreasonable belief

in our spirituality, our psychic ability, the powers of our imagination
and/or the level of our artistic inspiration, we are likely to have been
boastful and ostentatious about our supposed gifts.

Between lives we have had the opportunity to gain understanding
of the influence of the law of cause and effect upon our spirituality
and our psychic and imaginative faculties.

The karma:
1. To the extent that we are in tune with the law of cause and effect:
— We will possess a philosophical acceptance of disappointments
    in life and will be able to handle our problems with a sense of
    humour.
— We will possess good judgement as to the scope and soundness
    of our:
    - spirituality, whereby we become involved in practical and
      personally fulfilling altruistic and spiritual activities without
      exhausting our physical and emotional resources;
    - psychic ability, which enables us to use any gifts we possess
      constructively and to avoid dangerous psychic experiments;
    - imagination, which allows us to use this in positive artistic
      outlets and to avoid impractical flights of fancy.
— On the basis of our attunement to the source of universal love
    and beauty, we may now possess:
    - spiritual and psychic gifts;
    - empathy in human relations and caring skills;
    - the opportunity to further expand our intuitive faculties
      through contact with uplifting mystical teachings, often based
      on foreign cultures or involving foreign travel.

2. To the extent that we are not yet fully attuned to the law of cause
    and effect:
— We may possess poor judgement as to the scope and soundness
    of our:
    - spirituality, whereby we may over-commit ourselves in
      impractical and personally depleting altruistic and spiritual
      pursuits;
    - psychic ability, leading us to become involved in dangerous
      psychic experiments;
    - imagination, leading to self-delusion and the inability to spot
      when our imagination is playing tricks on us;
    - power to deceive or delude others.
— Our sensitivity, psychic faculties and imagination are likely to
    be over-active, resulting in:

- spiritual excesses;
- over-identification with others' problems and self-marytrdom;
- compulsive self-pity, escapism or fantasizing;
- in rare cases involuntary mediumship.
— We may be prone to restlessness and dissatisfaction in our attempts to develop our imaginative, psychic or spiritual faculties or to bring help to humanity. We may become involved in a fruitless search for the 'total' spiritual experience which leads us to wander from country to country and from one cult to another.
— Since we are unable to see the law of cause and effect at work in our lives, we may fail to learn from the difficulties we experience, assuming that these befall us 'unfairly' rather than as a result of our own attitudes.

The challenge:
1. To consider the extent to which we are repeating negative past-life patterns.
2. To take personal responsibility for difficulties arising from poor judgement, misuse of our imagination or psychic faculties; escapism; over-sensitivity; restlessness; dissatisfaction;
3. To consider how far we are aware that the development of spirituality, psychic ability and inspiration is governed by the law of cause and effect.

Suggested meditation affirmations
See Appendix II: 1(b).

Bach Flower Remedies
See Appendix III: 1(b), 6(a)(f), 8 (a)(d); 16(a)(l), 22(b), 29(o), 31(a)(k), 34(a)(j).

Links of Jupiter to the Pluto Principle,
to Scorpio and to the Eighth House
(See Appendix I)

In past lives
On the positive side, with the awareness that the ability to bring about change in our environment is acquired primarily by attunement to universal will, we have made efforts to overcome the desire for personal power and thereby serve as channels of divine power.

On the negative side we have been excessively self-confident, ostentatious and boastful about:

— the strength of our personal will and ability to wield personal power;
— the level of our skills in the fields of research, diagnosis and healing, believing these to be greater than they were in reality.

Between lives we have had the opportunity to gain understanding of the influence of the law of cause and effect upon our capacity to bring about change in our environment.

The karma:

1. To the extent that we are in tune with the law of cause and effect:
— We will possess a philosophical approach to life, which helps us to understand and accept painful experiences, especially those involving death or the ending of situations to which we are deeply committed.
— We will possess good judgement as to the scope and soundness of our:
    - capacity for self-investigation, self-diagnosis and self-transformation, which allows us to take advantage of opportunities to gain self-knowledge without pushing ourselves beyond the limits of our endurance;
    - capacity to diagnose and assist in the transformation of others, which permits us to sense when and where we may be of help and where we may not.
— The result of past efforts towards self-change and attunement to universal will may manifest as:
    - research skills in all areas (science, technology, psychology, the occult, detective work);
    - diagnostic skills, equipping us for work in the field of science, medicine and psychology;
    - the ability to heal at the psychic level — both ourselves and others — by throwing off negative forces and by attracting and channelling psychic power;
    - the ability to face change without fear and to encourage others to do so also, since we possess an instinctive understanding of the need for endings and new beginnings;
    - benefit from inheritances (probably the karmic outcome of having willingly surrendered our worldly goods in the past, particularly on death).

2. To the extent that we are not yet fully attuned to the law of cause and effect:
— We may possess poor judgement as to the scope and soundness of our:

- capacity for self-knowledge and self-change which leads to rash and misguided involvement in therapies which could prove psychologically harmful and/or to participation in self-destructive emotional/sexual relationships;
- capacity to diagnose and assist in the healing of others, whereby we make ill-considered promises and rapidly exhaust our emotional and psychic resources;
- ability to enforce our will, whereby we take on battles which we have little chance of winning.

— Excessive confidence in our capacity for conquest may lead to compulsive involvement in battles of will of all kinds — especially those of an emotional/sexual nature — and an inability to surrender, resulting in the rapid depletion of our material, physical and emotional resources. Also exaggerated is the tendency to blame outside sources for our difficulties rather than recognize that their origin lies within ourselves, and thus to maintain a vendetta of hate and revenge which will eventually take its toll on our health.

— Since we are unable to see the law of cause and effect at work in our lives, we fail to learn from the difficulties we experience as described above, imagining that life is treating us unfairly.

The challenge:
1. To consider the extent to which we are repeating negative past-life patterns.
2. To take personal responsibility for difficulties arising from misguided involvement in occult/sexual activities, over-confidence in our powers of diagnosis and healing and over-confidence in our personal power.
3. To consider how far we are aware that the development of our powers of diagnosis and healing — our ability to bring about positive change in our own and others' lives — is governed by the law of cause and effect.

Suggested meditation affirmations
See Appendix II: 1(k).

Bach Flower Remedies
See Appendix III: 6(a)(f), 13(a)(b)(d), 29(o)(p), 30(a)(d), 36(a)(k).

11.
THE SCHOOL OF SATURN

The essence of Saturn is a sense of universal responsibility based on understanding of universal law. It is the willingness to accept the difficulties we are faced with in life as the karmic outcome of our own past actions, words and thoughts. And it is the desire to co-operate with the law of grace and work towards cancelling out our karmic debts. Saturn teaches us to move away from sectarian morals and standards projected upon us by our culture and to overcome the inhibitions, anxieties and disease which result from excessive absorption with the status quo. The ultimate function of this planet is to help us to set aside the urge for material goals and to replace these by goals of a spiritual nature.

The general karma of Saturn consists in meeting with the outcome of a *past life-pattern* which has been composed *on the positive side* of:

— willingness to shoulder our responsibilities in life and persevere with our difficulties;
— the ability to remain true to our personal convictions regardless of social pressures or convention;

but *on the negative side* has been composed of:

— laziness, refusal to make an effort and a tendency to allow others to do things in our place; insufficient assumption of our responsibilities in society; *or*
— excessive personal ambition and pursuit of material goals;
— over-emphasis on social acceptance, status and respectability;
— a tendency to impose our own standards onto those in our care.

In the case of a positive past-life pattern the result of past perseverance and attention to duty will be stability of lifestyle and the ability to gain the natural respect of others and rise to a position of responsibility. Where we have resisted social pressures and have simply remained true to ourselves, we will possess qualities of self-containment, self-reliance and self-sufficiency so that our needs are met within and we are not dependent on others for fulfilment and happiness. We are likely to be blessed with good concentration and the capacity for sustained effort, resulting in the concrete realization of goals.

In the case of a negative past-life pattern, where our attitude towards responsibility has been out of balance:

— Past inertia may now manifest as some form of lack, for it is only by going without that we can realize the value of any commodity. Where in the past we have failed to pull our weight in society we may now meet with frustrations and setbacks due to lack of help from others.
— The outcome of over-emphasis on convention, respectability or status is likely to be felt as:
  - lack of self-confidence based on expectation of failure and fear of trying in case we are unsuccessful;
  - extreme self-consciousness, leading to difficulties in the spontaneous expression of drives;
  - a tendency to suffer anxiety and to display physical symptoms such as allergies, ulcers, etc., in response to challenges to our standing;
  - a tendency to become a workaholic whereby we drive ourselves mercilessly, with the possibility of exhaustion and breakdown.

The general challenge of Saturn is:
— To uplift — and to spiritualize — our entire concept of responsibility. Let us ask ourselves three questions concerning our approach to responsibility: (1) Are we willing to take on commitment in the world and to pull our weight? (2) Are we *over*-concerned with the notion of duty and achievement to the point that we are creating inhibitions or stress for ourselves? (3) Have we grasped the highest meaning of Saturn by accepting *spiritual* responsibility for ourselves and for our present and future destiny? When we begin to work at this level we automatically lessen the problems related to points (1) and (2).

Links of Saturn to the Sun Principle,
to Leo and to the Fifth House
(See Appendix I)

In past lives
On the positive side we have accepted that it is the duty of each of

us to give freely of ourselves and our special talents and thus we have
persevered in our own field — as shown by the sign and house placing
of our Sun or Saturn — even when the going was tough. At the same
time we have resisted the need to prove ourselves through status and
respectability and have continued calmly to play our part irrespective
of social approval.

On the negative side we may have neglected our duty to give of
ourselves in the area of life represented by the placing of the Sun
or Saturn. Alternatively we may have attached excessive importance
to social approval of our abilities by over-striving for material symbols
of success and respectability, often to the point of overwork and neglect
of our obligations in other directions. In addition we may have
demanded of our family and colleagues that they too should follow
our goals and ambitions, disciplining and restricting them to ensure
that they uphold our 'honour'.

Between lives we have had the opportunity to learn to develop a
balanced sense of responsibility for our self-expression. Thus we were
to learn the necessity for each of us to give freely of our unique talents
to the world, but with the sincere desire to make our personal
contribution rather than the urge for social acclaim and status.

The karma:
1. To the extent that we have been willing in the past to shoulder
    our responsibilities, we will now enjoy the possibility of
    continuing undisturbed in the same line of self-expression (as
    shown by the placing of the Sun or Saturn) for a sustained period,
    and thus of achieving long-term results whilst enjoying security
    of lifestyle. We will have the chance to rise to a position of
    responsibility in our field where we gain the respect of our
    colleagues for our commitment and hard work.
—   Where we have previously resisted the trappings of social
    conventions:
    –   we will now find our work totally fulfilling in its own right,
        regardless of whether we achieve social and material success
        or not — although the likelihood is that we will anyway;
    –   we will possess single-mindedness, which permits us to
        concentrate consistently on our special field without being
        distracted down non-productive alleys: thus we are able to
        achieve a steady output and actually bring our goals to
        fulfilment.
—   Male figures in our life — especially our father or male partner
    — will exert a supportive, stabilizing influence upon us, helping
    us to achieve self-discipline and to actualize our abilities whilst

providing us with security. Our male partner or male friends will often be older than ourselves, or at least mature and stable in their outlook on life.

2. Where in the past we have failed to put our natural talents to sufficient use we may find ourselves confronted with some constitutional weakness which makes it difficult for us to give full expression to our abilities. Since procreation is an important form of self-expression, we may find ourselves childless or faced with difficulties in having children. More likely, however, we will simply experience many setbacks in our attempts to make our mark on the world and a lack of opportunities or assistance. Sometimes we may feel we have to work twice as hard as others to attain the same results. Since our father represents a symbol of our own self-expression, we may suffer a lack of a father figure either in that we never know our father or in that he is frequently absent from home.

— Where in the past we have been excessively concerned with social approval and success we may now be prone to:
    - severe inhibitions about 'being ourselves' or giving expression to our talents, so that in expectation of failure we simply do not try and as a result may become increasingly introverted and frustrated;
    - extreme self-consciousness whenever we are called to 'perform' in front of others (along the lines of the placement of the Sun or Saturn) or to carry out any activities which will draw attention to ourselves;
    - the tendency to worry unnecessarily about the impression we have made on others, to be over-dependent on feedback and to develop anxiety symptoms expressed in chronic physical ailments;
    - the likelihood of taking on too much in the area of life ruled by the placement of our Sun or Saturn, leading to over-strain and health breakdowns; the likelihood of over-concern with providing for our children;
    - the possibility of meeting with male figures, especially our father or male partner, who are themselves overly concerned with duty and propriety and consequently are excessive disciplinarians or attempt to repress our creative drive in the interests of respectability.

The challenge:
1. To consider the extent to which we are repeating negative past-life patterns.

2. To take personal responsibility for difficulties we may experience
    as a result of lack of opportunity for self-expression; setbacks;
    inhibitions, shyness or self-consciousness; the tendency to worry
    and/or display physical anxiety symptoms; the tendency to
    become a workaholic; the absence of a father figure or an over-
    stern, over-conventional father.
3. To ask ourselves whether we are fulfilling our obligations in
    making full use of our unique talents; to further ask whether
    our sense of obligation (if any) results from true inner conviction
    or is governed simply by the need for material and social status.

We will be helped towards our goals by the cultivation of patience
and structured but well-moderated effort towards developing our
creativity and self-expression.

Suggested meditation affirmations:
See Appendix II: 2(a)

Bach Flower Remedies
See Appendix III: 2(a), 11(a)(b), 17(a), 18(a)(b), 20(a)(b), 25(a)(b),
33(a)(b).

Links of Saturn to the Moon Principle,
to Cancer and to the Fourth House
(See Appendix I)

In past lives
On the positive side we have been willing to fulfil our duties to our
family and to our friends even when the going was extremely tough.
In so doing we have been guided by our own convictions and have
shown no concern for the dictates of society or convention where
these ran counter to our personal beliefs.

On the negative side we have either neglected our responsibilities
to our children, family or others in our care, or else we have allowed
social conventions to determine the type and quality of our emotional
care, which in some cases will have resulted in as much neglect as
if we had completely relinquished responsibility. Often the emphasis
will have been on being *seen* to do our duty rather than on the actual
content of our emotional care. We may have sought to instil our
own notions of propriety into our offspring, attempting to discourage
or repress all emotional behaviour contrary to our own norm. We
may also have been excessively governed by social conventions in the
domestic arrangements we provided for our family, nagging them
unduly around the home.

Between lives we have had the opportunity to develop a more perfect sense of responsibility in the nurturing areas of our life. On the one hand we were to understand the need for each of us to fulfil our duties in caring for those who are emotionally dependent upon us. On the other hand we were to realize the mistake of placing allegiance to the social system before genuine love.

The karma:

1. To the extent that we are well-attuned to the notion of responsibility and have in the past given sustained emotional care to others, we will now enjoy a stable upbringing and continuous care from our parents upon which we can come to depend.

—   Past freedom from the pressure of social convention will bring the reward of a calm, well-balanced temperament which is happily self-contained, i.e. is able to meet its needs from within without excessive emotional dependence upon others. We are likely to gain respect for our self-possession and practicality.

—   Our mother or female partner will possess qualities of patience, endurance and dedication to her maternal duties, helping us to gain emotional stability and self-discipline in a loving way. Frequently our female partner or female friends will be older than ourselves or at any rate mature and stable in temperament.

2. Where in the past we have failed to give adequate nurturing care to others we may now find that we never know our true mother, or that our mother is frequently absent, leaves us to our own devices, or never has much time to give us.

—   Where we have allowed social convention to take precedence over genuine love and nurturing care we may find that:

    -   the quality of emotional rapport with our mother is poor in that spontaneous expression of feelings is avoided, too much emphasis is placed on running the household in an orderly and respectable way, or our mother may be of the type anxious to 'keep up with the Jones's', nagging us to do likewise;

    -   as adults we may suffer from diffidence in our emotional relationships and be mistrustful of our ability to give and receive love;

    -   self-consciousness and a fear of looking foolish may lead to suppression of feelings and as a result to stress-related mental and physical trouble;

    -   we may attract a female partner who places emotional self-control and domestic efficiency before genuine love and affection;

- worry and depression, especially about the family, which may descend upon us seemingly without cause, is often the greatest karmic problem we must bear;
- in other cases we may experience a compulsive urge to burden ourselves unduly with domestic duties which are undertaken cheerlessly and with a sense of resignation, essentially in order to keep up appearances.

The challenge:
1. To consider the extent to which we are repeating negative past-life patterns.
2. To take personal responsibility for difficulties we may experience as a result of lack of, or poor quality of, motherly care; emotional deprivation in childhood and emotional inhibitions in adulthood; self-consciousness; worry, depression and stress-related ailments; a tendency to become a workaholic in respect of domestic duties.
3. To ask ourselves whether we are fulfilling our obligations to give love and nurturing to those in our care; to further question whether our sense of obligation (if any) results from true inner conviction or is governed by the need for social respect.

The cultivation of patience and structured but well-moderated effort in some form of caring work, i.e. with children or old people, will help us towards our goals.

Suggested meditation affirmations:
See Appendix II: 2(b)

Bach Flower Remedies
See Appendix III: 2(a), 11(a), 17(a)(b)(e), 18(a)(c), 19(a), 20(a)(b), 25(a)(c), 32(a).

Links of Saturn to the Mercury Principle,
to Gemini and to the Third House
(See Appendix I)

In past lives
On the positive side we have shown ourselves willing to take responsibility for our mind and our speech by making the most of opportunities for study and academic achievement and displaying integrity in our verbal dealings with others. Ideally this sense of responsibility will have been based on our personal principles rather than an urge for status or concern for propriety.

On the negative side we may have neglected to fully exploit our intellectual ability by remaining mentally inert or we may have failed to communicate sufficiently with others due to laziness. Alternatively we may have over-involved ourselves in study with the motivation of constantly improving our intellectual status and/or indulged in pompous loquacity with a view to climbing the social ladder. Here we may also have imposed our own self-discipline and inhibitions onto those in our care, subjecting them to rigorous lessons, punishment in the event of academic failure and excessively strict rules of speech.

Between lives we have had the opportunity to develop a balanced sense of responsibility for our intellect and our speech. On the one hand we were to realize the need for each soul to maximize its mind power through study, application and concentration and to exploit to the full the gift of communication. On the other hand we were to realize that our use of these faculties should be motivated by a sincere desire to play our part rather than simply by the need for status.

The karma:
1. To the extent that we have been willing to discipline our minds in past lives, we will now enjoy a traditional, stable education which allows us the opportunity for uninterrupted study, good qualifications and the chance to put our minds to good use in our work.
—   Where we have resisted intellectual snobbery and preoccupation with intellectual status, we will find ourselves blessed with a mind which is remarkably self-contained and is able to find the answers it needs without external consultation since it does not depend on outside approval. We will possess excellent concentration and a brain which is able to approach any mental problem with single-mindedness. Our greatest assets are likely to be structured, organized thinking, giving an aptitude for maths and science, and conciseness and continence of speech.

2. To the extent that we have failed to exploit our intellectual potential we may find that facilities for our education are simply not available or that we are obliged to discontinue our schooling at an early age; in other cases, in spite of good opportunities, we may prove to be slow learners or to possess some learning impediment which prevents us from making headway equal to our peers and necessitates twice as much work on our part to achieve the same results.

— Where we have been excessively preoccupied with academic success as a means of gaining status, despite intelligence we may be held back by extreme lack of confidence, which leads to our losing interest in our schooling or giving up sooner than we might have done. Or occasionally we may be the seemingly opposite type — the 'bookworm' or 'swot', driving ourselves unstintingly in our studies, experiencing a compulsive need to improve our qualifications but finding it impossible to relax and thus risking a nervous breakdown. The whole area of academic achievement may be a cause for concern, leading to worry, depression and stress-related physical symptoms.

— Where in the past we have not fully exploited our powers of communication, we may now experience some speech impediment.

— Past over-concern with social approval may also inhibit our verbal self-expression, giving rise to self-consciousness or fear of saying the wrong thing.

— Our upbringing may be excessively disciplined both at home and at school. In some cases we may be expected to accomplish more than we are intellectually fitted for, subjected to academic pressure, and severely criticized or ridiculed in the event of failure. In other cases it is our speech which may be subjected to constant criticism.

The challenge:

1. To consider the extent to which we are repeating negative past-life patterns.

2. To take personal responsibility for problems we may experience as a result of learning difficulties or lack of education opportunities; lack of confidence and self-consciousness; a compulsive need to swot or improve our qualifications; worry, depression and stress-induced ailments relating to our intellectual status; an overdisciplined school or home upbringing.

3. To ask ourselves whether we are fulfilling our obligations to make full use of our intellectual and communicative faculties; to ask ourselves, further, whether our sense of obligation (if any) results from true inner conviction or is simply governed by the need for social respect.

The cultivation of patience and structured but moderated effort towards self-education will help us towards our goals.

Suggested meditation affirmations:
See Appendix II: 2(c)

Bach Flower Remedies
See Appendix III: 2(a), 10(a), 11(a), 17(a)(c), 18(a)(b)(d), 19(a), 20(a)(i), 25(a)(d)(e), 32(a), 33(a)(b)(c).

Links of Saturn to the Virgo Principle and to the Sixth House (See Appendix I)

In past lives
On the positive side we have displayed a sense of responsibility towards our work by persevering with our day-to-day duties even when the going became tough. Similarly we have shown ourselves capable of taking responsibility for our health by balanced diet, exercise and relaxation, rather than relying only on medical help from others. And our motivation in so doing has been the personal conviction that each of us should fend for ourselves, rather than the desire for social status and approval.

On the negative side, in some cases we may have channelled insufficient effort into our daily work or into the care of our health. In other cases we may have been *over*-concerned with gaining social respect for our physical self-discipline in terms of work or fitness. Here we may also have imposed our own self-discipline onto our family and those in our care.

Between lives we have had the opportunity to develop a more balanced sense of responsibility for our work and health. On the one hand we were to realize the need for each of us to attend to our daily work — whether in the home or the job — and to take responsibility for our bodily well-being. On the other hand we were to become aware that this sense of responsibility should not arise from an obsession with social approbation but from the understanding that by pulling our weight in the present we create for ourselves a healthy and fulfilling future.

The karma:
1. To the extent that we are correctly attuned to the principle of responsibility and have shown ourselves capable of perseverance, we will enjoy stable, regular work with the chance to rise to a position of responsibility and gain the respect of our co-workers. Equally we may possess a strong constitution and continuous good health which likewise attracts notice and admiration.
— Where we have avoided obsession with social approval in terms of work or health we are likely to be self-motivated in our work

and possibly work for ourselves, and we may be self-reliant in our health care with a natural instinct as to the needs of our body. Since we are independent of others' approval we are also serene and single-minded, allowing for ever greater efficiency in our work and our physical well-being.

2. To the extent that we have failed to channel sufficient effort into our daily work, we are likely to experience difficulties in finding stable employment or may be subject to frustrations and setbacks, finding ourselves called upon to put in double the effort and undergo double the drudgery of others.

—   Where in the past we have assumed insufficient responsibility for our bodily well-being, our health may be poor, resulting in continuous problems and the need for strict diets, exercises and tiresome or restrictive forms of treatment or therapy.

—   Past over-concern with social approval may now mean that:

    –   we will be lacking in confidence in our ability to do well at our work, which leads us to miss opportunities for advancement and to remain in a menial position;

    –   we may doubt our capacity for physical health, which reduces our confidence in ourselves and leads us to pass by many challenges which we might otherwise have been capable of;

    –   we may tend to worry unduly at the slightest cause for concern about our health or our work, which may give rise to depression or physical ailments (and thus may aggravate any existing health problems);

    –   in other cases we are likely to become workaholics, incapable of switching off from our work or doing so only under duress; this in turn is likely to lead to inadequate bodily care — in terms of rest, exercise and diet — and again may add to any inherent physical weakness we already possess;

    –   alternatively we may tend towards health mania — we may be fitness freaks who practise austerity and self-denial to an extreme which is outside of our control;

    –   as children we may be subjected by others to an over-disciplined daily regime or to an extreme, uninteresting 'health' diet.

The challenge:

1. To consider the extent to which we are repeating negative past-life patterns.

2. To take personal responsibility for difficulties we may experience as a result of lack of steady employment or difficult working conditions; poor health or the need for strict therapies; lack of

confidence and over-anxiety about our work or health often accompanied by stress-related ailments; the tendency to become a workaholic; excessive self-discipline in the cause of fitness.

3. To ask ourselves whether we are fulfilling our obligations to others in the area of work by building good health and efficiency; to ask ourselves, further, whether our sense of obligation (if any) results from true inner conviction or is governed simply by the need for social respect.

The cultivation of patience and structured but well-moderated effort towards achieving fitness will help us towards our goals.

Suggested meditation affirmations:
See Appendix II: 2(d)

Bach Flower Remedies
See Appendix III: 2(a), 10(a), 11(a)(d), 15(a), 17(a)(d), 18(a)(e), 19(a), 20(a)(h), 21(a), 25(a)(d)(f), 32(a), 33(f)(g)(j).

Links of Saturn to the Venus Principle, to Libra and to the Seventh House (See Appendix I)

In past lives
On the positive side we have displayed a sense of duty and commitment to our partners or close friends which has allowed us to remain loyal and faithful regardless of ups and downs and which has been motivated not by the pressure of convention or propriety but simply by personal conviction.

On the negative side we may have shirked responsibility at the one-to-one level either in that we have been unwilling to take on the encumbrance of a partner or in that we have allowed our spouse to shoulder all the responsibilities within the partnership. In other cases we may have married solely for material wealth or status, or may have allowed social convention to come before love in governing our choice of partner. Propriety may also have ruled our conduct within relationships, leading us to avoid any behaviour which might result in disgrace, regardless of the true needs of our partner or the relationship itself. We may have insisted that our children observe our own social standards and refrain from socially unacceptable associations.

Between lives we have had the opportunity to develop a more balanced sense of responsibility in our personal relationships. On the one hand we were to realize that peace on earth is dependent upon each of us playing our part to create and promote happy relationships. On the other hand we were to acquire a sense of proportion about our social obligations, refusing to allow our attitudes to relationships to be influenced by prevailing customs and conventions.

The karma:
1. Where we have displayed faithfulness and loyalty in our relationships, we will enjoy a stable romantic partnership, long-lasting and undisturbed by trauma or interruption.
— Where we have avoided bowing to convention we will find ourselves untroubled by others' opinions of our relationships or of our partner. Our relationship is likely to fill all of our needs in its own right, providing us with fulfilment and serenity and the chance to achieve something of worth in co-operation with our partner; indeed it is frequently a partnership which is highly productive in practical terms.
— Females in our life — and especially our mother or female partner — will tend to be patient, loyal, hard-working and of a practical bent and help us towards concrete attainment.

2. Where in the past we have 'passed' on relationship responsibilities, we may now discover that however much effort we put in, we find it hard to form relationships and in particular may have difficulties in finding a romantic partner. When we do find a partner, the relationship may suffer frustrations and setbacks: lack of funds, ill health, or other considerations may delay or prevent us getting together, or may impose hardships and extra obligations on our life together.
— Where we have been over-concerned with success and social approbation in terms of relationships:
    - we may now suffer inhibitions in our romantic and social contacts, to the point that we are often paralysed by self-consciousness and may suffer frustration and loneliness as a result;
    - in some cases we may find ourselves habitually attracted to older friends or lovers, probably because their maturity or status compensates for our sense of inadequacy;
    - we may worry unduly about the success of our relationships, becoming easily depressed or displaying physical stress symptoms at the least cause for doubt;

- we may take on too many duties and obligations in our relationships to the point of physical strain;
- we may resort to promiscuity to compensate for feelings of inadequacy;
- females in our life, and especially our mother or female partner, may be excessively motivated by ambition and desire for status, which they are likely to place before our happiness or the well-being of our relationship with them;
- our parents may impose restrictions on the sort of friends we may cultivate, discouraging contacts with those of the 'wrong' type.

The challenge:
1. To consider the extent to which we are repeating negative past-life patterns.
2. To take personal responsibility for difficulties we may experience as a result of lack of close friends or romantic partners; setbacks or hardships in our relationships; lack of confidence, self-consciousness and inhibitions in close contacts with others; frustration and loneliness; worry and anxiety about the success of our relationships; over-commitment; status-conscious females.
3. To ask ourselves whether we are fulfilling our obligations to create and promote harmonious personal relationships; to ask ourselves, further, whether our sense of obligation (if any) is governed simply by the need for social respect.

The cultivation of patience and structured moderated effort towards getting to know others on a one-to-one basis will help us towards these goals.

Suggested meditation affirmations:
See Appendix II: 2(e)

Bach Flower Remedies
See Appendix III: 11(a)(b)(e), 17(a)(f), 18(a)(f), 19(a), 20(a)(c), 25(a)(b)(g), 32(a).

Links of Saturn to the Venus Principle,
to Taurus and to the Second House
(See Appendix I)

In past lives
On the positive side we have been willing to fend for our own material needs rather than look to others for support, whilst avoiding an

obsessive desire for material status symbols. We have made efforts to develop practical, artistic skills, such as music, art, gardening, cooking, etc., through hard work and commitment.

On the negative side we may have failed to provide for our own needs, leaning on others for financial and material sustenance and/or we may have failed to pay our financial dues to the society of which we were part. At the other extreme we may have placed ambition and the desire for material status symbols before other considerations in our life, resulting in an obsession with pecuniary affairs. In some cases we may have behaved snobbishly in judging others by their material status rather than for their true selves.

Between lives we have had the opportunity to learn to approach the earth's resources with a balanced sense of responsibility. Thus we were to understand the need to fend for ourselves at the material level, but with the motivation of a sincere desire to pull our weight rather than the desire to amass wealth and possessions by way of status symbols.

The karma:
1. Where in the past we have assumed personal responsibility for our material needs, we will enjoy a stable regular income, free of worry or insecurity. We may rise to a position of authority in the field of finance or economics as a result of our natural aptitude in handling resources, and gain the respect of others on account of our abilities.
—   Where in the past we have resisted social pressure to strive for material status symbols, we will find that our material needs are easily satisfied and that we are materially and financially self-sufficient. We will be capable of approaching financial and material affairs single-mindedly and without distraction, and are likely to be considerably successful as a consequence.
—   To the extent that we have worked at developing practical, artistic skills, we may rise to a position of responsibility in fields such as art and design, music, cooking, gardening or the building trade amongst others, or we may be self-sufficient in any of these areas. Most important, we are likely to possess excellent concentration, perseverance and self-discipline which allows us to approach any work along these lines in a structured, organized way which yields good results.

2. Where in the past we have been insufficiently self-reliant as far as our material needs are concerned, we may now suffer a certain

amount of poverty, or financial frustrations and setbacks, and the need to work exceptionally hard for an average living.

— Past obsession with material success and status is likely to result in an unnatural fear of poverty and the drop in status this would entail, which in turn can manifest as:

 - involuntary frugality which leads us to deny ourselves even the smallest of life's luxuries, so as to provide for the future and guard against hard times; as a result we obtain hardly any real pleasure from the good things of the earth;

 - the tendency to overwork in order to build up a healthy bank balance, and as a result to risk the breakdown of bodily or mental health — again we deny ourselves the chance to take any pleasure from material affairs;

 - the tendency to worry (often subconsciously) at the slightest cause for financial concern, and as a result to suffer depression and stress-induced ailments.

— Where we have judged others by their wealth, we may now find that others judge us likewise — we may find ourselves on the receiving end of other people's snobbery.

The challenge:
1. To consider the extent to which we are repeating negative past-life patterns.
2. To take personal responsibility for difficulties we may experience as a result of poverty or financial hardship; anxiety about money; compulsive frugality and obsession with work.
3. To ask ourselves whether we are fulfilling our obligations to cater for our own material needs and to make full use of our practical abilities; to further ask ourselves whether our sense of obligation (if any) results from true inner conviction or is governed simply by the need for social respect.

A planned yet moderate approach to establishing our financial security and developing our practical artistic skills can help us towards these goals.

Suggested meditation affirmations:
See Appendix II: 2(f)

Bach Flower Remedies
See Appendix III: 11(a)(b)(f), 17(a)(g), 19(a), 20(a)(d), 25(a)(h), 32(a)(d), 33(f)(h)(j).

Links of Saturn to the Mars Principle,
to Aries, to the First House and to the Ascendant
(See Appendix I)

In past lives
On the positive side we have taken responsibility for ourselves by asserting ourselves where necessary and making appropriate use of our physical resources. We are likely to have been hard-working, courageous, and self-sufficient — as a result of our belief that each of us must fend for ourselves rather than as a result of any rules or regulations imposed upon us by others.

On the negative side, in some cases we may have failed to give sufficient expression to our physical resources. In other cases we may have over-concerned ourselves with proving our physical strength as a means of gaining status and may even have resorted to acts of cruelty, often against those weaker than us, in order to make the point; equally we may have over-concerned ourselves with gaining respect for our hard work and we may have attempted to instil our own standards of self-discipline into our family or colleagues by acting as slave-drivers in the home or at work.

Between lives we have had the opportunity to learn to develop a balanced sense of responsibility for our physical drives. Whilst we are certainly to recognize the need for each to exploit to the full his or her physical resources, our motive in so doing should be a sincere desire to play our part rather than the urge to gain status or respect.

The karma:
1. Where our use of our physical resources has been sensible and balanced, we will now enjoy a unique capacity for steady, sustained energy flow. Our remarkable stamina and strength will allow us to achieve any goal we have set ourselves without burning ourselves out. There may be great resourcefulness which allows us to tackle successfully all manner of practical tasks. Mechanical ability may be marked.
— Where in the past we have acted without concern for social approval, we may now find ourselves blessed with self-reliance and self-sufficiency.
— Male figures in our life, and especially our father and male partner, may themselves be hard-working and resourceful and may encourage us towards actualizing our goals.

2. Where, in the past, we have insufficiently exploited our physical resources, we may now find our drive is impaired either by a

physical disability or some form of weakness, or in that we are prone to accidents. This in turn is likely to lead to frustration, a sense of getting nowhere, and the need to put in greater than average effort to achieve an average result.

— To the extent that we have been over-concerned with proving our physical strength and endurance as a means to achieving status:

 – we may now lack confidence in our ability to assert ourselves and may experience a fear of attracting ridicule, which leads us to avoid confrontation situations where our weakness may be spotted; we may suffer impotence or a sense of sexual inadequacy and have difficulty in expressing passionate feelings;

 – in other cases we may become workaholics, unable to switch off our adrenalin flow even when we have reached the point of exhaustion, making us highly susceptible to physical and nervous breakdowns and to other forms of disease; similarly we may be prone to promiscuity in order to prove our capacity for sexual conquest;

 – there is the possibility of suffering cruelty at the hands of others who attempt to get the better of us when we have little chance of retaliation, and sometimes our father or male partner may behave in this way;

 – our upbringing may be excessively disciplined and may over-stress the importance of hard work, responsibility, physical endurance, the suppression of 'wasteful' forms of self-assertion such as anger, temper, tears, etc., and disapproval of sex;

 – male figures in our life — especially our father or male partner — may be workaholics and/or prone to excessive self-discipline and self-repression;

 – not surprisingly we are likely to suffer from physical stress symptoms, especially those involving inflammation such as eczema, ulcers, etc., since frustrated energy is constantly channelled inwards; periodic bitter outbursts may occasionally relieve the tension.

The challenge:
1. To consider the extent to which we are repeating negative past-life patterns.
2. To take personal responsibility for difficulties we may experience as a result of physical disability or accidents; a sense of frustration; feelings of personal inadequacy, self-consciousness or fear of appearing ineffective; inhibited self-expression or sexual hang-

ups; the tendency to become a workaholic; anxiety and stress-related ailments; cruelty at the hands of others; an excessively disciplined upbringing.

3. To ask ourselves whether we are fulfilling our obligations to express our physical resources; to ask ourselves, further, whether our sense of obligation (if any) is governed simply by the need for social respect.

The cultivation of patience and a structured yet moderate effort to build our physical strength, endurance and our ability to assert ourselves will help us towards these goals.

Suggested meditation affirmations:
See Appendix II: 2(g)

Bach Flower Remedies
See Appendix III: 2(a), 10(a), 11(a)(b), 17(a), 18(a)(h), 19(a), 20(a)(h), 21(a), 25(a)(i), 32(a), 33(a)(b)(j).

Links of Saturn to the Jupiter Principle, to Sagittarius and to the Ninth House
(See Appendix I)

In past lives
On the positive side we have taken personal responsibility for our philosophical or religious beliefs and moral values. Thus we have put effort into thinking about the meaning of life and arriving at our own conclusions rather than acquiescing in the dogma represented by the religious background into which we have been born.

On the negative side we have taken insufficient responsibility for arriving at our own philosophy of life. In many cases we have depended on the prevailing religious or political views without giving them much personal consideration, and have rigidly allied ourselves with the associated morality as a means of gaining social respect. Here outer form would have taken the place of inner belief. Furthermore we may have attempted to instil our own attitudes into others, being quick to condemn those who did not obey conventional religious or moral ideas.

Between lives we have had the opportunity to learn the importance of taking personal responsibility for our beliefs in life so as to avoid being too easily swayed by prevailing religious/political views and accompanying morals and conventions. Above all things, we were to learn that our religion or philosophy should not represent a mere status symbol whereby we gain respect and position in society.

The karma:
1. Where in the past we have given thought to the meaning of life, we may be born into a secure religious or moral background which, albeit conventional, is likely to provide us with stable guidelines by which we may evaluate life.
— The unshakeability of our beliefs may lead us to a position of responsibility within the Church, the law or politics, or at least will gain us the respect and confidence of others.
— To the extent that we have resisted the urge to lean too heavily on conventional morality we will find that our philosophical/religious needs are met from within. Thus we will be morally self-reliant and are unlikely to be troubled by doubts and anxieties over moral issues.

2. Where we have given insufficient thought to the purpose of life, we may experience difficulty in finding a viable philosophy — we may be compulsive agnostics or atheists despite a subconscious longing to find some belief to hold on to.
— Where in the past we have attached undue weight to conventional religious teachings and morality, we may find ourselves confronted with anxiety arising from the need to conform to accepted religious doctrine. Problems often start with a strict spiritual upbringing in which religion is an obligation based on fear. As adults, the whole question of morality may cause us anxiety (often unrecognized) in that we are afraid of disobeying traditional religious teachings which have remained impressed in our subconscious not merely from childhood but also from past-life experiences. One reaction is to entirely 'pass' on the whole issue of faith to avoid confronting our sense of obligation and the inner struggle that will ensue. Another is to over-immerse ourselves in ritualistic religious ceremony in order to prove to ourselves and others that we know where we stand. In either case our true needs are unlikely to be met, and depression and stress-related ailments may ensue.

The challenge:
1. To consider the extent to which we are repeating negative past-life patterns.
2. To take personal responsibility for difficulties we may experience

as a result of lack of faith; an over-strict religious upbringing; spiritual and moral questioning; fear and depression.

3. To ask ourselves whether we are fulfilling our obligation to find a meaningful explanation to life; to question, further, whether we are willing to come to our own conclusions or whether we continue to cling to traditional religious/philosophical thinking. Only when we find our own answer are our true needs likely to be met. A systematic, organized study of religion and philosophy — kept within the bounds of moderation — will help us towards this goal.

Suggested meditation affirmations:
See Appendix II: 2(h)

Bach Flower Remedies
See Appendix III: 2(a), 11(a)(i), 12(a)(c); 17(a)(h), 18(a)(i), 19(a), 20(a)(e), 25(a)(j), 32(a)(b).

Links of Saturn to Capricorn, the Tenth House and the Midheaven
(See Appendix I)

In past lives
On the positive side we have shown ourselves willing to assume and fulfil responsibilities in the society to which we belonged by displaying a conscientious approach to our public duties and persevering in the face of difficulty and frustration. At the same time we have resisted the desire for status in that we have performed our duties not so much for acclaim or honour but simply on the basis of our personal convictions.

On the negative side we may have shirked our social responsibilities or public duties, allowing others to 'carry' us. Alternatively we may have swung in the opposite direction and displayed excessive ambition in pursuit of respect and standing, in which case we are likely to have channelled a disproportionate amount of time and energy into our public duties, neglecting other aspects of our life. We may also have attempted to instil into those in our care this self-same concern for social approbation through the medium of an outwardly successful, conventional career.

Between lives we have had the opportunity to develop a more balanced approach to the assumption of wordly responsibilities. On the one hand we were to understand the need for each of us to make our own contribution to society but on the other hand we were to realize that this contribution is only of true value when motivated by a sincere desire to serve as opposed to ambition for social acclaim or status.

The karma:

1. To the extent that we have willingly fulfilled our duties to society we will now enjoy a stable and secure career life which eventually leads us to a position of authority, albeit from humble beginnings, whereby we gain the natural respect of others.

— Where we have resisted an excessive desire for respect and status, we will now possess an enviably self-contained approach to our career in that our job satisfaction is unaffected by criticism or approval. We will enjoy the capacity for excellent concentration and single-mindedness in our approach to our career, leading to sustained effort and thus to even greater achievement.

— The parent who exerts the greatest influence on our social attitudes — frequently our mother — will encourage us and help us towards a fulfilling career with prospects and personal satisfaction.

2. Where in the past we have failed to fulfil our obligation to work within society, we may now find ourselves faced with perpetual frustrations and setbacks as we seek to 'get on' in the world. Regardless of our efforts we may feel we are denied 'breaks' or a helping hand along the way, and may have the impression that however hard we work, we remain at a standstill.

— Past over-concern with career success and status may now manifest as:
   - an inborn lack of confidence in our ability to take on responsibility in our work;
   - self-consciousness and diffidence leading to the loss of opportunities for promotion and advancement;
   - worry about the impression we are making in our career and about the possibility of failure, criticism and demotion, resulting in mental depression and physical stress-related ailments.

— Alternatively, we may become workaholics, in that our minds and bodies are incessantly preoccupied with our work and career prospects; we cannot switch off, however much we long to do so, and our health and family/social life are likely to suffer as a result.

— The parent who exerts the greatest influence on our social attitudes — frequently our mother — may reinforce our sense of inadequacy by criticism and disapproval, and may over-emphasize the importance of wordly achievement and the need to gain acceptance within the status quo.

The challenge:
1. To consider the extent to which we are repeating negative past-life patterns.
2. To take personal responsibility for difficulties we may experience due to lack of career opportunities or career setbacks; self-consciousness and diffidence; worry and anxiety in respect of our career prospects; the tendency to become a workaholic; over-critical parents.
3. To ask ourselves whether we are fulfilling our obligations to pull our weight in the society we live in; to question, further, whether our sense of obligation (if any) results from true inner conviction or is governed simply by the need for material status and gain. A structured, patient approach towards developing a career for ourselves will help us towards this goal.

Suggested meditation affirmations:
See Appendix II: 2(i)

Bach Flower Remedies
See Appendix III: 10(a), 11(a)(b)(j), 15(a), 17(a)(l), 18(a)(j), 19(a), 20(a)(g)(h), 25(a)(b)(k), 33(a)(b)(d).

Links of Saturn to the Uranus Principle, to Aquarius and to the Eleventh House
(See Appendix I)

In past lives
On the positive side we have shown ourselves willing to play our own special part within our community yet in co-operation with others. We have worked towards breaking down social barriers by respecting the value and rights of all the members of our community and putting effort into building good relations with our friends and neighbours. And in so doing we have been motivated by the urge to promote the community spirit rather than by the desire to gain status.

On the negative side we may have channelled insufficient effort into our community and may have shown disrespect or prejudice towards our neighbours. Alternatively we may have outwardly appeared to play our part in community life, but with the motivation of gaining status rather than with any true desire to promote community relations.

Between lives we have had the opportunity to develop a sense of personal responsibility towards bringing into being a social environment in which each of us is true to ourselves yet functions in co-operation with each other member. Thus our motivation towards 'social work' of all descriptions should be based upon sincere convictions rather than the desire to gain social status for the aggrandizement of our own ego.

The karma:
1. Where in the past we have willingly played our unique role, yet with respect for the group as a whole, we will now find ourselves capable of gaining social acceptance for our original ideas, however unorthodox. In particular we may possess a gift for translating abstract insights into structured material form — thus equipping us for example for work in maths, science and technology. Whatever the nature of our originality, we have the ability to bring it down to earth so that it may yield tangible and practical results.
— Where we have put in effort towards furthering community relations, we will now enjoy stable relationships with our friends and neighbours, and in some cases may rise to a position of prominence in the group/community to which we belong, gaining respect for our 'social conscience' and services performed to society.
— To the extent that we have resisted the desire for social status or approval in our group or community activities, we will now find ourselves unaffected by others' opinions, enabling us to function self-reliantly, single-mindedly, and with a capacity for group organization and leadership.

2. Where in the past we have shown disrespect or contempt for co-members of our group or community, we may feel ourselves to be 'outsiders' amongst our peers. We may find that we are unaccepted for what we represent and that our original ideas — however inspired — are rejected.
— Where we have channelled insufficient effort into promoting good social relations and a community spirit, we may now find we have to work very hard to make friends — and that even so our friends remain few.

— Where we have in fact made some contribution to our community but with the motivation of gaining a good reputation rather than a true desire to be sociable, we may now be subject to anxieties and compulsions which reflect our excessive concern for what others think of us. Thus we may be prone to diffidence and self-consciousness in groups due to a fear of 'doing the wrong thing' or of being singled out and laughed at. As a result we are likely to avoid group activities, and to suffer depression due to the blockage of this vital aspect of human life. Note, however, that we may be drawn to older friends whose maturity makes us feel less self-conscious. Where we do persevere in social involvement we may find ourselves prone to anxiety about our social standing (and to stress-related ailments) or to excessive social commitment and thus to exhaustion and strain.

The challenge:
1. To consider the extent to which we are repeating negative past-life patterns.
2. To take personal responsibility for difficulties we may experience in terms of group participation or lack of friends.
3. To ask ourselves whether we are fulfilling our obligation to play our part in our community; to further question whether our sense of obligation (if any) results from true inner conviction or is governed simply by the need for social respect and status.

Some form of regular commitment to a group or club, or work in the local community will help us towards our goal.

Suggested meditation affirmations:
See Appendix II: 2(j)

Bach Flower Remedies
See Appendix III: 3(a)(j), 11(a)(e), 17(a)(i), 18(a)(k), 19(a), 20(a)(f), 33(a)(b)(e)(j).

Links of Saturn to the Neptune Principle,
to Pisces and to the Twelfth House
(See Appendix I)

In past lives
On the positive side we have worked hard to develop spiritual qualities, attempting to show selfless love to others and striving to remain true to our ideals even in the face of disillusionment. Our

motivation in so doing has been a personal conviction of the need to build a better world rather than any desire to gain 'moral' status or a 'good' reputation.

On the negative side we have disregarded the need for spiritual values and ideals, for humanitarianism and compassion, and may also have shunned the worth of the imagination, artistry, etc. Or in some cases we may have gone through the motions of being seen to be 'spiritual' and to do good works, but with the motivation of gaining status as a 'good person' rather than any real desire to express love for others.

Between lives we have had the opportunity to acquire a sense of personal responsibility to express love and beauty in our lives.

The karma:
1. Where we have already put in effort to attune ourselves to universal love and beauty we may enjoy:
    - strong spiritual values, in particular the ability to draw on our beliefs in everyday life and to make spirituality a living reality;
    - notably practical talents in music and the arts, which allow us to translate inspiration into concrete creations;
    - organizing skills in the field of humanitarian and charity work which again help us to achieve practical results.
—   Where our past endeavours have been inspired by personal conviction rather than the desire for social approval, we will now find ourselves unworried by others' reactions or criticism, allowing us self-containment and self-reliance in:
    - our spiritual life, in that our spiritual needs are met within and we don't need to look outside of ourselves for spiritual guidance; particularly marked is our capacity for concentration and perseverance in meditation, yoga and prayer;
    - inspired artistic activities, providing us with excellent concentration and sticking power, and the ability to pursue our work single-mindedly regardless of public opinion;
    - humanitarian work, which we will pursue unconcerned by outside criticism.
2. Where in the past we have spurned the need to feel at-one with others — through whatever means — we may now find that:
    - we are prone to a sense of loneliness even in the midst of a crowd;
    - there may be general difficulties in identifying with the way

others feel and a lack of imagination, which makes for
problems in human relations;
- sometimes this difficulty in 'losing ourselves' can result in
spells of insomnia;
- through the law of cause and effect we may now find ourselves
compelled to confront the inner life we have previously
neglected, in that circumstances confine us to spells of
isolation, possibly in hospitals, institutions or the like, where
we have no alternative but to be alone with our deepest
feelings;
- often we may suffer from fear of being alone, and of having
to confront our own feelings, ideals and disappointments;
- at other times we may be prone to overwhelming and
uncontrollable surges of self-pity, a sense of victimization,
imagined slights or treachery and feelings of guilt;
- in rare cases the repressed intuitive side of ourselves may
manifest as bouts of involuntary mediumship.
— Where there has been some recognition of the need for an active
spiritual life but our participation has been over-dependent on
social approval:
- we may long to experience religious ecstasy yet feel at a loss
as to how to do so or feel self-conscious about participating
in spiritual activities;
- in some cases spiritual ambition may manifest as anxiety about
our 'spiritual status', resulting in tension, depression and stress-
induced ailments;
- in other cases we may be prone to asceticism and excessive
spiritual self-discipline or we may be compulsive do-gooders
who literally wear ourselves out.

The challenge:
1. To consider the extent to which we are repeating negative past-
life patterns.
2. To take personal responsibility for difficulties we may experience
as a result of loneliness; periods of confinement; problems in
gaining satisfaction from our spiritual life; depression; asceticism
and self-martyrdom.
3. To ask ourselves whether we are attempting to build a sense of
at-oneness with the universe by learning to transcend the ego
in an organized, structured way. Suggestions for working towards
this include:
- Regular commitment to yoga or meditation based on clearly
defined steps. Patience is vital since results must be worked for.

- Some form of charity work in which we can develop compassion for others.
- Attempts to stimulate the imagination through reading or involvement with drama/music/art.

Suggested meditation affirmations:
See Appendix II: 2(k)

Bach Flower Remedies
See Appendix III: 2(a), 11(a)(g), 17(a)(j), 18(a)(l), 19(a), 20(a)(b), 22(a), 25(a)(l), 32(a)(c), 33(f)(i)(j).

Links of Saturn to the Pluto Principle, to Scorpio and to the Eighth House (See Appendix I)

In past lives
On the positive side we have resisted the urge to prove the strength of our will-power in order to gain in standing. In all power issues, and in particular in emotional and sexual relationships, we have looked first to ourselves in the case of conflict and have displayed restraint and responsibility in wielding personal power.

On the negative side we have used personal power irresponsibly in order to overpower others, especially at the emotional and sexual level, to defend our status or gain in standing. In other cases we may have over-emphasized the importance of emotional and sexual continence and rigidly instilled our beliefs into our dependents, thus giving rise to future inhibitions on their part.

Between lives we have had the opportunity to learn to take personal responsibility to channel our will not so as to achieve status but so as to bring maximum help to others (alignment to universal will).

The karma:
1. To the extent that we have shown restraint and responsibility in the use of personal power and are thus attuned to universal will, we may now possess:
   - a talent for research and diagnosis, equipping us for work in the fields of science, psychology and all forms of medicine, with the emphasis on the practical application of knowledge and the possibility of reaching a position of authority;
   - accurate self-knowledge;

- a gift for spiritual (psychic) healing, with a particular aptitude for concentration and persistence;
- genuine emotional self-containment and sexual continence which enhances and conserves any healing power we may possess.

2. Where we have sought status by wielding personal power, we may be subject to fear that our will may be overpowered and that we may be judged weak or ineffective. In particular this may manifest as:
   - lack of confidence in asserting our will or sex drive in case we are considered inadequate or attract ridicule, leading to the possibility of frigidity or impotence, or alternatively:
   - unnatural persistence in proving the strength of our will, both in general and in particular in emotional/sexual relationships and in matters relating to joint finances; this extremism is likely to be accompanied by exceptional bitterness when our desires are denied or blocked and an obsessive desire for revenge on those who get the better of us;
   - a fear of losing control and of self-surrender, which takes the form of: insecurity and defensiveness, especially in emotional/sexual relationships in which we hold back our deepest feelings and thereby suffer a sense of emotional isolation; fear of confronting and releasing subconscious emotions and drives leading to a build-up of frustrated energy and possible physical/mental illness; fear of all forms of change, especially death.

— Our upbringing may over-emphasize the need for emotional and sexual self-discipline with the possibility of emotional deprivation in childhood and sexual inhibitions in adulthood.

— In some cases we may suffer emotional or sexual abuse at the hands of individuals who seek to impose their will upon us in order to bolster their sense of personal power.

The challenge:
1. To consider the extent to which we are repeating negative past-life patterns.
2. To take spiritual responsibility for emotional deprivation or sexual frustration; feelings of general or sexual inadequacy; fears of all kinds; difficulties arising from our inability to give in or accept defeat.
3. To work in a planned and structured way to counter the attitudes and habits from which these problems originate. It would be

of value to explore systematically the subjects of sex, death and psychic energy through the study of psychology, the occult and healing. Therapies which allow us to confront and release repressed drives and emotions can also help us to break free from inhibitions and open ourselves to greater fulfilment.

Suggested meditation affirmations:
See Appendix II: 2(l)

Bach Flower Remedies
See Appendix III: 2(a), 9(a), 11(a)(h), 13(a)(b)(d), 17(a)(k), 19(a), 25(a)(m), 30(a)(b), 36(a)(e).

12.
THE SCHOOL OF URANUS

The essence of Uranus consists of developing our attunement to universal mind, which may provide us with access to unlimited knowledge and communication. Thus we are challenged to break down the barriers which impede such limitless vision in that they deny the at-oneness of the universe and lead to self-important attitudes and actions and to a lack of respect for others.

The general karma of Uranus consists in meeting with the outcome of a past-life pattern which has been composed *on the positive side* of:

— uninhibited individuality accompanied by a sense of humility, equal respect for all other beings, and a balanced exercise of personal freedom which is non-detrimental to others;

but *on the negative side* has been composed of:

— arrogance, self-importance and prejudice against those who differ from our norm, accompanied by disagreeable eccentricity, unpredictability, erratic fluctuation and the pursuit of freedom to the detriment of others.

In the case of a positive past-life pattern, past respect for others and a sense of personal humility will now bring the reward of popularity, originality and creativity (possibly to the point of inventiveness or ESP). A balanced exercise of personal freedom will now result in an agreeably unusual life filled with exciting changes.

In the case of a negative past-life pattern, the outcome of past inability to tolerate and accept those who differed from our norm may be that we now suffer through being 'odd' in some way so that we feel ourselves to be outsiders or are mocked by our contemporaries. Past unpredictability and misuse of freedom may now rebound upon us in that we find ourselves the victim of unforeseen, unwelcome and uncontrollable change, either in terms of our personal feelings or attitudes or in terms of circumstances or other individuals.

The general challenge of Uranus is:
— To achieve a balance between respect for our own individuality both at a personal level and in terms of the group to which we belong, and respect for others' individuality even where this differs vastly from our own.
— To strike a balance between our insistence on personal rights or the rights of our group, and the freedom of others to pursue their own path.
— To ensure that our urge for personal liberty is non-detrimental to the welfare of those for whom we are responsible.
— To learn to distinguish between change for the sake of change, and purposive change which will effectively develop our understanding and tolerance.

Links of Uranus to the Sun Principle, to Leo and to the Fifth House (See Appendix I)

In past lives we have experienced a strong awareness of our personal identity and of the role we were to play in the world.

On the positive side we have played our part in tune with others whose individuality we respected and valued. We have followed our path unaffected by the status quo, free of those attachments which might trap us in a rut, and adaptable to changes which would bring interest and variety to ourselves and those close to us.

On the negative side we have developed a sense of self-importance, seeing our own talents as superior to those of others, and scorning or mocking the way of being, goals and ambitions of others. We may also have placed our need to be free to make our mark on the world before our commitments to those dependent upon us, resulting in unwelcome upheaval in their lives. And we may have pursued purposeless change simply in order to avoid losing our independence.

Between lives we have had the opportunity to learn to overcome a sense of superiority as regards our own talents and abilities compared to other people's. In so doing we stimulate our capacity to tap universal mind in the form of hunches and flashes which will help us to find our true niche in life and release all of our potential in the most beneficial way possible.

The karma:
1. To the extent that we have acquired tolerance of others and respect

for their talents, we will now find ourselves endowed with original and futuristic abilities — particularly in the areas of life represented by the placing of the Sun and Uranus — for which we will be respected by our contemporaries.

— Where we have developed a sense of independence which has been based on a sincere quest to explore all of our potential and which has been non-detrimental to others, we will gain many opportunities to do different and exciting things in life, thus enabling us to use our talents to the full. Our life is likely to be full of agreeable changes and pleasant surprises.

— Our father may be delightfully different, humanitarian, and a source of inspiration to us to develop our own originality.

2. Where in the past we have displayed arrogance and intolerance of those who differed from our norm, we will now find that despite a strong sense of identity and highly developed abilities, our talents go unrecognized or unappreciated. Indeed we may find ourselves mocked or scorned by our contemporaries.

— Where in the past we have behaved unpredictably towards others, have indulged unreasonably in personal freedom, or have pursued purposeless change simply to avoid losing our independence:

    - we may find ourselves prone to an innate restlessness which prevents us from specializing in any branch and leads to much pointless chopping and changing in our life;

    - we may find our lives disrupted by changes over which we have little control — e.g. unforeseen changes in circumstances which result in constant moves and prevent us from settling to any one goal for long;

    - we may find our lives entangled with males (especially our father or male partner) who are considered by others to be eccentric, who are arrogant and scornful of our interests and efforts, or who place their own freedom before our welfare, act unpredictably and involve us in frequent and unwelcome change.

The challenge:

1. To consider the extent to which we are repeating negative past-life patterns.

2. To take personal responsibility for difficulties we may experience as a result of mockery or lack of recognition; restlessness; unforeseen changes; unpredictable male figures in our life.

3. To consider whether we are using our powers of self-expression

with humility, with respect for the ways of others where these differ from our own, and with a sense of independence which is non-detrimental to others and is based on expanding our horizons rather than avoiding commitment.

In practical terms we may benefit from involvement in a variety of different creative interests, not so much with a view to specialization but so as to gain appreciation of the value of each in its own right. The study of astrology can develop our awareness of the creative potential of each sign.

Suggested meditation affirmations:
See Appendix II: 3, 4(a)

Bach Flower Remedies
See Appendix III: 3(a)(b), 5(a)(b), 16(a)(b)(c), 26(a)(b), 29(a)(b), 32(a).

Links of Uranus to the Moon Principle, to Cancer and to the Fourth House (See Appendix I)

In past lives we have been strongly individualistic in our emotional response to life.

On the positive side we have also been able to accommodate the reactions of those who viewed things differently to us, and have seen interest and value in the many different outlooks and backgrounds of other people. We have expressed our feelings spontaneously, with a delightful freedom from convention and an original sense of humour — but never to the detriment of others.

On the negative side we have been intolerant of those who did not see things our way or who responded to life differently to us. Our sense of humour has been cynical, based on mockery or mimicry of those whose attitudes, mannerisms or habits did not conform to our own. Often implied here was prejudice against the home background or roots of others from whence they derived their characteristics. We may also have been prone to self-indulgent and unpredictable emotional outbursts, oblivious to their impact on others.

Between lives we have had the opportunity to learn to overcome a sense of superiority as regards our own roots, attitudes and mannerisms compared to other people's. In so doing we stimulate our capacity to tap universal mind in the form of intuition and hunches, and our ability to acquire understanding of others at the emotional level.

The karma:

1. To the extent that we have acquired tolerance and respect for others:
    - we will now possess a sparkling, unusual personality and sharp wits;
    - we will enjoy popularity and widespread social acceptance in that we have a natural rapport with people from all walks of life;
    - our home background may be exciting and unusual, involving interesting moves and changes which give us plenty of opportunity to widen our horizons and develop our understanding of life;
    - our ESP may be highly developed and we may benefit from helpful intuitive flashes.

— Where we have developed an emotional independence which is non-detrimental to others, we will be blessed with an adaptable objective disposition.

— Our mother may be egalitarian in outlook with many interesting social contacts from which we benefit. She may be highly original in her own right, encouraging and inspiring us to develop our own speciality.

2. Where we have displayed arrogance and intolerance of those who differed from our norm, although we may be considered unusual, we are unlikely to gain admiration or acceptance from our peers. We may find that certain of our mannerisms or habits over which we have little control are ridiculed, or we may be born into an unconventional home background for which we are scorned. In any case we may feel something of an outsider and find difficulty in fitting into society.

— Where in the past we have behaved inconsistently and unpredictably towards others and have indulged unreasonably in emotional freedom:
    - our disposition may be highly strung, plunging us into unwelcome highs and lows which occur without rhyme or reason; this emotional instability may be accompanied by tremendous restlessness, a tendency to be easily bored and an insatiable craving for emotional excitement; nervous debility can result;
    - our life may be subject to change, especially changes of

residence, which occur in particular in childhood and which shatter our emotional security;
– we may find our lives involved with females (especially our mother or female partner) who are considered to be eccentric, who are intolerant of our emotional reactions where these differ from their own, and/or who are themselves emotionally unstable and indulge in emotional outbursts detrimental to our emotional security.

The challenge:
1. To consider the extent to which we are repeating negative past-life patterns.
2. To take personal responsibility for difficulties we may experience as a result of emotional instability; restlessness and a tendency to boredom; nervous debility; unforeseeable changes; unpredictable female figures in our life.
3. To consider whether we are approaching life with sufficient humility, with respect for the ways of other people where these differ from our own, and with a sense of independence which is non-detrimental to others and is based on expanding our horizons rather than simply avoiding commitment.

In practical terms we may gain benefit from developing as many personal contacts as possible, and from frequently changing our home base so as to widen our understanding of people in general. The study of astrology can develop our awareness of the emotional characteristics of each sign mode.

Suggested meditation affirmations:
See Appendix II: 3, 4(b)

Bach Flower Remedies
See Appendix III: 3(a)(i), 5(a)(c), 16(a)(d), 26(a)(c), 29(a)(d), 32(a).

Links of Uranus to the Mercury Principle to Gemini and to the Third House (See Appendix I)

In past lives we have expressed independence in our thinking and in our speech.

On the positive side we have remained humble about our mental abilities, respecting the ability of others to achieve valuable insights in their own right. We have stated our opinions without concern for the conventions of the status quo, but never so as to embarrass or hurt others unduly, and with the ability to change our mind as and when more meaningful ideas came to light.

On the negative side we may have arrogantly considered our own mentality superior to that of others and argued with or belittled those whose opinions or intelligence did not — as we saw it — measure up to our own. We may have pursued the need for freedom of speech selfishly and to extremes, often simply as a gesture of rebellion. We may have been prone to change our mind frequently and unpredictably, resulting in confusion for others.

Between lives we have had the opportunity to learn to overcome a sense of superiority as regards our own intellect and communicative skills as opposed to other people's, and thus to stimulate our attunement to universal understanding and our ability to acquire total knowledge.

The karma:
1. To the extent that we have acquired tolerance and respect for others, we will now find ourselves endowed with an original, high-speed intellect which is able to grasp novel or abstract ideas, has a multi-faceted approach to problems and is thus capable of new insights. We may find we have a special talent for writing and speaking, with the ability to find the right word at the right moment, and in some cases we may possess ESP. We are likely to be respected for our brilliance and enjoy a good rapport with our peers at the intellectual and communicative levels.
— Where we have developed an independent mind which is motivated by a sincere quest for knowledge, we will possess the ability to change the direction of our thoughts at will, to focus rapidly upon one topic after another and thus constantly to expand our breadth of vision.

2. Where we have displayed arrogance and intolerance of those who differed from our norm, we may possess a mind and speech which, although exceptionally quick-witted, are judged by our contemporaries to be bizarre or over-complicated.
— Where we have pursued freedom of thought and freedom of speech simply as a gesture of rebellion:
    - the speed of our speech may be a hindrance rather than a help since it is often not understood and detracts from our ability to communicate clearly with others;
    - we may find it difficult to cope with the high-speed activity of our mind which swings erratically from one opinion to

another with little chance for follow-through, resulting in inconsistencies in our reasoning;
- our ideas may be extreme to the point of impracticability and our mind may be highly strung, incessantly active and subject to extreme tension;
- the outcome is that we feel ourselves to be outsiders and are unable to make effective use of our intellectual abilities.

The challenge:
1. To consider the extent to which we are repeating negative past-life patterns.
2. To take personal responsibility for difficulties we may experience as a result of a hyperactive intellect, mind and speech one step ahead of themselves, inconsistencies in thinking, problems in concentration and communication, and mental tension.
3. To consider whether or not we are using our powers of thought and speech with humility, with respect for the ways of others where these differ from our own, and with a sense of independence which is non-detrimental to others and is based on expanding our understanding rather than a gesture of rebellion.

In practical terms we may gain benefit from involvement in a variety of studies, from widespread reading, and from meetings with diverse individuals in the form of discussion groups. This will help to broaden our mind and increase our tolerance of different viewpoints. The study of astrology can develop our awareness of the reasoning and communicative faculties of each sign mode.

Suggested meditation affirmations:
See Appendix II: 3, 4(c)

Bach Flower Remedies
See Appendix III: 3(a)(b), 16(a)(e), 26(a)(d), 29(a)(c), 32(a)(e).

Links of Uranus to the Virgo Principle
and to the Sixth House
(See Appendix I)

In past lives we have been involved in work of an unusual nature or have possessed an independent approach to health care.

On the positive side this individuality will have been accompanied by a sense of respect for others' working skills and approaches to health care where these contrasted with our own. We are likely to have exhibited adaptability, flexibility and a positive receptivity to new ideas.

On the negative side we have displayed an arrogant insistence that our ways were the right ways and intolerance and scorn for those unable to concur with us. We are likely to have behaved unpredictably and irresponsibly in our work due to lack of commitment and/or been liable to purposeless dabbling in a succession of health fads, motivated simply by the desire to be 'different'.

Between lives we have had the opportunity to learn to overcome a sense of superiority as regards our own approach to health and work compared to other people's. In so doing we stimulate our attunement to universal understanding and our ability to uncover the knowledge which governs mankind's well-being of body and of mind and which will one day be freely available to us all.

The karma:
1.   Where we have displayed tolerance of others' working skills, we will be able to relate easily to new skills and technology, may be inventive in our own right, and at the same time enjoy the respect of our colleagues.
—   Past adaptability will now endow us with an ability to turn our hand to many different fields, and an exciting working routine, offering many opportunities for change which serve to further develop our skills.
—   Where we have shown respect for all facets of health-care we will now find ourselves resourceful in curing ourselves and others, with good understanding of alternative treatments and the appropriate use of each. Our specialized field — and in some cases our own insights — will be recognized by our peers, and we may receive opportunities to expand our understanding further.

2.   Where in the past we have displayed arrogance and intolerance of those who differed from our norm:
     –   although we may well possess skills or inventive ability in our own right, these may not be acknowledged or given sufficient scope, or may be rejected as being too way-out;
     –   we may be mocked as cranks for our interest in health and fitness or for our unusual daily regime.
—   Past chopping and changing in our work simply as a means of evading commitment or to avoid submission to authority may now manifest as unforeseen and unwelcome changes in our

working life, as restlessness and as incessant boredom with mundane routine.
— Past inconsistencies in health care may manifest as ups and downs in our physical well-being, making it difficult for us to achieve continuity in our daily lives. In some cases the nervous system may be prone to weakness.

The challenge:
1. To consider the extent to which we are repeating negative past-life patterns.
2. To take personal responsibility for difficulties we may experience as a result of lack of scope and fulfilment in our working life; unforeseen job changes; boredom with everyday life; ups and downs in health, and nerve problems.
3. To consider whether we are approaching day-to-day life and health care with respect for the ways of others where these differ from our own, and with a sense of independence which is based on expanding our horizons rather than evading commitment.

In practical terms we may gain benefit from:
— varied job experience, especially in the fields of new technology and alternatives,
— the study of various approaches to health care, especially alternative medicine.

Suggested meditation affirmations:
See Appendix II: 3, 4(d)

Bach Flower Remedies
See Appendix III: 3(a)(c), 16(a)(f), 26(a)(e), 29(a)(f).

Links of Uranus to the Venus Principle, to Libra and to the Seventh House
(See Appendix I)

In past lives our approach to relationships has been strongly individualistic.
On the positive side we have succeeded in doing our own thing whilst simultaneously accepting and tolerating the ways of others even where these were totally opposed to our own. We have expressed the need for freedom in relationships constructively, enjoying varied social liaisons whilst honouring our obligations to our dependents.
On the negative side we may have expressed intolerance of 'different' forms of relationship, and prejudice against or mockery

of those who participated in such relationships. We may have placed our desire to enjoy multiple relationships before our responsibilities to our existing partner or to our other dependents.

Between lives we have had the opportunity to learn to overcome prejudice and self-importance in our attitude towards relationships. In so doing we stimulate our attunement to universal mind, and our ability to acquire an instinctive understanding of others and the purpose of human interaction.

The karma:
1.   To the extent that we have acquired tolerance of the way others approach relationships, we will be blessed with an attractive personality which draws others towards us, resulting in popularity, and many unusual and interesting friends from all quarters of life.
—   Where we have developed a sense of independence which is based on a sincere quest to understand people and which is non-detrimental to others, we will now enjoy an exciting love life and social life.

2.   Where we have displayed arrogance and intolerance of those whose approach to relationships differed from our own, we may be compulsively attracted to individuals considered to be strange or unsuitable by our parents and/or peers, and there is the possibility of being outcast from our family or group on the basis of our relationships.
—   Where in the past we have deliberately chosen change as the main priority in our relationships, our partnerships and friendships may now be governed by change in a way which is quite beyond our control. Thus we may be subject to constantly fluctuating feelings towards our partners, to an incessant desire for excitement, and to sudden infatuations which quickly peter out, or else circumstances over which we have no influence may result in frequent and enforced partings from our lover.
—   Where we have behaved inconsistently and unpredictably towards others in the past, we may find ourselves involved with a partner who places the need for personal freedom before our interests.

The challenge:
1.   To consider the extent to which we are repeating negative past-life patterns.
2.   To take personal responsibility for difficulties we may experience as a result of compulsive infatuations — often with un-

conventional types — and lack of social acceptance; restlessness and changeable feelings in relationships; involuntary partings; partners who place their own freedom before our happiness.

3. To consider whether we are approaching personal relationships with humility, with respect for the ways of others where these differ from our own, and with a sense of independence which is non-detrimental to others and which is based on expanding our horizons rather than simply evading commitment.

In practical terms we may gain benefit from cultivating a wide cross-section of personal contacts in order to increase our acceptance of others. Even when we are committed to a steady partner, it is helpful to have plenty of friends from as many different backgrounds as possible. The study of astrology can develop our awareness of the manner of relating of each sign mode.

Suggested meditation affirmations:
See Appendix II: 3, 4(e)

Bach Flower Remedies
See Appendix III: 3(a), 6(a)(b), 26(a)(f), 29(a)(d), 34(a)(g).

Links of Uranus to the Venus Principle, to Taurus and to the Second House (See Appendix I)

In past lives we have adopted an individualistic approach to the resources of the earth, to material possessions and to the arts.

On the positive side we have developed the ability to accept and tolerate others' handling of money and resources, even where this differed vastly from our own; in the field of music and art we have given respect to the genre of others whilst remaining true to our own mode. We have shown ourselves capable of adapting to changing material circumstances, and have remained detached from excessive material bonds whilst honouring our financial obligations to our dependents.

On the negative side we have ridiculed those whose approach to money and possessions differed from our own or have scorned those who did not share our aesthetic tastes. Financial irresponsibility and refusal to take on material commitment may have plunged our family into unforeseen financial crises. Our artistic expression may have been motivated primarily by the desire to shock and outrage and by contempt for those not on our wavelength.

Between lives we have had the opportunity to learn to overcome a sense of superiority as regards our own approach to money, resources and the arts compared to other people's. In so doing we stimulate our ability to gain insight into the workings of matter, especially in terms of the earth's resources, and to tap inspiration in music and the arts.

The karma:
1. Where we have acquired tolerance and respect for others:
    - we may now possess valuable insights in the fields of economics, food production, science and technology;
    - we may be blessed with originality and inspiration in our expression of music or the arts;
    - we are likely to be respected and admired for our talents and enjoy good rapport with our colleagues.
— The outcome of past adaptability at the material level is likely to be unexpected strokes of fortune in the acquisition of wealth, land or real estate. In the field of the arts we may enjoy exciting and unexpected opportunities to express our artistic abilities in a number of different ways.

2. Where in the past we have displayed arrogance and intolerance of those whose approach to material affairs or to the arts differed from our own:
    - we may be scorned or mocked because of our financial status or our outlook on material values;
    - skills we possess in the areas of resources or technology may remain unrecognized;
    - we may feel ourselves to be out on a limb in terms of our musical or aesthetic tastes, and where we possess artistic talent, this may not be acknowledged as it should be.
— Where we have indulged unreasonably in personal freedom simply to avoid commitment:
    - we may suffer from restlessness which prevents us from settling down to a steady living — and consequently may find ourselves frequently without funds;
    - unforeseen strokes of fate may periodically disrupt our material security;
    - where we are involved in the arts, our careers may suffer many ups and downs.
— Where in the past we have behaved inconsistently and unpredictably towards others, we may now find our lives entangled with those of women (especially our mother or female

partner) who are themselves unconventional or unpredictable in their approach to money or the arts.

The challenge:
1. To consider the extent to which we are repeating negative past-life patterns.
2. To take personal responsibility for difficulties we may experience in terms of finance and resources — or in the arts — resulting from our unconventional outlook, restlessness, impulsiveness or unforeseen reversals in fortune; unpredictable behaviour on the part of females in our life.
3. To consider whether we are approaching material affairs (and the arts) with humility, with respect for the ways of others where these differ from our own, and with a sense of independence which is non-detrimental to others and which is based on expanding our horizons rather than evading commitment.

In practical terms we may gain benefit from diverse economic/ ecological studies and involvement in various forms of music and art, seeking always to see quality or purpose in every different approach. The study of astrology can develop our awareness of the unique approach to matter of each sign mode.

Suggested meditation affirmations:
See Appendix II: 3, 4(f)

Bach Flower Remedies
See Appendix III: 3(a), 29(a)(e).

Links of Uranus to the Mars Principle, to Aries, to the First House and to the Ascendant (See Appendix I)

In past lives a strong feature of our character has been the urge to assert ourselves in accordance with the dictates of our own mind, free from all restrictions.

On the positive side our nonconformist actions have been motivated by a desire to widen our horizons and to experience as much as possible in life whilst also taking into account repercussions to others.

On the negative side, however, our desire for liberty has represented little more than a gesture of rebellion against authority. Thus we have reacted in the form of reckless outbursts, uncontrolled use of force and unpredictable changes of course in response to attempts

to curb our freedom. In some cases the urge for liberty of action will
have played out not only at the individual level but at the group
level also, resulting in our active involvement with campaigns for
partisan rights or revolution, often to the detriment of other groups
or sectors of society.

Between lives we have had the opportunity to refine our ability to
be true to ourselves in our actions and self-assertion whilst bearing
in mind the inevitable repercussions to the well-being of the whole.
In so doing, we develop our ability to act in accordance with universal
mind, leading to original, inspired use and direction of energy forces.

The karma:
1. The outcome of positive individualistic action performed in the
    past is likely to consist in:
    - a magnetic, quick-witted personality and an unusual,
      attractive appearance;
    - a predisposition to behave decisively and effectively, to be
      resourceful and to demonstrate an inspired application of
      energy resulting in scientific/technological ability, or
      inventiveness;
    - a general capacity to summon up energy at will and to channel
      it in short intensive bursts as and when needed;
    - the possibility of finding ourselves presented with many
      different opportunities to pursue exciting activities which
      widen our horizons.

2. The result of previous thoughtless and erratic direction of energy
    may be that:
    - we may be mocked or scorned by others on account of unusual
      personality traits or an unusual appearance;
    - we may find ourselves accident-prone, due either to our own
      actions, to recklessness on the part of others or to circumstances
      outside of our control;
    - where in the past we have self-indulgently given vent to our
      anger, we may now find ourselves prone to involuntary temper
      fits which come and go unpredictably, which we may find
      extraordinarily difficult to contain and which in some cases
      may lead to senseless destruction;
    - restlessness may be a problem, manifesting as an insatiable
      craving for excitement, boredom with the mundane, and a
      penchant for dangerous hobbies and sports;
    - we may be subject to a spasmodic energy flow which takes

the form of periods of terrific activity followed by spells of
lethargy and which can prove taxing to the nervous system
and lead to difficulties in completing projects;
- there is a likelihood of clashes with authority — we may find
  ourselves singled out seemingly unfairly;
- in a small minority of cases we may suffer harm at the hands
  of gangs or activist groups;
- we may find our lives entangled with males (especially our
  father or male partner) whose erratic or reckless behaviour
  brings us fear and unhappiness.

The challenge:
1. To consider the extent to which we are repeating negative past-
   life patterns.
2. To take personal responsibility for difficulties we may experience
   as a result of accidents; temper fits; restlessness; a spasmodic
   energy flow; clashes with authority; contact with erratic males.
3. To consider whether we are channelling and using our energy
   drive with a sense of independence which is non-detrimental
   to others and which is based on expanding our experience of
   life rather than simply evading restriction and authority.

In practical terms we may gain benefit from involvement with as
many different types of energetic activity as possible. The study of
astrology can help develop our awareness of the unique energy drive
of each sign mode.

Suggested meditation affirmations:
See Appendix II: 3, 4(g)

Bach Flower Remedies
See Appendix III: 5(a)(d), 6(a)(c), 16(a)(g), 26(i), 29(a)(f).

Links of Uranus to the Jupiter Principle,
to Sagittarius and to the Ninth House
(See Appendix I)

In past lives our individuality has expressed itself through our
philosophy of life.

On the positive side we have acquired the ability to be true to
our own beliefs and code of morality whilst showing a healthy respect
for those of others. We have expanded our understanding of universal
law by opening ourselves to different ideas and philosophies — often
by travel — and deriving something of value from each.

On the negative side we have allowed ourselves to feel superior to or be derisive of those whose creed or morality differed from ours. In other cases we may have become fanatically involved with a succession of religious or philosophical movements — or indulged in a series of erratic journeys — mainly in order to avoid commitment and without understanding, purpose or gain.

Between lives we have had the opportunity to further refine our understanding of universal law through the study of the truth embodied in different religions or philosophies. Knowledge, as represented by the principles of universal law, can be gained only by overcoming the barriers of prejudice against ideas which are unfamiliar. Thus our task is to increase our tolerance of each and every belief.

The karma:
1. Where we have acquired tolerance and respect for others, we will possess a strongly developed philosophy of life which derives from inner conviction rather than external teachings. In some instances we are able to pass on inspired insights to others, in which case our ideas receive recognition and are accepted as of value to humanity.
— As a result of past adaptability we will gain the opportunity to engage in wide-ranging study of philosophy, religion, etc., either via institutions of learning or through travel, which further expands our wisdom.

2. Where in the past we have been unable to accommodate the vast cross-section of human belief and the essential part to be played by each idea within the whole, we may find ourselves out on a limb in terms of our religious or philosophical thinking. In some way our beliefs will conflict with those of our peers and may lead to our being considered eccentric or scorned.
— Where we have erratically changed course simply in order to avoid commitment, we may find ourselves subject to restlessness and instability in our search to find meaning to life. Almost beyond our control we may find ourselves plunging from one extreme of belief to another, which follow no pattern and bring us little satisfaction. Travel may likewise represent a source of frustration rather than expansion, in that we may find ourselves obliged to engage in many unforeseen and unwelcome journeys which bring instability into our lives.

The challenge:
1. To consider the extent to which we are repeating negative past-life patterns.
2. To take personal responsibility for difficulties we may experience as a result of our unusual beliefs, inconsistency of belief or extremes of belief, or in terms of travel.
3. To consider whether or not we are working constructively to break down all barriers of intolerance and prejudice in our understanding of the many different ways in which mankind finds meaning in life.

In practical terms we may gain benefit from a comprehensive study of the many different philosophies and religions of the world, with a view to obtaining something of value from each rather than expecting to find the whole truth in one belief system.

Suggested meditation affirmations:
See Appendix II: 3, 4(h)

Bach Flower Remedies
See Appendix III: 3(a)(e)(k), 16(a)(i), 29(a)(g), 32(a)(b), 34(a)(c).

Links of Uranus to the Saturn Principle, to Capricorn, to the Tenth House and to the Midheaven (See Appendix I)

In past lives we have been keenly aware of the nature and value of the contribution we were most suited to make to society in terms of our career and public duties.

On the positive side we have achieved a sense of balance about our own importance in relation to the contributions of others, viewing our personal contribution as part of a team effort, and our own field of activity as just one equal part of the whole. We have been adaptable in respect of the duties we were capable of fulfilling, resulting in personal expansion and co-operation with co-workers.

On the negative side we have been arrogant about our own status or our own area of responsibility, showing contempt for others. In other cases we have expressed an aversion to authority and an urge to evade commitment, resulting in difficulties for our colleagues.

Between lives we have received instruction as to how to introduce new ideas beneficial to the advancement of mankind through our role in society. We were to learn that our success in this respect is directly dependent upon overcoming a sense of self-importance or superiority as regards our status, since it is this which impedes access to universal mind and thus to inspiration.

The karma:

1. Where we have expressed humility with regard to our status in life together with a sound respect for others, we will possess a strong sense of purpose in our career, a good rapport with our colleagues, opportunities to work in the field of new ideas or advanced technology, and the ability to receive original insights and to put these into practice.

— Where in the past we have proved ourselves adaptable in our public duties, we will now experience many opportunities to diversify within the framework of our career, and where we undergo change this will be of an exciting and mind-broadening nature.

2. Where in the past we have expressed arrogance in respect of our public status, we may now well possess advanced ideas — or believe that we do so — but find it extremely difficult to discover a channel through which they can be pursued or fulfilled. As a result there is the likelihood of feeling oneself to be a misfit or of being considered eccentric by one's colleagues or the public at large.

— Where in the past we have pursued change in our career simply in order to avoid responsibility and commitment, we may now be prone to inherent restlessness and boredom in our work. Due to circumstances beyond our control we may be subject to changes in our career which are disagreeably sudden, and disruptive to what we are currently attempting to achieve.

The challenge:

1. To consider the extent to which we are repeating negative past-life patterns.
2. To take personal responsibility for difficulties we may experience as a result of problems in finding our niche in society; restlessness and boredom; unwelcome changes in our career.
3. To consider whether or not we are approaching our career with humility, with respect for the ways of others where these differ from our own, and with a sense of independence which is non-detrimental to others and is based on expanding our experience of life rather than simply evading restriction and authority.

In practical terms we may gain benefit by attempting to achieve greater versatility in our career or public duties.

Suggested meditation affirmations:
See Appendix II: 3, 4(i)

Bach Flower Remedies
See Appendix III: 3(a)(d), 16(a)(j), 26(a)(j), 29(a)(h), 34(a)(d).

Links of Uranus to Aquarius and to the Eleventh House
(See Appendix I)

In past lives
On the positive side we have shown ourselves capable of functioning as individuals yet with awareness of being part of a greater whole. Thus we are likely to have played our part in our community with a sense of independence and personal detachment, yet with humility and concern for the rights of all other individuals and all other groups.

On the negative side we may have arrogantly considered ourselves superior to other members of our group — or considered our own group superior to other groups within the community — and may have displayed prejudice against individuals or organizations differing from our norm. The need for personal freedom may have come before our responsibilities to other individuals or other groups and may have led to reckless and unpredictable actions towards other individuals and towards other groups.

Between lives we have had the opportunity to develop a more balanced attitude towards our sense of importance within the group or community to which we belong, and greater tolerance and acceptance of our friends and associates. Equally we were to learn to express freedom as a means of broadening our horizons rather than a means of avoiding responsibility and commitment. As we break down the barriers of arrogance and prejudice and refine our expression of personal independence, slowly but surely we expand our attunement to universal mind, and our social and cosmic awareness.

The karma:
1. Where in the past we have expressed tolerance and humility in our group and community life:
    - within our circle we are likely to be accepted for ourselves, no matter how unusual our interests may be, and where we belong to a specific group we are likely to enjoy easy relations with other groups or associations;

- we may have an aptitude for social work, social studies or political activities;
- we may be capable of insights in the field of science and the occult;

— To the extent that we have developed the adaptability necessary to move freely within society, we will now enjoy an exciting social life, with many opportunities to meet unusual, interesting individuals. We will feel at ease in the company of others, possessing the ability to get on with anyone from any walk of life and to attract friends of all types.

2. Where in the past we have displayed self-importance and prejudice in our community relations, we may now find that we are 'outsiders' in the circle to which we belong and that we are ridiculed for our unusual views.

— Where in the past our expression of freedom has been reckless and detrimental to others, we may now find ourselves on the receiving end of sudden, unexpected and disruptive attitudes and actions on the part of other people within our group or community, or on the part of conflicting groups or social movements.

— We may be subject to boredom, restlessness and constant changes of attitude in our personal or group associations and in our general social aspirations.

The challenge:
1. To consider how far we may be repeating the attitudes and traits described in connection with the negative past-life pattern.
2. To take personal responsibility for difficulties we may encounter arising from ridicule or lack of acceptance by our peers; restlessness and boredom in our social interactions; unpredictable, disruptive behaviour on the part of friends or associates.
3. To consider whether we are playing our part in the group or community to which we belong with understanding and tolerance and a balanced approach to freedom.

We may be helped towards this goal by active participation in all types of clubs, groups and social activities, preferably those which bring us into contact with individuals who differ from ourselves in some way.

Suggested meditation affirmations:
See Appendix II: 3, 4(j)

Bach Flower Remedies
See Appendix III: 3(a)(f), 5(a)(b), 16(a)(b)(h), 26(a)(g), 29(a)(i).

Links of Uranus to the Neptune Principle, to Pisces and to the Twelfth House (See Appendix I)

In past lives
On the positive side we have established our own way of attempting to transcend the ego through:
— spiritual activities, e.g. prayer, meditation or monastic life,
— charity or humanitarian work,
— the arts (music, dance, painting, drama, etc.)
whilst accepting and tolerating others' methods of 'stepping out of themselves', even where these differed vastly from ours.

On the negative side we may have expressed intolerance and scorn for those who sought 'escape' from life through the medium of drugs/alcohol/suicide/seclusion/religion. In other cases we ourselves may have indulged in random experimentation with the self-same activities with the motivation of avoiding commitment or simply in order to be 'different' and regardless of the unhappiness our actions may have brought to others. We may also have caused problems for others through sudden and unpredictable acts of deception or treachery.

Between lives our studies were intended to develop our understanding and tolerance of all forms of activity which provide a release from personal suffering, but at the same time to guide us particularly towards those experiences which are enlightening and purposive rather than those which are destructive and erratic.

The karma:
1. To the extent that we have shown tolerance and acceptance of all methods of transcending the ego:
    - we may possess a talent for mediumship and clairvoyance, manifesting in particular as messages received in sudden flashes, often in the unconscious state;
    - we may possess good understanding of the workings of the unconscious and of spiritual concepts, and the ability to explain these to others along scientific lines;
    - other gifts may include artistic inspiration and the ability to conceive of original ideas on helping humanity;
    - we are likely to be accepted and respected for our abilities.
— Where in the past we have shown a sincere desire for mystical

or super-conscious experience, we may now meet with opportunities to further develop our psychic and spiritual awareness, leading to exciting insights.

2. Where in the past we have ridiculed those who indulged in escapist activities, we may now find that we ourselves are laughed at, criticized or rejected in respect of our:
    - drug/alcohol dependency,
    - strong urge to be alone,
    - spiritual leanings or practices,
    - good works and humanitarian interests,
    - artistic bent.
    We may find ourselves in an environment in which these tendencies are not understood or accepted, and in which we feel ourselves to be outsiders.

— Where in the past we have experimented irresponsibly and erratically with activities which take us 'out of ourselves', we may now find ourselves subject to unexpected and sometimes upsetting experiences in respect of:
    - sudden, unwelcome psychic manifestations, such as hallucinations, involuntary mediumship or tricks of the imagination;
    - sudden bouts of religious idealism and rash participation in religious cults and mass movements, which lead to little fulfilment since they are without continuity or purpose;
    - sudden irrational impulses to be free of the real world through forms of escape such as drugs, alcohol, sex, retreat, and in a small minority of cases suicide;
    - involuntary confinement, which may occur suddenly and as a result of accidents caused by rash actions on the part of ourselves or others;
    - totally unexpected deceptions and let-downs by other people.

The challenge:
1. To consider how far we are repeating the negative traits described in association with our past-life pattern.
2. To take personal responsibility for difficulties we may encounter arising from lack of acceptance and ridicule, or from sudden unpredictable impulses and events.
3. To consider whether or not we are working to break down all barriers of intolerance and prejudice in our understanding of the ways in which the ego may be transcended and whether we are conducting our own lives so as to further this understanding.

Suggested meditation affirmations:
See Appendix II: 3, 4(k)

Bach Flower Remedies
See Appendix III: 2(a), 3(a)(g), 5(a)(e), 8(a), 26(a)(h)(c), 27(a), 31(a)(b).

Links of Uranus to the Pluto Principle, to Scorpio and to the Eighth House (See Appendix I)

In past lives we have been strongly aware of our personal power and in particular our sexual and psychic power.

On the positive side we have channelled this power into the direction of our choice whilst simultaneously respecting the ways of others where these differed from ours. We have attempted to develop our understanding in the areas of sexuality, psychology and the occult constructively and in a way that does not harm others.

On the negative side we have harboured a sense of arrogance as to our personal power, scorning those who were less powerful. We may have been prone to prejudice against or ridicule of those who differed from us sexually or psychologically. In other cases we may have indulged in random sexual experimentation or reckless dabbling in the occult, oblivious of any pain this may have brought to others. We may have been prone to unpredictable and reckless use of power or associations with power groups, characterized by a blatant refusal to submit to authority.

Between lives we have had the opportunity to learn that access to universal knowledge regarding the application of power can be gained only when we have broken down all barriers of prejudice. Only then may the secrets of life's deepest mysteries begin to unfold.

The karma:
1. Where in the past we have shown tolerance and acceptance of others at the sexual and psychological levels, we may possess:
   - an aptitude for research, in some cases leading to insights and discoveries (which may come in the form of sudden flashes) in particular in the field of science and medicine;
   - diagnostic skills;

- insight in the areas of sexuality and life after death;
- psychic ability, in particular in the form of sudden hunches;
- the ability to understand the psychological root of particular diseases and the correct treatment required, giving aptitude in the field of healing; there may be particular aptitude for the healing of nervous and mental illness;
- these abilities are likely to be recognized and respected by others working in similar fields and to lead to exciting and unusual opportunities to further expand our understanding.

2. Where in the past we have ridiculed those whose sexual or psychological characteristics differed from ours, we may ourselves undergo ridicule or rejection due to our unconventional sexual identity or on account of psychological problems.

— Where our handling of power has been irresponsible or reckless, we may find ourselves subject to:
- sudden inexplicable emotional and sexual impulses, such as unpredictable outbursts of rage or tears, or uncontrollable sexual attractions to individuals who are unsuitable for us as permanent companions;
- erratic psychological disturbances or sudden and unwelcome psychic phenomena;
- sudden losses of power, and in a small minority of cases sudden death (representing the ultimate loss of control).

The challenge:
1. To consider how far we may be repeating the negative traits described in association with our past-life pattern.
2. To take personal responsibility for difficulties we may encounter arising from lack of acceptance and ridicule, or from sudden unpredictable impulses and events.
3. To consider whether or not we are working to break down all barriers of intolerance and prejudice in our understanding of sexual/psychic/psychological matters, and whether we are conducting our own life in these areas in order to further this understanding.

In practical terms a wide-ranging study of psychology would be our greatest asset. Equally it may be beneficial to research into and participate in all forms of orthodox and alternative healing, the accent being on variety rather than exclusive specialization.

Suggested meditation affirmations:
See Appendix II: 3, 4(l)

Bach Flower Remedies
See Appendix III: 3(a)(g), 5(a)(d), 13(a)(b), 16(a)(k), 29(a)(k), 30(a), 36(a)(e)(f).

13.
THE SCHOOL OF NEPTUNE

The essence of Neptune consists of developing attunement to universal love and universal beauty and thereby building a sense of at-oneness with the entire universe which will ultimately bring us perfect peace and joy.

The general karma of Neptune consists of meeting with the outcome of a past-life pattern which has been composed *on the positive side* of:

— strongly developed ideals and the capacity to keep these alive in spite of disappointments, always believing that things will eventually improve;

— the ability to look for the good in others without dwelling on the bad;

— the willingness to express love towards others without necessarily seeking affection in return;

— a level of compassion which has permitted us to sympathize with others' feelings and thus make allowances for their misdemeanours;

but *on the negative side* has been composed of:

— the betrayal of our ideals manifesting as: disillusionment and despondency; cynicism, whereby we registered only the negative in our environment; withdrawal from the real world via escapism; treachery and deception;

— the inability to look at things from the other person's point of view, leading to a tendency to take things personally and condemnation of others.

In the case of a positive past-life pattern the outcome will be strong attunement to the source of universal love and beauty, manifesting as artistic/musical inspiration and a creative imagination — through having kept beautiful ideals in mind we now serve as channels for the expression of beauty. Past work in developing a sense of at-oneness with others will now bear the fruits of psychic/spiritual gifts, sometimes endowing us with clairvoyant, mediumistic or telepathic ability, sometimes enabling us to undergo euphoric experiences in meditation and yoga. Above all, our blessing will be that of happiness which allows us to experience a close rapport with our family, friends and others, untroubled by self-pity and extending beyond the barriers of space and time.

In the case of a negative past-life pattern, past betrayal of our ideals may result in a tendency to be constantly and unreasonably dissatisfied even though we no longer have real cause for disappointment. A past tendency to focus only on the bad in our environment may manifest as a negative or morbid imagination. Past escapist habit patterns may now result in addiction problems, mental confusion and absent-mindedness, low energy levels or hard-to-diagnose illnesses arising due to toxic conditions of the body. Past inability to sympathize with others and a tendency to take everything personally may mean that we are now prone to compulsive self-pity and in some cases a persecution complex. Past acts of treachery or deception may be met with in the present as a tendency to self-deception or experiencing deception or treachery at the hands of others.

The general challenge of Neptune is:
— To learn to love without asking for anything in return; to overcome personal sensitivity and develop compassion for others; to train our minds to focus on the potential goodness of all living creatures (positive visualization) and thus to overcome the tendency towards cynicism and negativity.
— To guard against the tendency to project our own thoughts, feelings and attitudes onto others, or to over-identify with others' difficulties and suffering whereby we become liable to misplaced compassion, guilt and martyrdom.

Links of Neptune to the Sun Principle, to Leo and to the Fifth House
(See Appendix I)

In past lives our desire has been to give of the very best of ourselves in work of an altruistic or worthwhile nature, and to obtain recognition and fulfilment from our efforts.

On the positive side we have succeeded in keeping our ideals alive in spite of the absence of immediate results, continuing to believe in ourselves when others were unable to and making allowances for those who failed to acknowledge our good intent.

On the negative side we have betrayed our ideals by succumbing to a deep sense of disillusionment, both in ourselves and in the feedback we obtained from others; by giving way to cynicism with regard to our prospects; by withdrawing from the real world via escapist thought patterns or activities; by deceiving others through projecting a false image for purposes of self-gain.

Between lives we have had the opportunity to develop a sense of universal love which would enable us to give of ourselves without needing to receive acknowledgement in return, to overcome the tendency to feel disillusioned with life and seek escapism, and to begin to translate our ideals into reality. Only in this way can we begin to tap inspiration and start to experience the euphoria we crave.

The karma:
1. Where in the past we have kept our ideals alive, we will now possess the potential for inspired self-expression in the arts and music, in the service of the handicapped and underprivileged or in spiritual affairs.
—   Where we have avoided self-pity, have attempted to sympathize with others' feelings and have thereby built up a sense of at-oneness with the world about us, we may find we possess psychic gifts, such as clairvoyance or mediumship, and the ability to experience ecstasy through mystical activities.
—   Our father — or male figures in our life — will represent a source of inspiration, being involved in spiritual affairs, in the arts, or in good works of some type. Our children may also be artistically or spiritually gifted.

2. Where in the past we have betrayed our ideals:
    -   we may undergo an illogical tendency to feel persistently discontented whatever we attempt to do in life and fail to gain satisfaction from our efforts;
    -   we may suffer from feelings of worthlessness and self-pity and be liable to addiction problems;
    -   we may suffer confusion concerning our identity, being unsure about our role in life, and we may be prone to self-deception, imagining ourselves to be of greater or lesser value than we really are;
    -   we may find ourselves in contact with over-idealistic, impractical and confused males who experience disillusionment and who are prone to escapism; in particular our father or

male partner may exhibit these traits, or we may consider our father to be 'weak' and may feel disappointed in him as a parent;
- we may also suffer disappointment through our children.
— Where in past lives we have deceived or betrayed others for our own advantage, we may now ourselves undergo deception or betrayal, especially at the hands of men who project a false image and subsequently turn out to be other than they originally appeared to be.

The challenge:

1. To consider the extent to which we are repeating negative past-life patterns.
2. To take personal responsibility for difficulties we may experience as a result of dissatisfaction; addiction problems; confusion regarding our identity and goals in life; weak males in our life; disappointments with children; deception, especially at the hands of males.
3. To give of ourselves without necessarily seeking recognition in return and to overcome self-pity and escapism resulting from lack of recognition. In practical terms we may be helped towards this goal by meditation; by a moderate degree of service, particularly voluntary work with children; and through some form of artistic activity which will bring us closer to the source of universal love and beauty.
4. To guard against over-identifying with others and their difficulties, and thus reduce our liability to misplaced compassion, guilt and martyrdom.

Suggested meditation affirmations:
See Appendix II: 5, 6(a)

Bach Flower Remedies
See Appendix III: 8(a), 12(a), 22(a)(b)(c), 31(a)(c), 34(a)(e), 35(a).

Links of Neptune to the Moon Principle, to Cancer and to the Fourth House
(See Appendix I)

In past lives we have longed for a world in which human beings express sincere love for one another and are in tune with each others' feelings. Our test has consisted of balancing these ideals against the lack of emotional response we have received from others.

On the positive side we have clung to our vision and have attempted to look for the good rather than the bad in the world about us. We have displayed compassion for others by relating to their difficulties and thus making allowances for their lack of response.

On the negative side we have betrayed our ideals by succumbing to a sense of disillusionment with man's inhumanity to man, to cynicism and to escapism, often to the detriment of our dependants. We have been critical of others for their inability to sympathize with us, failing to appreciate their own problems. We may also have deceived others by masking our true feelings and indulging in pretence, especially in family matters, for our personal gain.

Between lives we have had the opportunity to develop a sense of universal love, in the light of which we may become better able to overcome our personal hurts and disappointments and sympathize more fully with the feelings of others. In this way we begin to develop a true sense of at-oneness with creation as a whole and thus to gain access to divine inspiration.

The karma:
1. Where in the past we have attempted to sympathize with others' feelings:
   - we may now find we enjoy an empathetic rapport with others which extends beyond the barriers of space, time or death, often manifesting through gifts of ESP, mediumship or clairvoyance;
   - our capacity to tap inspiration may be well-developed, leading to gifts in the arts or music;
   - we may look up to our mother as the epitome of gentle womanhood — intuitive, compassionate and selfless, and our childhood home may be a place of beauty and happiness.

2. Where in the past we have betrayed our ideals:
   - we may feel persistently and unreasonably disappointed in the emotional rapport we are able to achieve with others;
   - in particular we may feel we receive insufficient sympathy from others, especially our family, and be subject to self-pity as a result;
   - we may be heavily dependent on cigarettes, drink, pills, etc., in order to help us cope with life;
   - we may be unable to control our tendency to 'dream' or fantasize which impairs our ability to concentrate and to make rational decisions;

- we may suffer from a negative imagination in that we find ourselves involuntarily dwelling on fears and worries which seem as real to us as if they were actually true;
- as a by-product of the process of attunement to Neptune we may tend to project our own feelings and motives onto others, and thus suffer from emotional confusion;
- we are likely to find ourselves involved with females, such as our mother or female partner, who find life hard to cope with and have withdrawn from the real world in some way; we may feel our mother is a disappointment in that she is unable to live up to our expectations (possibly through no fault of her own).

— Where in the past we have deceived or betrayed others for our own advantage, we may now ourselves be deceived or betrayed, especially in relation to family matters or by women who are insincere, play on our feelings, or exploit shared confidences for their own gain.

The challenge:

1. To consider the extent to which we are repeating negative past-life patterns.
2. To take personal responsibility for difficulties we may experience as a result of a persistent sense of emotional disappointment; addiction problems; a negative or morbid imagination; confusion; disappointments with females; deception or betrayal.
3. To guard against projection.
4. To give love and care to others without necessarily seeking an emotional response in return, and to overcome self-pity and escapist tendencies deriving from lack of satisfaction in our emotional or family life. In practical terms we may be helped towards this goal by meditation; by a moderate degree of service, particularly within the family circle or to young or old people; and through some form of artistic activity which will bring us closer to the source of universal love and beauty.
5. To guard against over-identifying with others' sufferings and thus reduce our liability to misplaced compassion, guilt and martyrdom.

Suggested meditation affirmations:
See Appendix II: 5, 6(b)

Bach Flower Remedies
See Appendix III: 4(a)(b), 5(a)(e)(g), 8(a)(e), 22(a)(c), 23(a)(b), 31(a)(d), 35(a).

Links of Neptune to the Mercury Principle, to Gemini and to the Third House
(See Appendix I)

In past lives our ideal has been a world in which communication reflects love and understanding between mankind. Inevitably we have suffered disappointment in the verbal response we gained from other people, which failed to meet the high standards we expected.

On the positive side we have kept our ideals alive by making allowances for others when their speech has been hurtful to us.

On the negative side we have given up trying to make ourselves understood and withdrawn from reality by cutting off from the words we did not wish to hear. Our extreme sensitivity may also have led us to speak untruths, generally in order to protect ourselves. Similarly we may have criticized others behind their backs rather than confront them face-to-face. In other cases we may have betrayed confidences for purposes of self-gain.

Between lives we have had the opportunity to learn to express universal love in all our communications with others and thus to concern ourselves only with the joy and help our words can bring to others rather than the response they are likely to generate. In this way we begin to gain access to divine inspiration.

The karma:
1. Where in the past we have attempted to empathize with others at the mental level and build a sense of at-oneness with the world about us:
   - we will be blessed with an inspired, creative mind which will express itself particularly through the medium of words — fiction, poetry, playwriting, acting;
   - our ESP may be strongly developed, thus permitting communication which extends beyond the three dimensions.

2. Where in the past we have practised mental escapism:
   - we may have difficulty in carrying through logical thought processes and suffer from poor concentration, absent-mindedness and forgetfulness; in rare cases the mind may completely lose its grip on the division between fact and fiction, resulting in mental disorders;
   - we may have problems in expressing ourselves succinctly or we may find ourselves prone to unwitting disclosal of information that we fully intended to keep secret;

— We may tend to project our own thoughts and opinions onto others and thus be liable to misconstrue verbal messages and incur verbal misunderstandings. This does not represent karma as such, but is a by-product of our attunement to Neptune.

— Where in the past we have bent the truth either inadvertently or deliberately:

 - we may now find ourselves on the receiving end of confused or misleading communications from others; in most cases other people will not deliberately set out to deceive us, but will do so simply as a result of their own confused thinking;

 - we may find that words we spoke to others in confidence are repeated elsewhere in a way that is detrimental to us, or we may discover that we are frequently the subject of gossip.

The challenge:
1. To consider the extent to which we are repeating negative past-life patterns.
2. To take personal responsibility for difficulties we may experience as a result of muddled thinking and absent-mindedness; communication problems; verbal deception or betrayal.
3. To guard against projection.
4. To consider whether we are using our faculties of mind and speech without necessarily seeking a favourable response in return, and to overcome mental and verbal escapist tendencies.

In practical terms we may be helped towards our goals by meditation; by service to others, particularly where help is needed with mental or speech disorders; or through some form of artistic activity which will bring us closer to the source of universal love and beauty, especially reading, writing or acting.

Suggested meditation affirmations:
See Appendix II: 5, 6(c)

Bach Flower Remedies
See Appendix III: 4(a)(c), 6(a)(d), 8(a)(f), 26(a), 31(a)(e).

Links of Neptune to the Virgo Principle
and to the Sixth House
(See Appendix I)

In past lives our ideals have centred around the importance of a fulfilling working life accompanied by perfect health. Confronted with the banality of day-to-day existence and the prevalence of physical illness, we have reacted in one of two ways.

On the positive side we have resisted disillusionment and replaced self-pity by genuine compassion and service.

On the negative side we have betrayed our ideals in that we have given way to a sense of hopelessness, apathy and cynicism or have withdrawn from the real world via escapism. In other cases we may have:

— behaved deceptively towards or let down working colleagues;
— deceived others as to the true state of our health for purposes of self gain;
— deceived others as to the nature of medicines we have administered to them.

Between lives we have had the opportunity to learn to express universal love in the areas of work and health care, and thus to gain access to divine inspiration.

The karma:

1. To the extent that we are attuned to universal love and beauty:
   - we will express this in our daily work through an aptitude for the arts or music, or through work in the caring professions or in the health sector;
   - relationships with working colleagues will be marked by empathy and mutual co-operation.

2. Where in the past we have betrayed our ideals:
   - we may be subject to a continuous and unreasonable sense of dissatisfaction with our day-to-day existence and our work;
   - we may feel persistently discontented with our level of fitness and may become easily depressed by minor health problems;
   - we may be dependent upon alcohol or drugs of various types to see us through what we experience as the dreariness of the day;
   - we may experience a lack of ambition or uncertainty as to our goals in life;
   - we may be subject to muddles in our work, due either to our own lack of organization or to inefficiency on the part of others;
   - our imagination may dwell morbidly on matters of health; we may suffer from hypochondria or from psychosomatic illnesses;
   - our illnesses may be hard to diagnose and may arise from toxic conditions of the body.

— Where in the past we have let down or betrayed others to our own advantage:
  - we face the possibility of being let down by colleagues who act behind our back for their own devices;
  - we may be 'let down' by medicines or drugs which react upon us in a manner which is entirely different to that which we expected and in some cases we may be susceptible to drug poisoning or allergies.

The challenge:
1. To consider the extent to which we are repeating negative past-life patterns.
2. To take personal responsibility for difficulties we may experience as a result of dissatisfaction, confusion or disappointment in the areas of work or health.
3. To avoid self-pity in our daily working routine and in our approach to health, and to practise positive visualization of a fit and healthy body.

In practical terms we may be helped towards our goals by meditation; by service work, particularly in the area of health care, care of the disabled, and care of animals; or by activities in the realm of the arts, e.g. music, drama, films, painting etc., which bring us into touch with universal emotion.

Suggested meditation affirmations:
See Appendix II: 5, 6(d)

Bach Flower Remedies
See Appendix III: 8(a)(b), 34(a)(f), 35(a)(b).

Links of Neptune to the Venus Principle, to Libra and to the Seventh House
(See Appendix I)

In past lives we have held lofty ideals regarding human relationships. Our dream has been that of a perfect love which would satisfy all our needs and fill us with ecstatic joy.

On the positive side we have upheld our ideals, despite disappointments, and have attempted to keep in mind only the good times with others. Our compassion has also been strongly developed, allowing us to sympathize with human weaknesses and in particular to make allowances for those who have mistreated us.

On the negative side we have betrayed our ideals by succumbing to a sense of disillusionment and cynicism which prevented us from translating our ideal relationship into reality; by withdrawing from the real world via romantic and sexual escapism; by deceiving or letting down our partner, in some cases through unfaithfulness.

Between lives we have had the opportunity to develop a sense of selfless love which would help us to approach all relationships — and especially our close partnerships — with concern for what we can give rather than what we can receive. By adopting this attitude we attune ourselves to the Source of Love and Beauty from whence we may derive artistic inspiration and a sense of peace and joy.

The karma:
1. To the extent that we have built a sense of at-oneness with others:
    - we will experience truly loving relationships based on mutual concern and devotion;
    - we may possess artistic/musical inspiration which is particularly stimulated by work in partnership.

2. Where in the past we have betrayed our ideals we may be subject to:
    - an inexplicable inability to find satisfaction in our love-life, feelings of discontent, persistent self-pity and a sense of confusion;
    - obsessive fantasy relationships or a tendency towards multiple unstable relationships which we feel unable to control and which bring us little or no fulfilment;
    - the possibility of finding our lives entangled with women, especially our mother or female partner, who themselves display escapist or evasive tendencies.
—   Where in the past we have deceived or let down others in relationships, we may now undergo deception or let-down at the hands of loved ones who may carry on activities (possibly love affairs) behind our back.
—   As a general by-product of attunement to Neptune, we may tend to project our own feelings onto partners and close friends or to over-identify with their sufferings.

The challenge:
1. To consider the extent to which we are repeating negative past-life patterns.
2. To take personal responsibility for difficulties we may experience

as a result of dissatisfaction; fantasy relationships; multiple, unstable relationships; contact with evasive or escapist females; deception by partners or loved ones.

3. To guard against projection.
4. To attempt to avoid self-pity and express universal love and compassion in personal relationships. In practical terms we may be helped towards this goal by meditation; by moderate involvement in voluntary work, especially in the field of counselling; or by involvement in any form of art or music.
5. To guard against over-identifying with others and their sufferings in one-to-one relationships and thus reduce our liability to misplaced compassion, guilt and martyrdom.

Suggested meditation affirmations:
See Appendix II: 5, 6(e)

Bach Flower Remedies
See Appendix III: 4(a)(h), 8(d), 14(a)(b), 22(a)(d), 31(a)(c), 34(a)(g), 35(a)(c).

Links of Neptune to the Venus Principle,
to Taurus and to the Second House
(See Appendix I)

In past lives we have laid great store by the beauty and joy to be experienced through the five senses and through material resources. Inevitably we have faced disillusionment in view of the widespread deprivation and suffering which exists in the world at the material level.

On the positive side we have nevertheless adhered to our ideals, attempting to play our own part in the alleviation of poverty and feeling grateful for our own material resources.

On the negative side we have betrayed our ideals by retreating into a state of despondency and cynicism regarding the distribution of money and resources; by succumbing to self-pity with regard to our own financial plight; by practising deception or betrayal in financial dealings as a means of self-gain.

Between lives we have had the opportunity to learn to express universal love in our dealings with matter and resources and to develop our attunement to universal beauty, thus allowing ourselves access to divine inspiration.

The karma:
1. To the extent that we have kept our ideals alive and have resisted disillusionment:
    - we may be artistically or musically gifted;
    - we may possess a talent for inspired financial investment;
    - we may be green-fingered or possess a special rapport with nature.

2. Where in the past we have betrayed our ideals:
    - we may feel persistently dissatisfied with our material assets in that whatever we acquire eventually proves disappointing;
    - this in turn may lead us into an incessant and fruitless search for sensual satisfaction, increasing despondency and a tendency towards escapism;
    - we may be disorganized and prone to confusion in money matters, resulting in financial scrapes and problems in making ends meet;
    - we may repeatedly meet with females who are themselves financially feckless or muddle-headed.
—   Where in the past we have deceived others for our own gain we may now find ourselves misled or duped over money matters or resources.

The challenge:
1. To consider the extent to which we are repeating negative past-life patterns.
2. To take personal responsibility for difficulties we may experience as a result of dissatisfaction and despondency; financial confusion and monetary dilemmas; deception or treachery in monetary affairs.
3. To attempt to avoid self-pity and express universal love in our approach to material resources.

In practical terms we may be helped towards our goals by meditation; by moderate involvement in voluntary work for charities devoted to the alleviation of poverty; and through music and art which help us tune into universal beauty.

Suggested meditation affirmations:
See Appendix II: 5, 6(f)

Bach Flower Remedies
See Appendix III: 8(a)(c), 22(a)(e), 35(a)(d).

Links of Neptune to the Mars Principle, to Aries, to the First House and to the Ascendant (See Appendix I)

In past lives our ideals have centred upon a world in which all expended energy and all actions result in personal fulfilment and benefit to others.

On the positive side we have overcome disillusionment by seeking to *embody* our ideals and busy ourselves with compassionate activities, thus leaving little time for self-pity.

On the negative side we have betrayed our ideals by succumbing to a sense of despair that our efforts count for so little or by giving up trying and withdrawing from the real world via escapism. In some cases we may have indulged in deception and underhandedness in the belief that we could achieve our goals more readily by subterfuge than by honesty.

Between lives we have had the opportunity to learn to use our physical resources to spread love and beauty in the world rather than merely to gain personal satisfaction. Only in this way can we experience the euphoria which we crave from life and gain access to the source of divine inspiration.

The karma:
1. To the extent that we are attuned to universal love and beauty, have kept our ideals alive and have resisted disillusionment:
    - our personality is likely to reflect a romantic, mystical charisma and we may possess unusual powers of empathy which attract others towards us;
    - we may possess artistic or imaginative flair, which will seek expression especially through active energetic media; thus in addition to ability in art, music, literature or drama, we may possess a particular aptitude for dance which provides an excellent outlet for the Martian energy;
    - our psychic ability may be marked, manifesting as a gift for clairvoyance or mediumship, or as a capacity for heightened spiritual experiences.
    - we may find ourselves in contact with males (e.g. our father or male partner) who are idealistic, gifted in music or the arts, or involved in work of a spiritual or humanitarian nature and who serve as a source of inspiration to us.

2. Where in the past we have betrayed our ideals:
    - we may undergo persistent and unreasonable discontent with

the outcome of our efforts in that however much energy we channel into a project, satisfaction eludes us; we may come to view all forms of self-assertion as pointless and this attitude may be coupled with low energy levels and lack of drive;

- we may derive little satisfaction from sex (a major outlet for our physical drive);
- in the case of Neptune in the First House, we may feel illogically dissatisfied with our physical appearance;
- we may be prone to addiction to drink and/or drugs;
- we may suffer from illnesses which are hard to diagnose, and which result from toxic conditions of the body;
- we may suffer from a sense of confusion regarding our goals in life, which may cause us difficulties in a society in which lack of ambition is interpreted as weakness of character;
- our imagination may be unusually active, often in a way that is difficult for us to handle; for example we may find ourselves engulfed by morbid fears, may suspect others of plotting against us, and in some cases may be prone to obsessive sexual fantasies and desires;
- we may involuntarily pursue objectives in an oblique, ill-defined and disorganized fashion, resulting in total confusion;
- we may find ourselves in contact with males (e.g. our father or male partner) who are themselves prone to escapism and confusion and whom we may find disappointing.
— Where in the past we have deceived or betrayed others for our own gain, we may now find that others act behind our backs to achieve their own ends, thereby deceiving us or betraying us in some way.

The challenge:
1. To consider the extent to which we are repeating negative past-life patterns.
2. To take personal responsibility for difficulties we may experience as a result of lack of satisfaction with our activities or with ourselves; low energy levels; strong escapist urges; lack of ambition or confused goals; an over-active or morbid imagination; a sense of persecution; disappointing or weak males; deception or betrayal by others.
3. To attempt to avoid self-pity and express universal love in the use of our energy drive. In practical terms we may be helped towards this goal by meditation; by moderate involvement in any form of service or charity work; and by music, art, drama and especially dance.

4. To guard against over-identifying with others' suffering and thus reduce our liability to misplaced compassion, guilt and martyrdom.

Suggested meditation affirmations:
See Appendix II: 5, 6(g)

Bach Flower Remedies
See Appendix III: 4(a)(d), 8(a), 22(a)(f), 23(a)(e), 31(a)(d), 33(f)(k)(j), 35(a).

Links of Neptune to the Jupiter Principle, to Sagittarius and to the Ninth House
(See Appendix I)

In past lives we have held high hopes of our religion and our church which we expected to prove totally fulfilling and to satisfy all our needs. When confronted with the inadequacies of our faith and the insincerity and corruption which taints most religious institutions, we have reacted in one of two ways.

On the positive side we have overcome our disillusionment by making allowances for cases of religious hypocrisy and attempting to focus on the good rather than the bad in our belief and in our fellow seekers.

On the negative side we have betrayed our ideals by becoming cynical towards all religions and devotees, and in some cases we have opted out completely from any form of religious involvement. In other cases we may have misused religion to mislead or dupe others, thereby ourselves indulging in hypocrisy.

Between lives we have had the opportunity to learn to see beauty and goodness in all religions, over and above the imperfections to which they may be subject. We will find this considerably easier if our attunement to Uranus is well-developed and we are able to see the essential value of the many different facets of the whole.

The karma:
1. Where in the past we have upheld our religious ideals:
    - we may possess an inspired understanding of universal law and the ability to pass this on to others through religious or philosophical teaching;
    - our capacity for meditation may be highly developed, enabling us to experience spiritual joy;

- we are likely to achieve spiritual fulfilment from the study of religion and philosophy — in many cases through travel.

2. Where in the past we have betrayed our religious ideals:
    - we may undergo difficulties in finding a belief or faith which proves fully satisfactory; we may find ourselves involved in a never-ending search for something to hold on to in life, often comprising much travelling or study of various philosophies and religions, which invariably prove disappointing;
    - we may experience confusion as to what we really believe in, or our sense of morality may be muddled and ill-defined;
    - although the desire to travel may be strong, our journeys may be subject to mix-ups and involve us in strange, confused situations.
— Where in the past we have behaved deceptively or deviously in the area of faith, we may find ourselves taken in by religious cults or organizations which prove to be other than they initially appeared, and which lead to extreme disappointment on our part.

The challenge:
1. To check the extent to which we are re-enacting negative past-life patterns.
2. To take personal responsibility for difficulties we may face arising from religious dissatisfaction or agnosticism; moral and philosophical confusion; disappointments in the area of religion or travel.
3. To attempt to overcome self-pity and disillusionment in our experience of religious and philosophic beliefs.

In practical terms we may be helped by meditation or by voluntary service abroad or in religious institutions.

Suggested meditation affirmations:
See Appendix II: 5, 6(h)

Bach Flower Remedies
See Appendix III: 4(a)(e), 34(a)(i), 35(a).

Links of Neptune to the Saturn Principle,
to Capricorn, to the Tenth House and to the Midheaven
(See Appendix I)

In past lives our ideals have centred around the fulfilment to be gained from achievement and the taking on of responsibilities in life.

On the positive side we have upheld our ideals in spite of disappointments and have carried out our obligations regardless.

On the negative side we have betrayed our ideals by giving way to a sense of despondency and cynicism; by opting out from our responsibilities in public life or in our job of work and in some cases indulging in escapist activities; by practising deception in our career or dealings with the public for purposes of self-gain.

Between lives we have had the opportunity to learn to fulfil our obligations to society without seeking status in return. In this way we begin to gain access to divine inspiration and the possibility of experiencing true satisfaction in our work.

The karma:
1. To the extent that we have kept our ideals alive and have resisted disillusionment, we may possess artistic, psychic, or caring skills which we are able to put to use in the form of a career. Thus we may find ourselves gifted in the fields of music, art, literature, drama, dance — or any other field calling for an active imagination — or we may be drawn to work in the Church, as a medium or clairvoyant, or in the caring professions.

2. Where in the past we have betrayed our ideals:
    -   we may feel persistently and unreasonably disappointed in whatever career we adopt; in fact the higher we climb in standing the less satisfied we are likely to feel; in other cases status, achievement or material assets seem to hold little attraction for us;
    -   we may suffer from a sense of confusion as to our goals in life, which may cause us difficulties in a society in which lack of ambition is seen as weakness of character and lack of status is regarded as failure; we may find it hard to stick with any job that we undertake in that we become easily discouraged and lack organization and a sense of career structure;
    -   we may be addicted to alcohol, drugs or fantasy, in some cases resulting in public disgrace where these interfere with or impair our public duties.
    —   Where in the past we have deceived others for our own gain, we may find ourselves on the receiving end of deceptive or treacherous behaviour by our colleagues, whose motive is to further their own ends by fair means or foul.

The challenge:
1. To check the extent to which we are re-enacting negative past-life patterns.
2. To take personal responsibility for difficulties we may experience resulting from disillusionment; self-pity; escapism; confused ambitions; treachery/deception in our career.
3. To attempt to avoid self-pity and express universal love in our approach to our career or our public duties.

In practical terms we may be assisted by meditation; by a career or hobby involving service to the underprivileged, to the handicapped or in any capacity where our compassion may grow; or by a career or hobby involving the arts, such as music, painting, dance, drama, writing, etc.

Suggested meditation affirmations:
See Appendix II: 5, 6(i)

Bach Flower Remedies
See Appendix III: 8(a)(f)(b), 22(a)(g), 34(a)(d), 35(a).

Links of Neptune to the Uranus Principle, to Aquarius and to the Eleventh House (See Appendix I)

In past lives our ideal has been that of a true brotherhood of mankind based on mutual respect, freedom and equality. When confronted with social realities, *on the positive side* we have been able to keep our ideal alive by playing our part to bring the perfect world a little nearer into being. *On the negative side* we have betrayed our ideal by giving way to a sense of hopelessness and to cynical disbelief that an ideal society may ever exist. In other cases we may have misled or deceived other members of the group or society to which we belonged, since we feared the results that straightforward dealings might produce for us.

Between lives we have had the opportunity to learn to overcome disillusionment and uphold our ideals in our group or community. In this way we begin to gain access to divine inspiration which can help us to put into effect the social changes we seek.

The karma:
1. To the extent that we are attuned to universal love and beauty:

- we will enjoy happy friendships and group associations based on empathy;
- we will be drawn towards groups based on:
  - altruistic goals (such as work for the underprivileged),
  - spiritual goals,
  - artistic activities (music, painting, dance, drama, writing, etc.)

2. Where in the past we have betrayed our ideals:
   - we may now undergo persistent disappointment with the social conditions which prevail in our community, our country or in the world at large;
   - we may experience disappointment with our friends and acquaintances in that they fail to live up to the high expectations we have of them;
   - this despondency with friends or with the world at large may lead us into escapist activities;
   - we may be subject to confusion about our social obligations — to society as a whole or to friends and acquaintances; we may approach group activities in a well-meaning but totally disorganized way, resulting in muddles for ourselves and others.
— Where in the past we have deceived or betrayed others, members of our group or community or personal acquaintances may deceive us, cheat us or betray us in some way.
— Additionally, we may be liable to over-concern with suffering produced by social inequalities, leading to a compulsive urge to serve; this represents a general problem of attunement to Neptune.

The challenge:
1. To check to what extent we are re-enacting negative past-life patterns.
2. To take personal responsibility for difficulties we may experience arising from disillusionment and despondency; confusion; deception.
3. To attempt to avoid self-pity and express universal love in our relations with other members of our group or community. Practical steps we can take in this respect consist in:
   - participating in groups and organizations which correspond to our own particular ideals and which aim to bring about fairer and more humanitarian social conditions;
   - making an effort to become a better member of our own

community and striving to treat others in accordance with our own ideals;

- involvement in group activities of drama, music, art, literature, etc. or charity work which help us to express universal love and beauty at the group level.

4. To guard against over-involvement with suffering produced by social inequalities and thus reduce our liability to martyrdom.

Suggested meditation affirmations:
See Appendix II: 5, 6(j)

Bach Flower Remedies
See Appendix III: 4(a)(f), 8(a)(g), 22(a)(f), 35(a).

Links of Neptune to Pisces and to the Twelfth House
(See Appendix I)

In past lives we have been idealists of the highest order, believing in the need for a world filled with love, peace and beauty. *On the positive side* we have developed the ability to reconcile such ideals with the realities of human life without submitting to despair and disillusionment. Thus we have made a contribution to the establishment of a more perfect world by showing compassion for others, giving selflessly of ourselves whilst seeking nothing in return and being prepared to look for the good in others without dwelling on the bad. *On the negative side* we have betrayed our ideals by giving way to a sense of hopelessness in the face of man's inhumanity to man; by withdrawing from the real world via escapism; or by focusing only on the negative in our environment to the disregard of that which was noble and good. In other cases we may have exploited confidences gained from those who placed trust in us, by indulging in treachery, betrayal or deception.

Between lives we have had the opportunity to develop a selfless love for others. The greater our capacity to experience emotional at-oneness with the universe, the greater our ability to tap the source of divine inspiration.

The karma:
1. To the extent that we are already attuned to universal beauty, have kept our ideals alive and have resisted disillusionment, we are likely to possess a creative imagination capable of transmitting inspiration in many forms, such as music, art, literature or drama.

— To the extent that we are attuned to universal love:
  - our capacity to sympathize with the feelings of all other living creatures may endow us with an aptitude for caring work since others tend to place their trust in us;
  - our ability to experience at-oneness at a universal level may enable us to break through the three dimensions in the form of clairvoyance, mediumship or telepathy, or through spiritual experiences.

2. Where in the past we have been unable to uphold our ideals:
  - we may feel constantly disappointed with the quality of our emotional life, in particular with our ability to experience emotional closeness with others or our capacity to derive satisfaction from religious/spiritual activities;
  - we may be prone to compulsive self-pity, addiction to drugs, alcohol or sex, or compulsive fantasizing.

— Where we have sown the pattern of habitual negative thinking as opposed to positive thinking, we may now possess a morbidly over-active imagination or suffer from a sense of persecution which prevents us from experiencing joy in life.

— The karmic outcome of past deception or betrayal of others may be that:
  - we find ourselves on the receiving end of other people's treachery;
  - we tend towards self-delusion.

— As a general by-product of the process of attunement to Neptune we may tend to project our own feelings and motives onto others and thus suffer emotional confusion.

The challenge:
1. To check whether we are repeating attitudes and behaviour described in association with the negative past-life pattern.
2. To take personal responsibility for difficulties we may encounter arising from emotional dissatisfaction, escapist urges or compulsive fantasy; an over-active imagination or sense of persecution; deception.
3. To guard against projection.
4. To attempt to make a useful contribution to the expression of universal love and beauty in the world by means of:
  - positive visualization
  - involvement in art or music
  - a moderate degree of involvement in voluntary or paid service work

    – prayer, yoga or meditation.
5. To guard against over-identification with others' sufferings and thus reduce our liability to misplaced compassion, guilt and martyrdom.

Suggested meditation affirmations:
See Appendix II: 5, 6(k)

Bach Flower Remedies
See Appendix III: 4(a)(g), 5(a)(e)(g), 8(a)(e), 12(a), 14(a), 22(a)(f), 23(a)(b), 31(a)(d), 34(a)(e), 35(a).

Links of Neptune to the Pluto Principle, to Scorpio and to the Eighth House
(See Appendix I)

In past lives our ideals have centred around the use and misuse of power: it has been our belief that the human will should be used for healing and transformatory purposes rather than to promote personal power. When confronted with man's exploitation of power for his own gain:

On the positive side we have succeeded in maintaining our ideals in spite of our disillusionment. Thus we have been prepared to make allowances for man's greed and wilfulness and to keep in mind his capacity for regeneration. At the same time we have been prepared to relinquish personal power where this was of benefit to others.

On the negative side we have experienced overwhelming disappointment that man so often uses his will for selfish or destructive purposes. This is likely to have been accompanied by a lack of sympathy for the human weaknesses which lead to the misuse of power and a sense of cynicism about the possibility of world change. At a more personal level we are likely to have been engulfed by self-pity and despondency when abused by others' misuse of power, especially at the sexual level. In other cases we may have exploited intimate confidences or indulged in treachery or deception, particularly in sexual matters or shared finances, in order to increase our personal power. In a small number of cases we may have attempted to misuse occult power for our own purposes.

Between lives we have had the opportunity to learn to overcome personal disappointment by acquiring greater compassion for those human traits which result from over-development of self-will. We thus begin to gain access to the source of divine inspiration and increase our capacity for the inspired use of power.

The karma:

1. To the extent that we have maintained our ideals and ability for positive thinking and are attuned to universal love, we may possess:
   - an aptitude for diagnostic work, where our ability to identify with the fears, insecurities and attachments which lie at the roots of much disease helps others to gain self-knowledge and thus to begin to heal themselves;
   - healing potential, based on a non-judgemental, sympathetic approach with special aptitude for emotional problems and for using the technique of positive visualization successfully;
   - the gift of mediumship — itself an important form of healing since it helps us to overcome fear of the unknown and to adjust more easily to bereavement by providing proof of the afterlife;
   - the capacity for deep regenerative personal relationships which are beneficial both to ourselves and the other person and which have the possibility of enduring beyond physical death.

2. To the degree that we have succumbed to cynicism and disillusionment we may undergo:
   - a tendency to irrational disappointment and dissatisfaction in emotional/sexual relationships, which in some cases may lead to compulsive escapism, in particular sexual escapism;
   - the tendency to imagine that others are plotting to overpower our will, which may lead to a persecution complex.
— Where we have misused our power over others for self-gain we may now experience:
   - deception or betrayal by others, particularly in sexual affairs, joint finances or big business;
   - self-delusion regarding the strength of our will and the level of our psychic power, and in some cases the tendency to mistake hallucinations, tricks of the imagination or negative psychic phenomena for genuine spiritual visions.
— Even with the best of intent there is always the danger of projecting our own unacknowledged emotional and sexual behaviour patterns onto others or over-identifying with others' insecurities and traumas.

The challenge:

1. To check to what extent we are re-enacting negative attitudes and behaviour described in association with our past-life pattern.
2. To take personal responsibility for difficulties we may experience arising from disillusionment; escapism; an over-active ima-

gination; self-delusion; deception.
3.   To guard against projection.
4.   To avoid self-pity and express universal love in our use of sexual, financial and psychic power. Meditation is a useful practical aid, as is moderate involvement in the fields of spiritual healing, psychotherapy, counselling, or work in mental institutions, hospitals or hospices.
5.   To guard against over-identifying with others' sufferings and thus reduce our liability to misplaced compassion, guilt and martyrdom.

Suggested meditation affirmations:
See Appendix II: 5, 6(l)

Bach Flower Remedies
See Appendix III: 2(a), 5(a)(e)(g), 8(a), 9(a), 12(a), 22(a), 24(a), 31(a)(b)(d), 33(f)(k)(j), 34(a)(h), 35(a).

14.
THE SCHOOL OF PLUTO

The essence of Pluto consists of developing attunement to universal will, which allows us access to universal force in order to effect diagnosis and healing of dis-ease in ourselves and our environment.

The general karma of Pluto consists of meeting with the outcome of a past-life pattern which has been composed *on the positive side* of:

— a very strong will and the urge to bring about positive change in the world about us, but the ability to accept the universal plan and work in accordance with divine direction rather than personal desires;
— the ability to accept endings in our lives or in the lives of those close to us as part of the overall scheme of things rather than struggle against change;
— the willingness to look to ourselves and instigate personal change before condemning others or seeking to change others;

but *on the negative side* has been composed of:

— the tendency to use our strongly developed will-power to attempt to change individuals and situations to our own advantage without thought to what is beneficial to the *whole*;
— inability to accept change in our lives or in the lives of those close to us where this is contrary to our wishes;
— inability to see ourselves as we really are or to acknowledge when and where change is needed in ourselves.

In the case of a positive past-life pattern, the outcome will be an aptitude for diagnosis and the ability to restore well-being — the mark of the true healer. Thus we are likely to be adept in pin-pointing the source of sickness in that we are able to see clearly the underlying negative patterns which lie at the root of physical and mental dis-ease. We have the ability to recognize and throw off such 'negative' patterns relatively easily before they can wreak havoc with our mental and physical health, and to make a fresh start when this is necessary. This 'throwing off' ability also allows us to discard the negative energy we pick up from others — of particular advantage if we are working in the field of healing. Above all, we possess the potential to trigger change in our environment — not through the use of personal pressure but at a psychic level. That is to say, we ourselves do not bring about change but act as transmitters of divine energy which helps to bring about change in the manner most beneficial to the whole.

In the case of a negative past-life pattern, past insistence on having our own way will have given rise to patterns of rigidity and attachment, a fear of change, a deep sense of insecurity and defensive behaviour patterns. Inability to let go will mean that we experience difficulties in recognizing and discharging 'negative' feelings as and when they arise, leading to a build-up of frustrated emotions. Frequently we will meet with individuals who embody the self-same inflexibility we once meted out to others and which is still inherent in us, albeit unrecognized. In some cases we may find ourselves called upon to relinquish that to which we are (usually subconsciously) most attached.

The general challenge of Pluto is:
— To overcome the need to have our own way and the accompanying manipulative behaviour traits which we have built up over many incarnations and which are now firmly entrenched in our psyche.
— To overcome defensive behaviour patterns which cause us to hold back all emotions and drives which we believe others might use against us or might lead to unwelcome change in our lives — and thus to open ourselves more fully to others.
— To guard against projecting — and condemning in others — attitudes, emotions and behaviour patterns which we fail to acknowledge or fear to express in ourselves.
— To confront, discharge and transmute 'negative' feelings resulting from losses, blows to our will or threats to our security.

Links of Pluto to the Sun Principle,
to Leo and to the Fifth House
(See Appendix I)

In past lives we have channelled our will into developing our individual form of self-expression. As a result, our speciality — as represented by the sign and house placing of the Sun — will have become strongly defined and powerful, and we are likely to have achieved recognition in our field.

On the positive side we have been prepared to use our talents for universal good and have accepted changes which altered the course of our life as part of the cosmic plan. We may also have achieved some level of self-perception, enabling us to realize when our need for recognition grew out of balance.

On the negative side we have used our talents — and the recognition we obtained therefrom — to gain and maintain personal power over others. We are likely to have strongly resisted any threat to our self-esteem by intimidating or bullying those around us and in this way self-pride may have come before the well-being of those in our care. In the event of a blow to our pride, we may have been incapable of giving in gracefully, becoming bitter and seeking revenge on those we considered to be responsible for our fall. We may have been blind to the degree of our pride and its detrimental effect on our lives, believing our difficulties to be caused by others rather than by ourselves.

Between lives we have had the opportunity to learn to play our part in accordance with universal direction — to learn that there is no need for us to struggle in order to maintain a certain 'image' or to obtain recognition, since we will automatically gain the chance to express our talents to the world when we are attuned to universal will.

The karma:
1. To the extent that we possess good self-perception and a capacity for diagnosis we will now be endowed with the ability to see when a specific avenue of self-expression is outworn and when we need to take a new direction in life.
— To the extent that we are able to put the past behind us by discarding unproductive patterns of behaviour, we will find it relatively easy to recognize and discharge feelings of anger and grief caused by blows to our self-esteem, thus allowing us to adapt more comfortably to changes in our life.
— To the extent that we are attuned to universal will and are willing to serve as channels of divine energy:
    - our powers of charisma will bring us recognition in the area of our self-expression;
    - we may possess healing power inasmuch as we are able to trigger positive change in our environment through the medium of our self-expression, i.e. through the skill represented by the placing of our Sun or Pluto.

— Our father is likely to be strong and dependable and may himself possess some kind of healing power; at any rate he may encourage us towards positive self-change by example rather than by pressure.

2. To the extent that we are not yet in tune with universal will and fear losing control over our destiny:
   - we may undergo a strong but often unacknowledged sense of insecurity due to a compulsive need for recognition and a deep-seated fear that we may fail to gain such recognition or be made to feel worthless;
   - we may hold back from expressing our creative talents for fear of blows to our pride, resulting in inner tension and a sense of isolation;
   - we may fear losing our father or our male partner (since he symbolizes our self-expressive Sun urge).

— Where in the past we have used our will to overpower others for the purpose of personal gain, we may now meet with individuals, especially men, who place their personal self-esteem before our happiness. Frequently we may find ourselves at the mercy of an inflexible father whose will we feel unable to challenge. We may also be attracted to a male partner who reflects the same traits and who can continue to frustrate our self-expression.

— Where we have become inflexible due to our need to maintain our self-esteem (but are often unable to acknowledge our inflexibility):
   - we may undergo blows to our pride in that we are obliged to terminate the form of self-expression which means most to us or suffer humiliation in this area;
   - since procreation is an important form of self-expression, we may experience a rift or parting from our children;
   - the loss of our father or of male figures in our life may be experienced as exceptionally painful, since such male figures often symbolize our own Sun drive;
   - we may find it difficult to recognize and discharge anger or grief produced by blows to our self-esteem or relating to men, in particular our father, leading to a build-up of frustration and bitterness, and in some cases to illness.

The challenge:
1. To consider the extent to which we are repeating negative past-life patterns.

2. To take personal responsibility for difficulties we may experience as a result of our insecurity and defensiveness; blows to our self-esteem; loss of male figures; domination by father or male partner.

3. To consider whether we are guided by the desire to follow universal will — as opposed to the desire for personal power — in the use of our special talents and abilities and the recognition we gain from these.

4. To overcome the fear of losing control, to learn to trust and to open ourselves more fully to others in the expression of our creative talents.

5. To guard against projecting — and condemning in others — modes of self-expression which we fail to acknowledge or fear to express in ourselves.

6. To confront, discharge and transmute 'negative' feelings resulting from blows to our self-esteem. Self-awareness studies and therapies, and participation in healing groups will help us towards this goal.

Suggested meditation affirmations:
See Appendix II: 7, 8(a), 9(a).

Bach Flower Remedies
See Appendix III: 2(a), 7(a)(b), 9(a)(b), 13(a)(b), 28(a), 30(a)(c), 36(a)(k).

Links of Pluto to the Moon Principle,
to Cancer and to the Fourth House
(See Appendix I)

In past lives we have developed strong and powerful emotions which have led to one of two responses:

On the positive side we have been willing to work for universal good and to use our inner strength to help and heal others; where we have experienced emotional crises we have accepted these as necessary for our growth. We may also have achieved some capacity for introspection, enabling us to pin-point the root of our emotional suffering as lying within ourselves rather than blaming others for our distress.

On the negative side we have channelled our will into achieving and maintaining our own emotional security to the disregard of others. In order to avoid relinquishing the people or things to which we have been attached, we may have manipulated others, particularly members of our family, into giving in to our wishes, generally by the use of emotional blackmail. When our will has been blocked by others or by fate, we may have harboured feelings of resentment, jealousy and hatred for long periods of time, whilst remaining blind to the emotional inflexibility which lay at the heart of our difficulties.

Between lives we have had the opportunity to attune ourselves to universal will so as to help us to accept the emotional upheavals which occur in our lives. We thereby acquire a true sense of security and develop our ability to serve as channels of divine healing power.

The karma:
1. To the extent that we possess good perception and a capacity for diagnosis, we will be endowed with depth of insight into our own and others' hidden 'negative' emotions which underlie so many of our mental and physical problems.
—   To the extent that we are able to put the past behind us by discarding outworn patterns of behaviour, we will find it comparatively easy to discharge such 'negative' emotions, which permits us to avoid a build-up of tension and sickness, and to adjust more readily to new circumstances.
—   To the extent that we are attuned to universal will and are capable of serving as channels of psychic energy:
    - we will possess unusual emotional strength by which we charismatically draw others towards us;
    - we may possess the power to heal by transferring energy at the psychic level, in particular to help others overcome their own emotional trauma.
—   We will possess a strong bond with our mother, who represents a source of emotional strength and healing power.

2. To the extent that we are not yet in tune with universal will and fear losing control over our own destiny we may be subject to general emotional insecurity manifesting as:
    - a nagging fear that people or things upon which we depend for our happiness and stability may suddenly be snatched from us;
    - in particular we may fear losing our home or the loss of our mother or female partner;
    - the tendency to mistrust others and hold back our emotions due to a sense of vulnerability and thus to feel emotionally isolated.
—   Where in the past we have used our will to overpower others for personal gain, we may now find our lives entangled with

individuals, especially women, who are themselves subtly manipulative. Typically our mother may exert a very strong hold over us, in that she seeks to control us, or simply in that we are greatly attached to her and find it difficult to break away from her influence. Equally we are often attracted to female partners who fit this pattern.

— To the extent that we have become inflexible due to our need to maintain our emotional security (and are often unable to recognize our inflexibility):
  - we may be predisposed towards painful emotional trauma involving or threatening loss of our emotional security;
  - in particular we may experience family upheaval during childhood;
  - our attachment to our mother — whatever the state of our relationship with her — may cause us considerable grief when we are parted from her as a result of separation or death;
  - we may find it hard to recognize and discharge feelings of grief and anger resulting from blows to our emotional security or relating to females, in particular our mother, which can lead to a build-up of frustration and in some cases to illness.

The challenge:

1. To consider the extent to which we are repeating negative past-life patterns.
2. To take personal responsibility for difficulties we may experience as a result of emotional insecurity; repression of emotions; emotional trauma; loss of home or of female figures; domination by mother or female partner.
3. To consider whether we are guided by the desire to serve in accordance with universal will — as opposed to the desire to retain personal power — in our emotional response to life.
4. To overcome the fear of losing control, to learn to trust and to open ourselves more fully to others at the emotional level.
5. To guard against projecting — and condemning in others — emotions which we fail to acknowledge or fear to express in ourselves.
6. To confront, discharge and transmute 'negative' feelings resulting from blows to our emotional security. Self-awareness studies and therapies and participation in healing groups will help us towards this goal.

Suggested meditation affirmations:
See Appendix II: 7, 8(b), 9(b).

Bach Flower Remedies
See Appendix III: 2(a), 7(a)(c), 9(a)(b), 13(a)(b), 14(a)(c), 23(a)(e), 28(a), 30(a), 31(f).

Links of Pluto to the Mercury Principle, to Gemini and to the Third House
(See Appendix I)

In past lives we have concentrated much energy into developing our intellectual and verbal skills.

On the positive side we have been willing to use our mental and verbal faculties for universal good and to change our mental attitudes as and when appropriate.

On the negative side it is likely that we have used our mental and verbal skills to enhance our personal power and have placed excessive emphasis on proving ourselves stronger than others in reasoning and debate. Thus we may have tended to pit our will against others in relentless and ruthless argument and to expose the intellectual weaknesses of others in order to prove our own superiority. It is likely that we have stubbornly refused to change our mental attitudes, even where such stubbornness was detrimental to our well-being and have tended to blame outside sources rather than ourselves for our troubles.

Between lives we have had the opportunity to learn to use our faculties of mind and speech in accordance with universal will rather than to enhance our personal power. In so doing we develop our attunement to universal force and our ability to serve as healers through the medium of the written and spoken word.

The karma:
1. To the extent that we possess good perception and a capacity for diagnosis we will now possess excellent powers of insight which allow us to cut straight through to the core of any problem.
— To the extent that we are readily able to cut our links with the past, we will be capable of discarding unproductive lines of thought as soon as they have exhausted themselves. A penetrating, ruthless mind of this kind enables us to constantly tackle fresh challenges rather than remain stuck in a rut; in particular it equips us for scientific, psychological or para-scientific research.
— To the extent that we are able to serve as channels of universal energy:
    - we may be charismatic writers and/or orators;

- we may find that we possess the capacity to heal through the medium of the written or spoken word, and it is especially in the area of mental 'dis-ease' that we may be most helpful to others.

2. To the extent that we are not yet in tune with universal will and fear losing control:
   - we may be subject to mental tension due to a compulsive urge to come out on top in any verbal or mental exchange;
   - we may hold back from expressing our true opinions due to a sense of vulnerability and thus suffer from mental tension and feelings of intellectual isolation;
   - we may find ourselves 'taken over' by worries or problems which we are unable to drop from our minds.

— Where in the past we have used our will to overpower others for personal aggrandizement, we may be attracted towards arguments with individuals who display the self-same tendencies as ourselves — and thus become drawn into bitter and protracted battles of minds.

— To the extent that our thinking patterns are excessively rigid and inflexible:
   - we may find it hard to recognize and discharge feelings of anger and grief resulting from the thwarting of our will at the intellectual level, leading to a build-up of bitterness and in some cases to illness;
   - we may be prone to periods of depression which impel us to acknowledge where our thinking has been wrong and to give way in terms of our attitudes and ideas; the longer we fight this depression without realizing that its origin lies in our own inflexibility, the greater our mental suffering.

The challenge:
1. To consider the extent to which we are repeating negative past-life patterns.
2. To take personal responsibility for difficulties we may experience as a result of intellectual conflicts, mental tension or depression.
3. To consider whether we are guided by the desire to serve in accordance with universal will — as opposed to the desire for personal power — in the way we use our mind and the way we speak.
4. To overcome our fear of losing control and to lower our intellectual and verbal defences.
5. To guard against projecting — and condemning in others —

mental attitudes which we fail to acknowledge or fear to express in ourselves.

6. To confront, discharge and transmute 'negative' feelings resulting from the thwarting of our will at the intellectual level. Self-awareness studies and therapies and participation in healing groups can help us towards this goal.

Suggested meditation affirmations:
See Appendix II: 7, 8(c), 9(c)

Bach Flower Remedies
See Appendix III: 2(a), 9(a)(b), 13(f)(h), 28(a), 29(a)(l), 30(a), 33(l).

Links of Pluto to the Virgo Principle and to the Sixth House
(See Appendix I)

In past lives we have poured great energy into our day-to-day work with the aim of achieving the perfect result.

On the positive side our motivation has been to use our skills for the universal good, and we have responded readily to the various directions in which our services have been channelled, understanding the purpose behind change.

On the negative side work has become an obsession which has taken precedence over all other factors. Not only have we been loth to tolerate any changes in our working life, but we may also have ridden roughshod over those who threatened our security. In other cases we may have been impossibly demanding taskmasters who imposed our own standards of perfection upon others.

We may also have channelled our will into the pursuit of physical health. Here, *on the positive side* we have accepted the ups and downs in our health as opportunities for spiritual growth and have been able to recognize and correct any tendency towards obsession. *On the negative side* we may have developed a rigid daily regime which we placed before all other considerations, possibly to the point of fanaticism. Here our unrelenting adherence to specific diets or health cures — or even the practice of celibacy — may have been damaging not only to ourselves but also to those close to us. Some of us may have worked as healers of various kinds who may certainly have brought help to others but may also have used our position to gain personal power.

Between lives we have had the opportunity to learn to overcome the obsessive need to prove our mastery of matter through compulsive dedication either to work or to health. In developing attunement to universal will we begin to gain access to divine healing power which assures the true well-being of ourselves and our environment at the physical and material levels.

The karma:

1. To the extent that we are attuned to universal will, possess good perception and are able to throw off that which is no longer useful to us:
    - we have the aptitude to work in the field of healing inasmuch as:
      - we are capable of accurate diagnosis;
      - we sense instinctively when a change in the method of treatment is required;
      - we have the ability to discard negative energy 'picked up' from the patient;
      - we may serve as channels of psychic healing power;
      - these talents allow us in particular to diagnose, discharge and heal our own sickness;
    - in our work we will manifest charismatic leadership qualities of supreme efficiency, strength and stamina inasmuch as:
      - we have the ability to immediately pin-point the source of problems;
      - we can effortlessly discard unproductive approaches and change course as and when needed;
      - our ability to discharge psychological tension permits us to remain calm and in control at all times;
      - we possess the power to transform, to regenerate and to achieve the 'impossible' in all matters relating to our work.

2. To the extent that we are not yet in tune with universal will and fear losing control over our own destiny:
    - we may be prone to work mania which drains us of mental and physical energy and can prove detrimental to our personal relationships;
    - we may be subject to compulsive but unrecognized worry regarding our work and our health, which is likely to exacerbate any sickness we may be suffering from;
    - we may be prone to compulsive secrecy and find it hard to trust others in matters of work and health.
    - Where in the past we have used our will to overpower others for the purpose of self-gain:

- we may meet with domineering individuals in our work situation who attempt to impose their own will upon us;
- we may find ourselves entangled with individuals who attempt to wield power over us through the condition of our health.
— To the extent that we have become inflexible due to our need to maintain our existing regime (and are often unable to recognize our inflexibility):
  - we may suffer from one or more interruptions in our working life and/or our health which we find hard to accept and against which we may put up a terrific fight;
  - we may find it difficult to recognize and discharge feelings of anger and grief resulting from loss of health or work or the thwarting of our will in these areas, which can lead to a build-up of bitterness and further increase our liability to ill-health.

The challenge:

1. To consider the extent to which we are repeating negative past-life patterns.
2. To take personal responsibility for difficulties we may experience as a result of work mania; insecurity regarding our job or our health; power conflicts in our work; physical breakdowns; loss of employment.
3. To consider whether we are guided by the desire to serve in accordance with universal will — as opposed to the desire for personal power — in our attitude to daily life, to our work and to our health.
4. To overcome the fear of losing control and to learn to trust others in matters of work and health.
5. To guard against projecting — and condemning in others — attitudes to work and health which we fail to acknowledge or fear to express in ourselves.
6. To confront, discharge and transmute 'negative' feelings resulting from the thwarting of our will in matters of work and health. Self-awareness studies and therapies and participation in healing groups can help us towards this goal.

Suggested meditation affirmations:
See Appendix II: 7, 8(d), 9(d).

Bach Flower Remedies
See Appendix III: 2(a), 3(h), 9(a)(b), 18(a)(m), 25(a)(n), 31(g), 36(a)(g).

Links of Pluto to the Venus Principle,
to Libra and to the Seventh House
(See Appendix I)

In past lives we have channelled great energy into our relationships.

On the positive side we have served as strong and dependable friends and/or lovers who have nevertheless accepted the need for endings as a result of partings or death. We may also have achieved good self-perception in our attitude towards relationships, being willing to look first to ourselves in the case of disagreements or tensions.

On the negative side we have become dependent upon the permanency of our relationships and have developed a compulsive need to wield power in contacts with others. Thus we may have behaved possessively and manipulatively towards close friends or partners, showing little concern for their own happiness and fulfilment. Where loved ones have nevertheless broken away from us, we are likely to have plotted and/or perpetrated acts of revenge.

Between lives we have had the opportunity to learn that personal will must be subjugated to universal will if hate and suffering are to be eliminated from relationships and that we express true love for others not by our attachment to them but by allowing them total freedom.

The karma:
1. To the extent that we are in tune with universal will we will possess unusual charisma by which others are attracted towards us. We will also possess a natural talent for healing relationship difficulties which manifests as follows:
   - through the capacity for diagnosis we have the ability to put our finger on the source of any difficulty and to see clearly where our own inflexibility is at fault;
   - through our ability to eliminate outworn behaviour patterns we will find it relatively easy to recognize and discharge our own feelings of anger and grief in relationships and to throw off negative energy picked up from others;
   - through our ability to place our own will on one side, we may serve as channels of psychic power, whereby positive transformation of relationship problems can be achieved.

2. To the extent that we are not yet in tune with universal will and fear losing control over our destiny we may suffer from a deep-seated sense of insecurity in close relationships manifesting as:

- defensiveness and extreme hesitancy to commit ourselves in a permanent relationship, resulting in the tendency to be a 'loner';
  - where we are committed to a permanent relationship, inability to surrender ourselves fully to our partner due to feelings of vulnerability and a resultant sense of emotional isolation;
  - lack of trust and a tendency towards groundless suspicion and compulsive jealousy, which can lead to the alienation of our partner and the destruction of the relationship.
- Where in the past we have used our will to overpower others for the purpose of personal gain:
  - we may attract towards us partners or close friends who themselves attempt to wield power over us and who may threaten us (physically or emotionally) if we fail to conduct the relationship on their terms;
  - our mother may display such tendencies in her relationship either with us or with our father.
- To the extent that we have become inflexible due to our need to maintain the permanency of relationships:
  - we may be obliged to let go of partners or close friends as a result of unavoidable partings, divorce or in some cases death;
  - we may find it difficult to recognize and discharge feelings of anger and grief resulting from the loss of partners or friends or the thwarting of our will in relationships, leading to a build-up of bitterness and in some cases to illness.

The challenge:
1. To consider the extent to which we are repeating negative past-life patterns.
2. To take personal responsibility for difficulties we may experience as a result of insecurity or jealousy; loneliness; relationship conflicts; loss of friends or partners.
3. To consider whether we are guided by the desire to follow universal will — as opposed to the desire for personal power — in our approach to personal relationships.
4. To overcome the fear of losing control, to learn to trust and to surrender ourselves more fully to others in personal relationships.
5. To guard against projecting — and condemning in others — modes of relating which we fail to acknowledge or fear to express in ourselves.
6. To confront, discharge and transmute 'negative' feelings resulting from the loss of partners or friends or the thwarting of our will in relationships. Self-awareness studies and therapies and

participation in healing groups will help us towards this goal.

Suggested meditation affirmations:
See Appendix II: 7, 8(e), 9(e).

Bach Flower Remedies
See Appendix III: 2(a), 7(a), 9(a)(c)(d), 13(a)(c), 28(a), 30(a), 36(a)(h).

Links of Pluto to the Venus Principle, to Taurus and to the Second House (See Appendix I)

In past lives we have channelled great will-power into building and maintaining our material security and comfort.

On the positive side we have considered our financial assets as God-given, to be used not simply to further our own interests but for the benefit of all. Thus we have been prepared to accept changes in our material circumstances, seeing these as chances to develop in spiritual strength and to explore new directions.

On the negative side we have developed an obsession with the achievement of material and financial power. We are likely to have envied others their wealth and luxuries and used any means at our disposal to increase our own assets. Our wealth may have served as a weapon which we used to gain our own way and to manipulate others to our ends. We have jealously guarded our possessions and may have sought revenge against those who took from us what we felt to be rightfully ours. Any changes in our material circumstances are likely to have been met with bitterness, yet we have been unable to realize that the source of our difficulties lay within ourselves.

Between lives we have had the opportunity to learn to assign the management of our resources to the dictates of universal will. We thereby ensure not only our own well-being but that of the planet as a whole, and simultaneously gain access to divine transformatory power.

The karma:
1. To the extent that we possess good perception and a capacity for diagnosis, we will be capable of shrewd insights in the area of finance and resources, which allow us to spot when a change of course would be to our advantage.
— To the extent that we are able to discard outworn attitudes and behaviour patterns, we will find it relatively easy to recognize

and discharge feelings of anger and grief at times of change in our material and financial affairs, and thus to adapt quickly to new circumstances.

— To the extent that we are capable of serving as channels of psychic energy:
  - we have the power to actualize our material goals and achieve a position of financial strength;
  - we will be capable of acting as catalysts where problems of resources are concerned, so as to help induce positive change in financial affairs.

2. To the degree that we are not yet in tune with universal will and fear losing control over our own destiny:
  - we may suffer from tension in financial affairs due to a subconscious fear of poverty or relinquishing possessions we hold dear;
  - we may be prone to compulsive secrecy and distrust of others in our financial affairs leading to a sense of isolation.

— Where in the past we have used our material resources to impose our will on others, we may meet with individuals who exploit their material strength or play upon our appetites to attempt to gain power over us. In particular our partner may use their greater financial strength as a bargaining weapon against us.

— To the extent that we have become inflexible due to our need to maintain our material security (and are generally unable to recognize our inflexibility):
  - we may undergo changes in our financial status which oblige us to part with possessions to which we are greatly attached;
  - we may suffer 'strokes of fate' which destroy our possessions or deprive us of sources of pleasure;
  - we may find it difficult to recognize and discharge feelings of anger and grief resulting from financial losses or the thwarting of our will in financial matters, which can lead to a build-up of bitterness and in some cases illness.

The challenge:
1. To consider the extent to which we are repeating negative past-life patterns.
2. To take personal responsibility for difficulties we may experience as a result of material/financial insecurity, losses or conflicts.
3. To consider whether we are guided by the desire to serve in accordance with universal will — as opposed to the desire for personal power — in our approach to material resources.

4. To overcome the fear of losing control, to learn to trust and to behave more openly in our financial affairs.
5. To guard against projecting — and condemning in others — attitudes towards resources which we fail to acknowledge or fear to express in ourselves.
6. To confront, discharge and transmute 'negative' feelings resulting from financial losses or the thwarting of our will in financial matters. Self-awareness studies and therapies and participation in healing groups can help us towards this goal.

Suggested meditation affirmations:
See Appendix II: 7, 8(f), 9(f).

Bach Flower Remedies
See Appendix III: 2(a), 9(a)(b), 13(a), 18(a)(n), 24(a)(c), 30(a), 36(a)(l).

Links of Pluto to the Mars Principle, to Aries, to the First House and to the Ascendant (See Appendix I)

In past lives we have developed our will, courage and fortitude to the point that we have been able fearlessly to tackle any goal with maximum energy levels. In so doing, *on the positive side* we have been guided by universal forces so that where our will has been blocked we have accepted this as having an essential purpose and consequently have given in gracefully. *On the negative side* we have become obsessed with the cause of winning, which may have led us ruthlessly to destroy that which came between us and victory and to use the force of our personality or physical strength to prove ourselves more powerful than others. In the event of defeat we are likely to have harboured bitterness and hatred or to have perpetrated acts of revenge, tending always to blame external circumstances for our difficulties rather than our own stubbornness.

Between lives we have had the opportunity to learn to abandon selfish goals in the cause of universal good. Thus we were to learn the importance of handing over conflicts to universal will rather than attempting to settle them as we see fit, since it is only by this means that the matter may be resolved to the good of all concerned.

The karma:

1. To the extent that we are attuned to universal will:
    - we are likely to possess a magnetic personality, sexual charisma and exceptional physical strength;
    - we will be capable of perceiving when drastic changes of course are needed in our lives and of making such changes without the need to look back;
    - we have the ability to recognize and discharge feelings of anger and grief experienced at times of personal defeat;
    - we thus maintain high energy levels which permit us to achieve all our goals;
    - we may expand this ability in the form of spiritual healing whereby we are able to draw out and discard the negative forces in others; of all the Pluto contacts it is the Mars–Pluto link which holds the greatest potential for healing ability since it implies the possibility of attuning our very life force with universal healing power.

2. To the extent that we are not yet in tune with universal will and fear losing control over our own destiny:
    - we may undergo considerable emotional tension whenever we find ourselves involved in a win or lose situation, due to a subconscious fear that our will may be overpowered;
    - we may hold back the expression of our deepest passions and drives due to feelings of vulnerability and thus suffer a sense of personal isolation;
    - the resultant stress can lead to physical and mental troubles and to periodic, uncontrollable outbursts.

—   Where in the past we have used our will to overpower others for personal gain, we may now meet with individuals, especially men, such as our father or male partner, who are excessively dominating, attempt to overpower our will, or emphasize their superior physical strength by physical or sexual violence towards us.

—   To the extent that we have become inflexible due to our need to gain our own way:
    - at some point in our life we may be subjected to defeat whereby our will is overpowered by other individuals or simply by circumstances;
    - we may suffer physical injury, inflicted deliberately or accidentally;
    - we may find it difficult to recognize and discharge feelings of anger and grief resulting from the thwarting of our will,

which can lead to a build-up of bitterness and in some cases to illness.

The challenge:
1. To consider the extent to which we are repeating negative past-life patterns.
2. To take personal responsibility for difficulties we may experience as a result of insecurity and tension; domination by male figures; defeat or loss.
3. To consider whether we are guided by the desire to serve in accordance with universal will — as opposed to the desire for personal power — in the use of our energy drive and our life force.
4. To overcome the fear of losing control, to learn to trust and to open ourselves more fully to others in the expression of our deepest passions and drives.
5. To guard against projecting — and condemning in others — drives or behaviour patterns which we fail to acknowledge or fear to express in ourselves.
6. To confront, discharge and transmute 'negative' feelings resulting from the thwarting of our will. Self-awareness studies and therapies and participation in healing groups can help us towards this goal.

Suggested meditation affirmations:
See Appendix II: 7, 8(g), 9(g).

Bach Flower Remedies
See Appendix III: 2(a), 5(a)(d), 9(a)(b), 13(a)(b)(d), 28(a), 30(a)(d).

Links of Pluto to the Jupiter Principle, to Sagittarius and to the Ninth House
(See Appendix I)

In past lives we have channelled our will into the development of powerful faith, generally in a particular religion or philosophy of life.

On the positive side we have been able to achieve flexibility within the framework of this intensity, which has allowed us to concede when our beliefs or moral values have been mistaken.

On the negative side we have been inflexible in respect of our beliefs and our code of morality. In addition we may have attacked others on the basis of their beliefs or moral values and attempted to convert them to our way of thinking, possibly through the use of force. In other cases we have been compulsive gamblers.

Between lives we have had the opportunity to learn to conform to universal will in the spreading of ideas or beliefs. Thus we were to understand that where our philosophy might be of help to others, we will be automatically provided with the chance to give guidance, but when 'spreading the word' becomes a fight — in any shape or form — clearly we are simply seeking personal power.

The karma:

1. To the extent that we possess good perception, we will be able to accept the need for alteration in our lives in the form of a change in our philosophical beliefs or moral values — or in the form of a change in culture — and to put such change into effect.

— To the extent that we are able to discard outworn behaviour patterns:
  - we will find it relatively easy to cast off moral attitudes deriving from our past, in particular from our childhood, and the fear and anxiety associated therewith;
  - we will find it relatively easy to cast off resentment or grief resulting from enforced changes of culture.

— To the extent that we are attuned to universal will and willing to serve as channels of divine energy:
  - the strength of our religious/philosophical beliefs will magnetically attract others towards us, and in some cases we may rise to the position of charismatic religious leaders;
  - the strength of our faith literally has the power to move mountains, i.e. it is essentially through our faith that we can trigger positive change in our environment;
  - we may bring about healing in others by helping them to free themselves of rigid and outworn moral attitudes and philosophical beliefs.

2. To the extent that we are not yet in tune with universal will and fear losing control over our own destiny:
  - we may be defensive about our beliefs and moral values and fearful of discussing these openly due to a sense of vulnerability — and may thus be liable to a sense of spiritual isolation;
  - we may feel insecure when confronted with a philosophy of life or code of morality which threatens to undermine our own convictions.

— Where in the past we have forcibly imposed our own philosophy, religion or code of morality upon others, we are likely to meet with individuals who themselves have inflexible beliefs or codes of morality and who attempt to impose these upon us. In some

cases we may grow up within the framework of a 'black and white' morality which operates by inspiring fear and from which we may find it difficult subsequently to break away.
— To the extent that we have become inflexible due to our need to maintain our existing philosophy and code of morality (and are often unable to recognize our inflexibility):
  – we may meet with situations where we are obliged to abandon our existing religious, moral or cultural ideas in that we find ourselves in a different country or in the company of people whose outlook differs greatly from our own;
  – we may find it difficult to recognize and discharge feelings of fear, anger and grief deriving from a rigid religious or moral upbringing, which may lead to a build-up of tension and in some cases to illness.

The challenge:
1. To consider the extent to which we are repeating negative past-life patterns.
2. To take personal responsibility for difficulties we may experience as a result of fear and insecurity; changes in culture or beliefs.
3. To consider whether we are guided by the desire to serve in accordance with universal will — as opposed to the desire for personal power — in the expression of our philosophical, religious or moral beliefs.
4. To overcome the fear of losing control, to learn to trust and to open ourselves more fully to others in the expression of our religious and moral beliefs whilst resisting the urge to 'convert' them.
5. To guard against projecting — and condemning in others — religious and moral attitudes which we fail to acknowledge or fear to express in ourselves.
6. To confront, discharge and transmute feelings of fear, grief and anger deriving from a rigid religious or moral upbringing. Self-awareness studies and therapies, and participation in healing groups will help us towards this goal.

Suggested meditation affirmations:
See Appendix II: 7, 8(h), 9(h).

Bach Flower Remedies
See Appendix III: 2(a), 29(m), 30(a)(e).

Links of Pluto to the Saturn Principle, to Capricorn, to the Tenth House and to the Midheaven
(See Appendix I)

In past lives we have laid great weight on the fulfilment of duty and conscientiousness, and have probably held a position of power in society.

On the positive side we have been prepared to follow divine guidance by accepting changes in our career or public life, even where this involved a loss of status.

On the negative side we have become obsessed with maintaining our status and/or we have used our social standing to bolster our personal power. We are likely to have gone to any lengths to gain and hold on to social status, and in the event of loss of status it is possible that we have experienced lingering resentment and a desire for revenge on those we considered responsible for our downfall.

Between lives we have had the opportunity to learn to follow our worldly responsibilities in accordance with universal direction. Whatever 'power' we gain in life is given to us for a specific purpose and will be withdrawn when that purpose has been fulfilled. The lesson to be learned here is that of cosmic responsibility over and above personal status.

The karma:
1. To the extent that we possess good perception, we will be able to sense instinctively when the time is ripe for a change in our career in that a situation has yielded to us everything it can offer; this permits us to avoid remaining in a rut and to achieve continuous advancement.
— To the extent that we are able to discard outworn attitudes and behaviour patterns, we will find it relatively easy to recognize and discharge feelings of anger and grief resulting from career endings or loss of status and will thus be able to adapt ourselves to new circumstances without the constant need to look back.
— To the extent that we are attuned to universal will and are capable of serving as channels of divine energy:
   - we may be drawn to a career involving research, science, medicine or healing, but whatever our choice of career, our powers of charisma may permit us to gain renown and to rise to a position of authority;
   - we have the power to transform, to regenerate and to achieve the 'impossible' in all matters relating to our career.

2. To the extent that we are not yet attuned to universal will and fear losing control over our own destiny, we may suffer from feelings of insecurity concerning our 'standing', manifesting as:
   - a fear that we will fail to succeed in our career;
   - a fear of change in our career or a fear that we may be demoted or lose face in some way;
   - defensiveness and compulsive secrecy in matters relating to our career, leading to a sense of personal isolation.
— Where in the past we have used our will to overpower others in order to achieve status, we may meet with ruthless authority figures who use their position and influence to overpower our will.
— One of our parents — often our mother — may possess a strongly developed will and exert a dominating influence upon us.
— To the extent that we have become inflexible due to our need to maintain our rank — and are often unable to recognize our inflexibility:
   - at some point in our life we are likely to lose our status or that which represents our status, such as position, material assets etc.;
   - we may find it difficult to recognize and discharge feelings of anger and grief resulting from the thwarting of our will in our career or blows to our public standing, which may lead to a build-up of bitterness and in some cases to illness.

The challenge:
1. To consider the extent to which we are repeating negative past-life patterns.
2. To take personal responsibility for difficulties we may experience as a result of insecurity and a sense of isolation; career conflicts; loss of status.
3. To consider whether we are guided by the desire to follow universal will — as opposed to the desire for personal power — in our approach to our career and the fulfilment of our public duties.
4. To overcome the fear of losing control and to develop greater trust in matters relating to our career or status.
5. To guard against projecting — and condemning in others — attitudes towards responsibility and duty which we fail to acknowledge or fear to express in ourselves.
6. To confront, discharge and transmute 'negative' feelings resulting from the thwarting of our will in terms of our career or status. Self-awareness studies and therapies, and participation in healing groups can help us towards this goal.

Suggested meditation affirmations:
See Appendix II: 7, 8(i), 9(i).

Bach Flower Remedies
See Appendix III: 2(a), 9(a)(c)(e), 13(a), 30(a)(g), 31(h)(i), 36(a)(i).

Links of Pluto to the Uranus Principle, to Aquarius and to the Eleventh House
(See Appendix I)

In past lives we have channelled great energy into establishing freedom at the individual level or group level and into bringing about social change.

On the positive side we have resisted the urge to impose our own will upon our peers and have been willing to follow universal direction, accepting changes and setbacks when these were inevitable.

On the negative side we are likely to have expressed a compulsive need to influence our community or society according to our own idea of truth and in some cases may have involved ourselves in violent political or revolutionary struggles. We may have become obsessed with maintaining our position of leadership amongst our associates and may have reacted ruthlessly and viciously to attempts to snatch control from us.

Between lives we have had the opportunity to learn to act as instruments of universal will in bringing about social change rather than to attempt to enforce our own social ideas on others. In so doing we gain access to universal healing power and the chance to help bring about truly positive transformation in society.

The karma:
1. To the extent that we possess good perception, we will instinctively understand when it is necessary to leave behind existing friends in order to make new ones, or to make changes in our social activities to avoid stagnation.
— To the extent that we are able to discard outworn attitudes and behaviour patterns, we will find it relatively easy to adapt to:
   - loss of friends or partings from friends;
   - drastic changes in social conditions or the balance of political power;
   and to recognize and discharge feelings of grief or resentment arising therefrom.
— To the extent that we are capable of serving as channels of divine energy:

- we are likely to exert a charismatic influence upon our friends and contemporaries, and consequently may rise to a position of power within our group, community or society, and in some cases within politics;
- we possess the power to heal through the medium of social change, i.e. we have the potential to trigger positive transformation in our social environment by virtue of our political or community activities;
- we may be particularly drawn to groups based on self-transformation or spiritual healing.

2. To the extent that we are not yet in tune with universal will and fear losing control over our own destiny:
   - we may experience a deep-seated fear of losing our rights within the society in which we live;
   - we may experience a sense of insecurity within our peer group due to fear of losing face or losing our supposed control over others; this may manifest as defensiveness, lack of trust and the tendency to hold back from others at the group level and thus to feel socially isolated.

— Where in the past we have become inflexible in terms of our social/political beliefs or have attempted to impose these beliefs on others:
   - as part of a generation born with a Uranus–Pluto aspect, we may find ourselves ruled by a political system which threatens our personal freedom or our group rights;
   - however, those of us who have Pluto in the Eleventh House or a planet in Aquarius in aspect with Pluto are more likely to experience the karma of being obliged to relinquish the power we hold within our group or community;
   - in a more general sense we are likely to find ourselves constantly parted from friends or acquaintances;
   - we may find it difficult to recognize and discharge feelings of anger and grief resulting from the loss of friends or from the thwarting of our will in group or community affairs; this may lead to a build-up of bitterness and in some cases to illness.

The challenge:
1. To consider the extent to which we are repeating negative past-life patterns.
2. To take personal responsibility for difficulties we may experience as a result of insecurity or upheavals in the society, community or circle to which we belong.

3. To consider whether we are guided by the desire to follow universal will — as opposed to the desire for personal power — in our work within society or our local community.
4. To overcome the fear of losing control, to learn to trust and to open ourselves more fully to others at the group level.
5. To guard against projecting — and condemning in others — social attitudes which we fail to acknowledge or fear to express in ourselves.
6. To confront, discharge and transmute 'negative' feelings resulting from the thwarting of our will in group or community matters. Self-awareness studies and therapies and participation in healing groups can help us towards this goal.

Suggested meditation affirmations:
See Appendix II: 7, 8(j), 9(j).

Bach Flower Remedies
See Appendix III: 7(a)(d), 13(a)(e), 29(n), 30(a)(f), 36(a)(j).

Links of Pluto to the Neptune Principle,
to Pisces and to the Twelfth House
(See Appendix I)

In past lives we have developed very strong ideals both for ourselves and for the human race as a whole. *On the positive side* we have avoided fanaticism or fixed ideas as to the manner and speed at which improvement should take place. *On the negative side* our idealism has become obsessive in that we have felt compelled to express our ideals on our own terms and without consideration for others. Where others' concept of perfection differed from ours we may have attempted to convert them to our way of thinking, in some cases by the use of force. In other cases we may have expressed our fanatical ideals by a compulsion to serve others in the way we believed they needed to be served, regardless of their true well-being. In yet other cases our obsessive idealism may have expressed itself by a compulsive urge to escape from reality through drugs, alcohol, retreat, fantasy or suicide. There is also the possibility that we may have sought to augment our personal power by acts of deception, betrayal or treachery.

Between lives we have had the opportunity to learn to play our part in bringing greater beauty into the world not by fanatical idealism but by developing our attunement to universal will. Since each individual's own ideals can only ever mirror a part of the perfection for which mankind is destined, it is only by means of universal direction that such perfection can come into being.

The karma:
1. To the extent that we possess good perception we will be quick to spot when excessive idealism threatens our balanced functioning, and will be able to promptly discard outworn spiritual aspirations.
— We will find it relatively easy to recognize and discharge feelings of disappointment, grief and anger resulting from situations in which our ideals have been thwarted or we have suffered let-down, deception or betrayal.
— To the extent that we are attuned to universal will:
  - we will exude a mystical charisma by which others are magnetically attracted towards us;
  - we have the potential to undergo powerful meditative/spiritual experiences (a) by which we ourselves are transformed and (b) by which we are able to transform our environment;
  - we may also express powers of healing within the framework of
    - clairvoyance/mediumship,
    - work in institutions,
    - work with the handicapped or underprivileged,
    - work with those suffering from compulsive escapist problems,
    - inspired artistic/musical creations.

2. To the extent that we are not yet in tune with universal will and are afraid of losing control we may fear:
   - having to reassess our ideals;
   - losing the escapist props which allow us to avoid confronting our ideals;
   - openly expressing our disappointments, grief and guilt — and thus our spiritual ideals — due to feelings of vulnerability;
   - spiritual practices which involve 'losing control';
   - the resultant defensiveness and self-repression can lead to emotional tension and a sense of spiritual isolation.
— Where in the past we have habitually let others down, we may now suffer profound disillusionment as a result of acts of deception, betrayal or treachery on the part of others.
— To the extent that our ideals have become inflexible and we have in the past attempted to impose our ideals upon others:
  - we may meet with situations in which we are obliged to re-

examine our existing ideals or in which others attempt to impose their ideals upon us. As far as aspects between Neptune and Pluto are concerned, certain generations of us will live through world conditions which serve to challenge what we believe to be right. For example, those born in the 1890s whose charts featured the Neptune–Pluto conjunction lived through a period when figureheads such as Mao Tsetung and Adolf Hitler symbolized widely diverse ideals which they attempted to impose on the world at large. At a more individual level, those of us whose charts contain Pluto in the Twelfth House or a planet in Pisces in aspect with Pluto may experience traumatic events in our personal lives which trigger profound emotional suffering, thereby challenging us to confront our ideals, and in some cases such events may involve spells of isolation from the mainstream of society;

– we may find it difficult to recognize and discharge feelings of guilt, grief or anger resulting from blows to or betrayal of our ideals, leading to a build-up of tension and in some cases to physical or mental illness; the tendency to suppress our feelings in this way can exacerbate existing escapist tendencies (drugs, alcohol, etc.).

The challenge:
1. To consider the extent to which we are repeating negative past-life patterns.
2. To take personal responsibility for difficulties we may experience as a result of:
   – compulsive self-pity or escapism;
   – a sense of spiritual isolation;
   – acts of betrayal and treachery on the part of others;
   – illnesses or crises which temporarily cut us off from the mainstream of life, seeing these as opportunities to come to terms with our inner selves.
3. To lower our spiritual defences and to open ourselves more fully to others in the expression of our ideals, disappointments and sorrows.
4. To guard against projecting — and condemning in others — idealism or escapism which we fail to acknowledge or fear to express in ourselves.
5. To be prepared to confront, discharge and transmute 'negative' feelings stemming from past disappointments.
6. To consider whether we are guided by the desire to serve in accordance with universal will — as opposed to personal will

— in our attempts to bring our ideals to fulfilment.

Suggested meditation affirmations:
See Appendix II: 7, 8(k), 9(k).

Bach Flower Remedies
See Appendix III: 1(a), 2(a), 4(a)(d), 6(a)(e), 8(a), 9(a)(b).

Links of Pluto to Scorpio
and to the Eighth House
(See Appendix I)

In past lives our will has been highly developed, and has expressed itself in the form of a strong desire for power, in particular at the sexual and psychic levels.

On the positive side we have been willing to relinquish personal power in order to bring help to others. Thus we are likely to have dedicated ourselves to the diagnosis and cure of dis-ease in all its forms so as to bring about positive change in the world. Most important, we have acknowledged the need to start with ourselves in the form of self-analysis, self-knowledge and self-change. *On the negative side* we have used our strong will to play power games so as to manipulate individuals and situations to our own advantage, especially in the area of sexual/emotional relationships or power politics, and in some cases through involvement with the occult. In order to maintain our power we are likely to have behaved rigidly and inflexibly, sometimes resorting to blackmail or violence. Where our will has been overpowered by other individuals or by 'fate' — especially where our deepest feelings were involved — we may have been incapable of accepting our destiny and may have succumbed to bitterness, hatred and a desire for revenge.

Between lives we have had the opportunity to learn to subjugate personal desires by accepting and adjusting to losses or changes which affect our security. For it is only by overcoming self-will that we begin to tap universal force and play our part in bringing into being a New Age world in which disease and suffering are eliminated and each individual uses his/her psychic energy to ensure the well-being of the whole.

The karma:
1. To the extent that we are already attuned to universal will:
   - we will possess an aptitude for diagnosis which gives us insight into the conditions which underlie all states of being. In

general terms this provides us with ability in research work, in the fields of medicine and science, or in investigatory work of all kinds. More specifically, it allows us to perceive the psychological patterns which lie at the source of all forms of disease, equipping us for work in the field of psychiatry or spiritual healing;

- we will find it relatively easy to acknowledge and discharge 'negative' feelings resulting from blows to our will or threats to our security before they can harm us mentally or physically;
- we will find it relatively easy to make fresh starts in life where necessary, especially following rifts in emotional or sexual relationships, bereavement, or any situation in which power or security is snatched from us;
- we will possess a powerful charisma by which others are attracted towards us and which may enable us to achieve a position of power;
- we may possess the ability to trigger positive change in our environment by acting as vehicles of psychic power; in particular we may inspire positive change in our environment through the medium of:
  - close emotional/sexual relationships,
  - scientific achievement,
  - healing of all kinds.

2. To the extent that we are not yet in tune with universal will and fear losing control over our own destiny:
   - we may be subject to insecurity and fear change, especially in sexual/emotional matters and in all situations where we may be called upon to let go; in particular we may fear death, the ultimate 'letting go';
   - we are liable to compulsive secrecy and distrust of others; in particular we may hold back from expressing our deepest feelings due to a sense of vulnerability and may find it difficult to surrender ourselves fully in sexual relationships; the result is likely to be a strong sense of emotional isolation.
— Where in the past we have attempted to manipulate others to our own advantage, we may now undergo ill-treatment at the hands of individuals who treat us with inflexibility or attempt to manipulate us or overpower our will, especially sexually or in the areas of joint finances or power politics.
— To the extent that we have become inflexible due to our need to exert control over others in all power issues and in particular in sexual matters:

- we may undergo involuntary changes in our life in which power is snatched from us seemingly without cause, especially in sexual/financial matters and we may experience difficulty in adapting ourselves to such change;
- we may find it difficult to recognize and discharge feelings of jealousy, anger and grief resulting from situations in which our will has been thwarted, especially in sexual matters, leading to a build-up of bitterness and in some cases to illness.

The challenge:
1. To consider the extent to which we are repeating negative past-life patterns.
2. To take spiritual responsibility for difficulties we may experience as a result of insecurity and a sense of emotional isolation; loss of power; cruel, manipulative treatment by others.
3. To consider whether in our life in general, and in particular in sexual/emotional relationships and our use of psychic energy, we are guided by the desire to serve others or by the desire for personal power.
4. To overcome the fear of losing control, to learn to trust, and to surrender ourselves more fully to others in the expression of our deepest feelings, in particular in sexual relationships.
5. To guard against projecting — and condemning in others — sexual and emotional attitudes, or attitudes towards power, which we fail to acknowledge or fear to express in ourselves.
6. To confront, discharge and transmute 'negative' feelings resulting from blows to our will or loss of power, in particular in sexual relationships. Self-awareness techniques and therapies and participation in healing groups can help us towards our goal.

Suggested meditation affirmations:
See Appendix II: 7, 8(l), 9(l).

Bach Flower Remedies
See Appendix III: 2(a), 7(a), 9(a), 13(a)(b), 14(a)(c), 28(a), 30(a)(d), 31(h)(j), 36(a)(k).

15.
THE BIRTH CHART OF JOHN LENNON — A KARMIC ANALYSIS

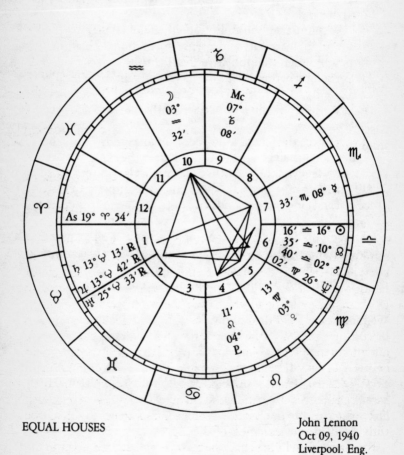

EQUAL HOUSES

John Lennon
Oct 09, 1940
Liverpool. Eng.
05:30:00p.m. GMT
Zone: +00:00
002W55'00"
53N25'00"

The following list shows the sign and house locations of each of the planets, and their aspects to non-personal planets:

The Sun falls in Libra and in the Sixth House and is quintile Pluto.
The Moon falls in Aquarius and in the Tenth House and is trine Uranus, trine Neptune and opposition Pluto.
Mercury falls in Scorpio and in the Seventh House and is opposition Jupiter, opposition Saturn and square Pluto.
Venus falls in Virgo and in the Fifth House, and is square Uranus and semi-sextile Pluto.
Mars falls in Libra and in the Sixth House, and is trine Uranus, in conjunction with Neptune and sextile Pluto.
Jupiter falls in Taurus and in the First House, and is in conjunction with Saturn.
Saturn falls in Taurus and in the First House.
Uranus falls in Taurus and in the Second House and is trine Neptune.
Neptune falls in Virgo and in the Sixth House and is septile Pluto.
Pluto falls in Leo and in the Fourth House.

(Aspects to the Ascendant and to the Midheaven have been omitted from this list since the birth time is not precise.)

In beginning the interpretation of a birth chart the astrologer is faced with a large number of factors which need to be classified in order of importance before any real meaning can be derived from the analysis.

The most essential point to remember is that if it is of any significance, a theme will be repeated several times; thus a highly relevant lesson may be expressed on the one hand by a certain planet falling in a specific sign or in a specific house, and on the other hand by a certain aspect (angle) which two planets form with one another. We may save a good deal of time-wasting and needless confusion by cutting through to the crux of the chart's message if we begin our interpretation by looking for the most frequently repeated links between a personal planetary principle (planet, sign or house) and a non-personal planetary principle. These links will reflect the basic karmic challenges of the individual in question. Where several such links exist, they can be classified in order of importance in accordance with the degree of exactness of the aspect.

For example, in John's chart the following challenges occur in the chart in more than one mode of expression:

1. Mercury square Pluto — orb 4° 22'
    Mercury in Scorpio

2. Venus square Uranus — orb 7° 40'
    Uranus in the Second House
3. Moon trine Uranus — orb 7° 59'
    Moon in Aquarius
4. Moon opposition Pluto — orb 0° 39'
    Pluto in the Fourth House

Although clearly all of major significance in terms of John's life pattern, these factors may be classified into the following order of importance by virtue of the aspect orbs:

1. Moon opposition Pluto;   A link between the Pluto
    Pluto in the Fourth House   principle and the Moon
                                   principle.

2. Mercury square Pluto;   A link between the Pluto
    Mercury in Scorpio   principle and the Mercury
                                   principle.

3. Venus square Uranus;   A link between the Uranus
    Uranus in the Second   principle and the Venus
    House   principle, Taurus and the
                                   Second House

4. Moon trine Uranus;   A link between the Uranus
    Moon in Aquarius   principle and the Moon
                                   principle.

The Moon–Pluto Link
This is borne out by an extremely tight opposition aspect between the Moon and Pluto and the position of Pluto in the Fourth House, the house ruled by the Moon. This factor points to the existence of strong and powerful emotions which in many cases can manifest as inner strength which helps the individual in question to accept and ride over emotional crises in his own life and to give out emotional support to others. At the highest level it enables us to let go of emotional wounds and tensions so that we can constantly move on to new experiences. Frequently there is a marked desire to dig down to the roots of our insecurities in order to effect self-healing.

Less attractively, this combination points to an inborn obsession with preserving our emotional security to the point of bullying or blackmailing those who threaten us. This tendency towards subtle manipulation — and since the Moon is involved it does very much play out at a subtle level — derives from unconscious fear of change, especially of the type that will threaten our emotional well-being. This self-same resistance to change is also likely to present us with difficulties in discharging and letting go of emotions, which can be especially harmful to ourselves and to others where 'negative' feelings, such as hatred and jealousy, are concerned.

Inevitably we will undergo some difficult karma inasmuch as any upheaval or threatened upheaval — and especially that involving our home or females in our life — will affect us at a deep emotional level and may take a good deal of time to come to terms with. Even where there is no definite prospect of change, a sense of emotional insecurity can nag away at the subconscious level, marring our well-being.

Since the Moon represents a female energy, there is the likelihood of attracting towards oneself powerful females who sometimes possess great charisma, inner strength and even healing power, but who in other cases can be of the manipulating, possessive type. One's mother or mother figure is particularly likely to exhibit certain of these characteristics, as is one's female partner or close female friends. Attachment to one's mother will be very strong, even where the relationship in itself is a difficult one, and parting from her, whether on the physical plane or through death, is likely to be experienced as exceptionally traumatic.

If we now look at John's life and character, we will see much that reflects the basic pattern of the Moon–Pluto link. He indeed possessed very powerful emotions, many of which derived from early childhood trauma, when he witnessed the tragic break-up of his parents' marriage at a time when transiting Saturn was conjunct the Fourth House Pluto, thus triggering the natal Moon–Pluto opposition. Following this event he was assigned to the care of his maternal aunt. Although the initial parting from his mother took place in 1946 just before John's sixth birthday, he maintained contact with her until her violent death in a road accident in 1958, with transiting Neptune square to the natal Moon–Pluto opposition, which in effect marked the ultimate letting go. It is clear that this early suffering remained indelibly imprinted in John's psyche, as is apparent from the obsessive concern with childhood emotional pain expressed in his song lyrics.

Neither can there be any doubt that John possessed great charisma which enabled him to gain a subtle control over others' emotions, and this he used to the full to maintain his domination of those close to him. Notwithstanding John's own emotional strength, the Moon–Pluto link was also reflected by the dominating women in his life — his mother, for example, who always held a deep fascination for John, the strong-willed Aunt Mimi, and his second partner Yoko Ono, herself a woman of powerful magnetism.

The challenge of any Moon–Pluto link is primarily to come to terms with events or behaviour which shatter our emotional security. Inevitably this involves coping with feelings such as grief, resentment and hatred, and difficulties in letting go of the past. However, as we learn to recognize these 'negative' emotions and discard them, we develop our ability to tap and transmit psychic energy at the emotional level.

John was certainly one who lived out the Moon–Pluto challenge at a profound level. Trapped by his emotions for a large part of his life, he nevertheless made great efforts to root out the source of his psychological suffering and to rid himself thereof. At the age of 29, with transiting Saturn square to his Moon–Pluto opposition, he underwent regression therapy, thereby re-enacting his childhood rejection in order to recognize and release the pain. This period was marked by an outpouring of tremendous hatred and bitterness, but eventually gave way to a phase of new-found creativity from mid-1971 onwards. Indeed, many would argue that John's best work, and most definitely his solo work, appeared only after psychological therapy. It seems likely that the elimination of much emotional dross provided the impetus for his most inspired compositions, such as the incomparable 'Imagine'.

The Mercury–Pluto Link

The characteristics of Mercury–Pluto consist, at the highest level, of penetrating mental faculties capable of deep insight. There is the ability to rapidly discard unproductive lines of thought and thus to make constant progress in our thinking rather than remain stuck in a rut. This can be the mind of the researcher or diagnostician which is able to cut straight through to the core of a problem. Speech is likewise liable to be direct and succinct, ungiven to flowery and unnecessary elaboration.

In its less agreeable form, this combination can tend towards inflexible, ruthless and domineering thinking and speaking patterns born of the desire to control others' minds. Thus there is often a crudeness and aggressiveness of speech which seeks to crush others' opinions and ideas.

The karma of the Mercury–Pluto link will usually manifest as periods during which our rigid thinking patterns need to be broken down and transformed. Needless to say, mental tension will be great at such times and there may be bouts of extreme depression before the old outworn thought-forms can be finally discarded. Our contacts with others are also likely to be marred by verbal conflict, and there is the possibility of protracted arguments with other individuals whose thinking is equally as fixed as our own.

John Lennon may well be remembered best for his blunt out-spokenness. Perhaps he more obviously personified the Mercury–Pluto link than any other factor in his chart. The famous *Rolling Stone* interview with Jann Wenner in January 1971, eventually published in book form, is a perfect example of John's mind at its hardest-hitting. When aroused he would spare no one in the cause of truth — in all its unsavoury details.

It is apparent that John suffered from the customary tendency towards inflexibility in that it took him a very long time to drop long-standing opinions and attitudes — particularly in one-to-one relationships since Mercury falls in the Seventh House. Consequently his life was filled with feuds and conflicts — with his partner Paul, his manager, his father, to name but a few.

Painstakingly, however, he succeeded in fulfilling the Mercury–Pluto challenge of gradually coming to look at situations with fresh understanding — albeit following lengthy absorption with his resentments. In each case it seemed that it was necessary for him to sink to the bottom of the pit of bitterness before he could begin to resurface. And those involved with him during these phases inevitably witnessed the pure venom of his tongue.

Not only did he manifest the self-transformatory side of Mercury–Pluto, but he also reflected the characteristic interest in deep study and research. From 1976 until his death in 1980 he shut himself away from the world in order to care for his son and to immerse himself in reading and learning, covering a large number of subjects and delving deeply into each. Most certainly John possessed a razor-sharp and keenly penetrating mind, but it was not until he had succeeded in discarding many of the old embittered thinking patterns that his true intellectual potential was released. Sadly the world will never know what the fruits of this rebirth might have yielded.

The Venus–Uranus Link

To consider this link firstly from the standpoint of relationships, the main challenge is to develop greater tolerance and understanding of others, even where they differ widely from ourselves. Thus we may be attracted towards partners or friends who differ from the norm, or we may find ourselves involved in unconventional relationships in order to learn to accept all individuals and all forms of contact with others as valuable in their own right. The aim of this planetary link is undoubtedly to develop our broad-mindedness.

A further test consists in learning to adopt a more balanced approach to freedom within relationships. Those of us born with this contact will invariably find it difficult to submit to restriction, which can frequently manifest as rejection of commitment or irresponsible behaviour towards those who are emotionally dependent upon us. The challenge here is to remain true to our need to be ourselves whilst simultaneously respecting the rights and expectations of others with whom our lives are linked. As with all Uranus contacts, it is a question of treading the middle road.

The difficult karma associated with this particular contact is often that of finding oneself inescapably drawn towards a person who is considered 'odd' or unsuitable by our family and friends and who may well be rejected by them on that count. The karma of Uranus is often to suffer ridicule or to feel oneself to be an outsider, and where Uranus contacts Venus it is in terms of one's relationships that this may happen.

At another level, there is sometimes the problem of finding oneself perpetually at the mercy of short-lived intense infatuations which effectively threaten our prospects of long-term happiness and test to the hilt our capacity to remain faithful.

In many ways John Lennon appeared to be harmoniously tuned to the Venus–Uranus principle, as reflected by his wide circle of friends from vastly differing backgrounds. Nevertheless, he encountered the commonplace Venus–Uranus challenge of falling in love with a woman who was considered by many to be 'unsuitable' and who was mercilessly criticized by the press on this score. The long-term refusal of his fans to accept the only woman he had ever truly loved was possibly one of the most painful experiences of John's life.

The problem of sudden attractions which quickly peter out but which threaten the well-being of permanent relationships was also a very real one for John. His need for sexual freedom was well known, and one particularly wild spell of libertine behaviour from 1973 to 1974 threatened to bring his marriage to Yoko to an end.

A link between Venus and Uranus is also indicative of a challenge regarding material values and the arts, and this is particularly so in John's case since Uranus falls in his Second House. Firstly it is a question of accepting and respecting manifold approaches to the use of resources and towards art and music, in the understanding that one's own outlook is only one small fraction of the greater whole. Secondly, the urge for financial and artistic freedom must be weighed against one's obligations and responsibilities to others.

The 'good karma' of this principle is originality and inspiration in music or the arts and the possibility of gaining the acceptance and respect of our contemporaries. Equally there is the possibility of exciting opportunities to express one's artistic abilities in a number of different ways. As far as money is concerned, unexpected strokes of fortune are possible in terms of the sudden acquisition of wealth.

It is hardly necessary to comment that John Lennon enjoyed 'breaks' of an extraordinary nature in both these areas. He was one of the most avant-garde artists of his era and contributed towards breaking down the barriers of conservatism as far as music and song-writing are concerned. His rise to millionaire status from modest beginnings likewise reflects the extremes to which Uranian karma can lead us.

In many ways he enjoyed the most positive of the features associated with the Venus–Uranus link — although it is possible that his reputation suffered rather than flourished on account of the ridicule attracted by Yoko Ono's wildly unconventional artistic ventures.

The Moon–Uranus Link

As far as this link is concerned, John was blessed with the unusual, attractive character, sparkle and wit represented by the positive side of the contact. Above all, he was typically unabashed in being himself and displaying his true feelings — the reason no doubt for the fascination he held for so many of us. His high-speed reactions, droll comments and talent for mimicry were well-known and added to his appeal as one of the outstanding personalities of our time. However, his humour was often at others' expense, and one of the least attractive traits in John was his tendency to make cruel fun of the disabled and afflicted. The talent for mimicry often degenerated into mockery and most certainly there was an air of arrogance about the man suggestive of his sense of superiority to others.

An important test associated with the Moon–Uranus link is to learn to curb a tendency towards emotional extremism and self-indulgence. Most certainly we are challenged to express our true feelings — and thus to be truly ourselves rather than conform to others' expectations of us. But at the same time it is necessary to avoid going over the top by allowing uncontrolled emotional outbursts to harm the well-being of those in our care.

Frequently the karma connected with this particular lesson is to be born to a mother who is herself emotionally uninhibited — at best delightfully unconventional, at worst an unstable nervous wreck. John's mother Julia was indeed an extraordinary character — a zany nonconformist with a most bizarre sense of humour. Much has been made of her personal instability, but the most difficult factor for John must surely have been her unpredictable behaviour towards him as a child. During his early years he suffered the changes and upheavals in his home-life characteristic of this link, which were later reflected in his own emotional instability as an adult.

This notwithstanding, John Lennon was an ardent campaigner for human rights both through the medium of his music and through the medium of publicity stunts. As such he was an important New Age prophet who held forth the vision of a brotherhood of man in which each and every human being will be released from the bondages of creed and class and will be respected as individuals in their own right. It is in this role that he may well be best remembered as the mouthpiece of Uranus — the great leveller and equalizer.

APPENDIX I

Links Between Planets

Links are present:
1. when two planets named are in aspect to each other; *or*
2. when the first planet named is in the sign of which the other is the ruler; *or*
3. when the first planet named is in the house of which the other is the ruler; *or*
4. when any personal planet or the Ascendant or Midheaven is in the sign ruled by the second planet named and forms an aspect with the first planet named.

(A weaker link exists when the second planet named is in the sign or house of which the other is the ruler; this kind of link should be taken into account only when other links are simultaneously present.)

Example:
Links would be present, for example, between Pluto and the Sun:
1. when Pluto and the Sun are in aspect to each other; *or*
2. when Pluto is in Leo; *or*
3. when Pluto is in the Fifth House; *or*
4. when any personal planet (Sun, Moon, Mercury, Venus or Mars) or the Ascendant or Midheaven is in Leo and forms an aspect with Pluto;

(A weaker link exists when the Sun is in Scorpio or in the Eighth House; take this into account only when one or more of the four above-mentioned links simultaneously applies.)

APPENDIX II

Suggested Meditation Affirmations

1. May I come to understand the system of justice which operates in everything that befalls me:
   (a) in terms of success and failure
   (b) at the emotional level
   (c) at the intellectual level
   (d) in my health and my work
   (e) in relationships
   (f) at the material level
   (g) at the physical level
   (h) at all levels
   (i) in my career
   (j) at the group level
   (k) at the sexual/psychic level.

2. May I free myself of the expectations and criticisms of the outside world in order to devote myself single-mindedly to:
   (a) giving fully of myself and my talents
   (b) the giving and receiving of love
   (c) the expression of my true thoughts and opinions
   (d) building good health and working efficiency
   (e) building and maintaining happy one-to-one relationships
   (f) achieving material security
   (g) asserting myself and exploiting my physical drives
   (h) expressing my true religious or philosophical beliefs
   (i) a career which is personally fulfilling
   (j) participation in social and community activities
   (k) achieving a sense of at-oneness with others
   (l) self-change in order to bring about world change.

3. I see myself as a soul, a tiny sparkling point of light which is merely using this body as a temporary vehicle. I feel myself flying away from this body through the dimensions until I become aware of the Source of Light and Truth from which I can obtain total understanding and absolute knowledge. I now absorb this Light and Truth.

4. May I be guided by that which is really to the advantage of myself and those close to me in my desire for freedom:
    (a) in the fulfilment of my ambitions
    (b) in my emotional reactions and home life
    (c) in my verbal reactions and my studies
    (d) in decisions concerning my work and health
    (e) in my one-to-one relationships
    (f) in material affairs and the arts
    (g) in the use of my energy drive
    (h) of religious/philosophical belief
    (i) in my career
    (j) in group and community relationships
    (k) in activities which allow me to step outside of myself
    (l) in the expression of my sexual and psychic energy.

5. I see myself as a soul, a tiny sparkling point of light which is merely using this body as a temporary vehicle. I now feel myself becoming at-one with the Source of Peace, Love and Beauty and thereby experience a sense of unity with all creation.

6. Focus on positive visualization of:
    (a) ourselves, playing our part in the world, happy and fulfilled, bringing help to others
    (b) personal contentment and peace; a compassionate, caring world in which all emotional needs are met
    (c) loving yet honest communication between ourselves and others
    (d) perfect personal health and working efficiency; a healthy contented world population engaged in mutual service
    (e) harmonious and joyful one-to-one relationships — either generalized or focusing on a specific relationship
    (f) material abundance both for ourselves and for the world as a whole
    (g) ourselves, full of radiant vitality, and capable of effectively asserting ourselves
    (h) the main religions of the world, encircled in light, seeing

each as positive and uplifting
(i) a fulfilling personal career; a world in which human beings have a perfectly developed sense of responsibility towards each other
(j) the group or community of which we are part; the brotherhood of man
(k) a New Age world, filled with indescribable beauty, love and light
(l) a world in which psychic energy is used for healing purposes — a world which is regenerating itself at all levels.

7. I see myself as a soul, a tiny sparkling point of light which is merely using this body as a temporary vehicle. In this consciousness I dedicate myself to the service of the whole of creation and ask that I may be used as a channel of divine healing power.

8. May I learn to follow universal will as opposed to personal will
(a) in the use of my talents and abilities
(b) in the acceptance of emotional upheavals
(c) in the use of my intellectual faculties
(d) in accepting what befalls me in terms of my health and my work
(e) in my one-to-one relationships
(f) in the use of my resources and possessions
(g) whenever I have a strong desire to win
(h) in accepting new ideas
(i) in my career in the outside world
(j) in my efforts to bring about universal freedom
(k) in my efforts to implement my ideals
(l) in all emotional/sexual/power conflicts.

9. Consciously hand over to the Forces of Light any conflict we may be involved in:
(a) which threatens our pride
(b) which threatens our emotional security and produces emotions such as jealousy
(c) which is based on an intellectual disagreement
(d) which threatens our working security or our health
(e) in the area of one-to-one relationships — here it's helpful to picture the other person and repeat the words 'I release you'
(f) which threatens our financial security

(g) in which we have the urge to prove ourselves stronger than the other person
(h) which relates to a difference of religious/philosophical belief
(i) which relates to our career ambitions and/or threatens our status
(j) which relates to injustice or the infringement of our rights
(k) which arises from disillusionment and results in self-pity on our part
(l) which threatens our personal power and sense of security.

APPENDIX III

Bach Flower Remedies

1. *Agrimony*
(a) when we sense we're putting up a cheerful front yet are suffering from torture at the same time
(b) for inner restlessness and worry, concealed by outer optimism, jokes and light-heartedness

2. *Aspen*
(a) for general anxiety and fear, sometimes blind panic, vague and undefined, based on no specific cause

3. *Beech*
(a) for mental arrogance, prejudice and intolerance
(b) of others' abilities or mentality
(c) of others' daily routine
(d) in accepting colleagues not on our wavelength and in attitude to career
(e) plus lack of understanding
(f) of other groups and individuals
(g) when others' ways differ from ours
(h) when we are over-critical of others
(i) of others' mannerisms
(j) of others within group or community
(k) of others' philosophy

4. *Centaury*
(a) when a compulsive urge to serve or too much gullibility
(b) impels us to run to the assistance of all and sundry
(c) leads us to give away confidences which we know we should not
(d) impels us to become slaves to others
(e) leads to disillusionment in our beliefs

(f) leads us to offer ourselves too readily to 'good causes'
(g) encourages a tendency to self-martyrdom
(h) leads others to take advantage of us

5. *Cherry Plum*
(a) for fear of losing control and a sense of desperation which might lead to
(b) rash and ill-considered decisions
(c) uncontrolled emotional outbursts
(d) uncontrollable actions
(e) a suicidal urge
(f) and fear of insecurity
(g) and fear of losing mind

6. *Chestnut Bud*
(a) for inability to break the pattern
(b) of repeated infatuations which come to no positive conclusion
(c) of a karma which we know to be harmful to our well-being
(d) of indiscreet speech
(e) however much we try
(f) and to learn when we make the same mistakes over and over again

7. *Chicory*
(a) for over-possessiveness
(b) which leads us to feel we are not getting enough attention from friends and family
(c) of those we care for and are anxious to keep close to us
(d) of our friends

8. *Clematis*
(a) for bouts of compulsive escapism
(b) which interfere with the efficiency of our work
(c) which causes financial problems
(d) for excessive fantasizing, especially romantically
(e) and a dreamy 'not with it' temperament
(f) and persistent absent-mindedness
(g) which prevents us from initiating concrete actions

9. *Crab Apple*
(a) for phases of self-hatred or self-disgust
(b) during Plutonic self-examination
(c) when we look penetratingly at our attitude towards
(d) relationships
(e) ourselves

10. *Elm*
(a) for those occupying positions of authority who become *temporarily* overwhelmed by their responsibilities

11. *Gentian*
(a) for occasions when we experience self-doubt, discouragement and shaken confidence
(b) due to frustrations and setbacks
(c) especially in studies
(d) especially in work or health matters
(e) especially in relationships
(f) especially financially
(g) in our attempts to meditate
(h) in sexual/emotional matters
(i) following a dissatisfying religious experience
(j) in our career

12. *Gorse*
(a) for hopelessness, despondency or despair we may suffer
(b) due to an affliction or shortcoming we have to bear in life or due to a chronic illness
(c) in trying to find a religion to believe in

13. *Holly*
(a) for jealousy and envy
(b) causing bitterness and hatred
(c) leading to bitterness or suspicion in a relationship
(d) leading to a need for revenge
(e) in the event of loss of power and authority
(f) for bitterness as a result of
(g) fear, insecurity or jealousy
(h) argument

14. *Honeysuckle*
(a) when our mind dwells on the past and what might have been
(b) in our love life
(c) and we cannot let go of a past sorrow

15. *Hornbeam*
(a) when we feel run down and unable to face our daily duties (especially the 'Monday morning feeling')

16. *Impatiens*
(a) for impatience
(b) and irritability
(c) when others' ways differ from ours

(d) when others' idiosyncrasies annoy us
(e) and when our argumentativeness inhibits communication
(f) with our work or medicine, which might cause us to give up too soon
(g) when we feel ourselves checked or restricted
(h) with other groups or associations and within our own group
(i) when a new study fails to satisfy all our requirements
(j) with boring aspects of our working routine or with colleagues not so quick on the uptake
(k) due to frustration of will
(l) and cutting corners when we want immediate results

17. *Larch*
(a) for lack of self-confidence due to expectation of failure or ridicule
(b) in emotional relationships
(c) in intellectual matters
(d) in work or health matters
(e) leading to inertia
(f) thus becoming loners through fear of rejection in personal relationships
(g) in material affairs
(h) which leads to shutting out religion as 'not for us'
(i) in group situations, leading to lack of involvement
(j) in spiritual matters, which deters from involvement
(k) in sexual matters
(l) leading to inertia and unwillingness to try

18. *Mimulus*
(a) for fear
(b) of doing something specific in front of others which will draw attention to us
(c) especially introversion or self-consciousness in relation to some specific situation
(d) e.g. exams or other forms of intellectual assessment
(e) especially worries about health
(f) of approaching others
(g) especially over financial situations
(h) especially of asserting ourselves
(i) especially of breaking moral codes
(j) of failing in career
(k) especially while participating in group activities
(l) of all things esoteric, which deters from involvement
(m) of losing our health or work
(n) of loss and for feelings of insecurity

19. *Mustard*
(a) for black depression which can suddenly descend upon us seemingly without cause and lift just as suddenly

20. *Oak*
(a) for strain and exhaustion due to taking on too many responsibilities out of a sense of duty
(b) pushing oneself beyond one's limits, plodding on regardless even when filled with despondency and carrying too much on one's shoulders
(c) especially with friends and partners
(d) to ensuring financial security
(e) in religious activities
(f) in community or club work
(g) and carrying others
(h) at work
(i) especially intellectually

21. *Olive*
(a) for physical and mental exhaustion which accompanies breakdowns

22. *Pine*
(a) for guilt or self-reproach
(b) when we feel disappointed in ourselves that we have been unable to live up to our ideals, thinking we should have done better
(c) and a sense of worthlessness
(d) in relationships
(e) about personal possessions in face of widespread deprivation
(f) that we can't do more for others or that others' troubles are somehow our fault
(g) that we haven't achieved more

23. *Red Chestnut*
(a) when a morbid or over-active imagination
(b) dwells on fears that it is unable to dislodge
(c) always fears the worst for others
(d) encourages negative thoughts
(e) makes us excessively afraid that some calamity will befall those dear to us

24. *Rock Rose*
(a) for terror or panic
(b) about losing health or work
(c) about insecurity or fear of loss

25. *Rock Water*
(a) for excessively strict self-discipline and self-repression
(b) which brings about an urge to follow too strict a code of conduct
(c) which affects our emotional responses
(d) which causes us to set ourselves too high standards
(e) in our speech and brain-work
(f) of physical fitness
(g) in relationships, leading to frigidity
(h) leading to excessive frugality and overwork to achieve financial security
(i) leaving no time for enjoyment
(j) of a religious nature
(k) in application to our career
(l) in spiritual matters making us over-concerned with doing the 'right thing'
(m) which is applied to our sexual desires, in some cases leading to impotence and frigidity
(n) which has caused us to become excessively rigid in our regime to the point of lack of balance

26. *Scleranthus*
(a) for uncertainty and indecision
(b) and chopping and changing in one's goals and ambitions
(c) causing alternating extremes of mood
(d) causing changefulness of mind
(e) over work problems and health care
(f) when torn between two relationships
(g) causing changeability and inconstancy in social relations
(h) as to which course to take
(i) in the case of spasmodic fluctuations of energy flow
(j) in our career between two alternatives

27. *Star of Bethlehem*
(a) for the after-effects of shock
(b) resulting from severe disappointment

28. *Sweet Chestnut*
(a) for periods of intense mental anguish, extreme loneliness or sense of being in a void

29. *Vervain*
(a) for nervous breakdown, exhaustion, stress or tension, caused by
(b) living life at breakneck speed
(c) over-activity of mind
(d) over-active emotions

(e) going to extremes
(f) extremes of activity
(g) extremes of involvement in religious or philosophical cults and beliefs
(h) over-taxing ourselves in our career
(i) extremism in social and political beliefs and over-enthusiastic involvement in group endeavours
(j) extremes of spiritual enthusiasm
(k) feeling impelled to go to extremes sexually or in the assertion of our will
(l) being worked up about converting someone to our way of thinking
(m) over-concern for proving to others that we are right, tending to force our view on others
(n) a fanatical desire to reform society or the circle of which we are part
(o) where we are likely to over-estimate our capabilities, become over-enthusiastic and take on too much
(p) becoming obsessed

30. *Vine*
(a) for inflexibility
(b) and an unyielding determination to win
(c) and rigidity when we tend to dominate those close to us demanding and expecting unquestioned obedience
(d) and a desire to force our will on others
(e) in our beliefs, when we expect others to follow our way of looking at things
(f) when power of leadership within our group means too much to us
(g) when ambition takes us over

31. *Walnut*
(a) gives protection against over-sensitivity
(b) to unwelcome psychic phenomena
(c) for others, which may lead to martyrdom
(d) causing over-identification with others' suffering to the point where we ourselves suffer
(e) to others' thoughts which we involuntarily pick up and which can cause us disturbance
(f) when we have to let go of someone or something dear to us
(g) when bitterness might set in at the time of redundancy
(h) is an excellent link-breaking remedy to be taken
(i) at the time of a change in direction
(j) at times of loss or change
(k) to outside influences

32. *Water Violet*
(a) when self-reliance and self-containment, however admirable, can manifest as aloofness, pride and a sense of superiority or off-handedness which alienates others
(b) when religious matters are concerned
(c) when spiritual matters are concerned
(d) who are deemed to be financially unreliant
(e) where intellectual matters are concerned

33. *White Chestnut*
(a) for persistent unwanted thoughts
(b) about the impression we have made on others
(c) especially verbally
(d) especially in our work
(e) especially in our group
(f) for persistent worry and preoccupation
(g) about work or health
(h) about money matters
(i) with feelings such as guilt, self-pity, or a sense of victimization
(j) which we are not able to switch off or dispel from our mind
(k) or delusion
(l) when we're unable to clear some episode or argument from our minds

34. *Wild Oat*
(a) for the dissatisfaction of being uncertain as to how to
(b) commit ourselves
(c) find a stable belief
(d) find a stable career and find our special niche
(e) find a goal in life
(f) find fulfilling employment
(g) find the right relationship in life
(h) find our heart's desire
(i) find a clearly defined faith
(j) settle in one path

35. *Wild Rose*
(a) for apathy and resignation
(b) with the monotony of our daily life
(c) and a sense of hopelessness about finding the right person
(d) and a sense of hopelessness about the sad state of the world

36. *Willow*
(a) for resentment and bitterness and an overwhelming feeling that life is treating us unfairly

(b) in financial matters
(c) when frustrated in career matters
(d) when our ideas don't gain acceptance
(e) in the face of defeat or loss
(f) following a bereavement
(g) following loss of employment or health breakdown
(h) when our partner breaks away from us against our will
(i) when we are passed over in some way
(j) when our friends apparently desert us
(k) when we suffer defeat and tend to blame others, not ourselves
(l) when forced to relinquish something we prized.

Note

The Bach Flower Remedies total thirty-eight in number (plus the composite remedy known as Rescue Remedy) of which only thirty-six have been referred to in this list. For further information on all the remedies and their uses, and for supplies, please contact:

> The Dr Bach Centre
> Mount Vernon
> Sotwell
> Wallingford
> Oxon
> OX10 0PZ
> England

(Please send a stamped, self-addressed envelope)

BIBLIOGRAPHY

Arroyo, Stephen, *Astrology, Karma and Transformation* (CRCS, 1978).

Bach, Edward, MB, BS, DPH. *Heal Thyself — An Explanation of the Real Cause and Cure of Disease* (C.W. Daniel, 1931).

Ballard, Juliet Brooke, *The Hidden Laws of Earth* (A.R.E. Press, 1979).

Cerminara, Gina, *Many Mansions* (New American Library, 1967).

Chancellor, Philip M., *The Handbook of the Bach Flower Remedies* (C.W. Daniel, 1971).

Gammon, Margaret H., *Astrology and the Edgar Cayce Readings* (A.R.E Press, 1974).

Greene, Liz, *Saturn — A New Look at an Old Devil* (Aquarian Press, 1977).

Hawken, Paul, *The Magic of Findhorn* (Fontana, 1976).

Hone, Margaret, D.F. Astrol S., *The Modern Text Book of Astrology* (Fowler, 1972).

Sechrist, Elsie, *Meditation — Gateway to Light* (A.R.E Press, 1976).

Spangler, David, *Revelation, The Birth of a New Age* (Findhorn Foundation, 1977).

Sugrue, Thomas, *There is a River — The Story of Edgar Cayce* (Dell Publishing, 1967).

White, Ruth and Swainson, Mary, *Gildas Communicates* (C.W. Daniel, 1978).

The *Edgar Cayce Readings* are on file at the Edgar Cayce Foundation, Atlantic Avenue at 67th Street, PO Box 595, Virginia Beach, Virginia 23451, USA.

INDEX TO THE INTERPRETATION SECTION